The Adolescent Psyche

Adolescence is recognized as a turbulent period of human development. Along with the physical changes of puberty, adolescents undergo significant transformations in the way they think, act, feel, and perceive the world. The disruption that is manifest in their behaviour is upsetting and often incomprehensible to the adults surrounding them.

Drawing on Jung's concept of individuation, Richard Frankel shows how this unique stage of human development expresses through its traumas and fantasies the adolescent's urge towards self-realization. He refers also to the work of Winnicott, Hillman and Lifton, who explore the dynamics of adolescence with a phenomenological eye.

At a time when the media are focusing attention on the statistics of adolescent crime, substance abuse, pregnancy, and suicide, an increasing number of adolescents are being referred for psychotherapy and/or psychiatric hospitalization. Through case studies, Frankel explores the impact of contemporary culture on the lives of young people, and illustrates the practical difficulties therapists face in their clinical work with clients in this age group.

Through its original amalgamation of the ideas of Jung and Winnicott, this book provides a new orientation to the theory and practice of adolescent psychology. The advice and guidelines Frankel provides will be welcomed by psychotherapists, parents, educators, and anyone working with adolescents.

Richard Frankel is a psychotherapist in private practice and a clinical social worker based in Massachusetts, USA, and has many years' experience of working with adolescents and their families in mental health clinics, schools, and hospitals.

The Adolescent Psyche

Jungian and Winnicottian Perspectives

Richard Frankel

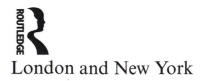

London and New York

First published 1998
by Routledge
11 New Fetter Lane, London EC4P 4EE

Simultaneously published in the USA and Canada
by Routledge
29 West 35th Street, New York, NY 10001

Typeset in Times by Routledge
Printed and bound in Great Britain by TJ International,
Padstow, Cornwall

British Library Cataloguing in Publication Data
A catalogue record for this book is available from the British Library

Library of Congress Cataloging in Publication Data
Frankel, Richard, 1961–
The adolescent psyche: Jungian and Winnicottian perspectives/
Richard Frankel.
p.   cm.
Includes bibliographical references and index.
1. Adolescent psychology. 2. Psychoanalysis. 3. Adolescent
psychotherapy. I. Title.
BF724.F66   1998
155.5–dc21   97–29591
                                                        CIP

ISBN 0–415–16798–1 (hbk)
ISBN 0–415–16799–X (pbk)

To Lisa,

For Nurturing The Unformed In Me

Contents

Figures

Foreword

The adolescent girl who cuts herself in secret rituals, the teen-age boy who affiliates himself with a violence ridden gang, the fifteen-year-old girl who rages at her parents when moments before she had expressed sweet feelings toward them, the ones attracted to cultish religious groups, the ones preoccupied by thoughts of death and suicide, the bizzarely dressed and oddly pierced young people, the teen-agers held up in their rooms, watching endless hours of television . . . what does psychological theory have to offer us to help us understand and witness the disturbing manifestations of adolescence? Richard Frankel—trained in phenomenology and depth psychology—brilliantly exposes most of our current theories as reducing adolescence to a rehashing of the dynamics of early childhood. In this book he releases us from this reductive circling back as the only explanation of the adolescent and attempts, instead, to lay bare the archetypal landscape of adolescence itself.

Following Jung, he asks what is the teleology of this part of the life cycle. What is adolescence aiming toward? Is there anything in the often odd and dangerous, frequently idealistic, and spiritually probing behavior and attitudes of adolescents to respect, to nurture, to understand on its own terms? In this heterogeneous American culture that has eroded common custom, ritual, and expectation, is there a way for us to see adolescents fashioning—in guises that are often hard for us to recognize—their own transition rituals and offerings? Frankel asserts that much of what we witness with adolescents are their attempts—often desperate—at self-initiation; efforts to shatter their innocence through wounding; efforts to build their capacity to endure losses through the navigation of betrayals, separations, and symbolic deaths; efforts to express the purity of their idealistic visions of the possible. He argues that the extremes of adolesence are intrinsic to it, and must be insighted on their own terms, not through the lenses of childhood or adulthood.

Those familiar with Jungian psychology know that Jung and post-Jungians have had little to offer clinicians regarding adolescence. Jung's developmental interests were largely confined to mid- and later life. Yet through Frankel's careful harvesting of the scattered insights into adolescence—provided by Jung, Hillman, Guggenbühl-Craig, Bosnak, Wickes, Allan—he is able to present a coherent, convincing alternative to the psychoanalytic visions which have dominated clinical thinking about adolescence. Having steeped himself in both clinical experience with adolescents and Jungian psychology, Frankel is able to expose and articulate those parts of Jung's thoughts that are invaluable when considering adolescence— for instance, the emphasis on telos, the encounter with the shadow, the ways in which adolescents engage the individuation process, the need for ritual in a culture that provides little ritual coherence, the function of trying on various personas in the search for an individual self. He succeeds in bringing adolescence out of a state of neglect in Jungian and post-Jungian psychology, showing us that it can be a fertile site for the application of Jungian theory and practice.

Winnicott is also included here as an insightful theorist of the adolescent psyche. His recognition of the value of non-compliance in adolescence for the unfolding of the personality is given voice throughout the book. Despite Winnicott's overt lack of respect for Jung, many depth psychologists work with a profound appreciation for both Jung and Winnicott. Frankel deftly weaves between Winnicott's astute sensitivity regarding adolescence and Jungian approaches, exposing their compatibility and capacity to mutually enrich each other.

Frankel's book has a therapeutic effect on the reader, as it helps us discern our own countertransference reactions to adolescents. It tutors those who want to understand adolescence to reconnect with their own transit through this tumultuous period. Our adult dreams point us back over and over again to adolescence and the puer side of ourselves. Frankel queries us: "What was born there that needs to be recalled and remembered?" As well, he helps us sort through our own "adult" emotional reactions that are overly quick to negate, deride, pathologize, and condescend to the expressions of adolescence, seeing through these as senex reactions deeply alienated from the spirit of youthfulness, the puer. Through building in us a respect for the psychological work that is being done in adolescence, and by helping us see the barrier created by our own envy of youth's vision and energy, Frankel is able to help the reader step toward what he or she initially judged as outlandish, horrific, developmentally off-track.

I especially appreciate Frankel's affirmation of therapy with adolescents, and his careful outlining of the functions of a therapeutic relationship in adolescence such as internalizing the reflective voice of the therapist, witnessing and taking an active interest in the many aspects of the teen-ager's personality, modeling how to dialogue with and reflect upon them, helping the patient engage a crisis in a meaningful way so that its inherent potential for transformation can unfold, reflecting back to the adolescent the grace, beauty, and power of her engagement with the spirit of youth. Through careful and interesting clinical vignettes, he is able to tutor us in the kind of therapeutic insighting and presence that can make a difference to the adolescents we work with.

Frankel's work illustrates the fruits of a deconstructionist approach to psychological theory and practice. Apart from its manifest theme of adolescence, Frankel teaches us how to work with theory. As he works the theories of adolescence he lays bare the way in which psychological theory is a creative process of the culture, each theory revealing aspects of the phenomenon under study while concealing others, each carrying its own set of implicit values. To see adolescence in a way that allows us to manifest our caring toward the youth traversing it, he beckons us to see with clarity first from one vantage point, then from another—Freud, Jones, Anna Freud, Blos, Hillman, and so forth. Only in this way do our theories begin to serve the young people and their experience, rather than subjugating their experience to a monocular vision of our own. I am very moved by the fruits of Richard Frankel's sustained gaze on adolescence. He has not succumbed to segmenting theory from practice, the imaginal from the lived, the causal from the teleological, the deconstruction of theory from the construction of it. As you can see, I am happy to invite you into this book, and eager for its sensitivities to grow within the much needed relationships we form with adolescents.

Mary Watkins, Ph.D.
Pacifica Graduate Institute
Santa Barbara, California

Acknowledgements

This book has taken shape over many years and many voices have contributed to it. I would like to express my thanks and gratitude to the following people who were an invaluable source of support: Charles Scott, who first disclosed to me the fruitfulness in wedding phenomenology and archetypal psychology—he was an early reader of my manuscript and his insights have been incorporated into the final text; Thomas Moore's eloquent presentations at the Archetypal Psycholgy Study Group stimulated my thinking, and led me to discover the links between the psychology of the puer–senex archetype and the work with adolescents; Robert Bosnak and Andrew Samuels, who read my work and offered me strong encouragement to "send it off"; my dear friend, Gregory Shaw, who was readily available for conversation and an exchange of ideas whenever I reached a snag; my editor, Roseann Cain; Mary Watkins, whose persistent voice would not let me forget that I was sitting on a manuscript which needed to go out into the world before I moved on to other pursuits—Mary has been my mentor as a psychological thinker, writer, and practioneer and has generously given of herself over the years, encouraging and inspiring the unfolding of my own thinking; and my wife, Lisa Bloom, to whom I dedicate the book. In addition to her unflagging support while writing, she has painstakingly gone over every word, phrase and idea contained in it. Her creativity, intelligence and inventiveness are sprinkled throughout these pages as she is the true *sine qua non* of this work.

Excerpt from RULE OF THE BONE by Russell Banks. Copyright ©1995 by Russell Banks. Reprinted by permission of HarperCollins Publishers, Inc.

Excerpts from ON ADOLESCENCE: A PSYCHOANALYTIC INTERPRETATION by Peter Blos. Copyright © 1962 by The Free Press, a Division of Simon & Schuster. Reprinted with permission of the publisher.

Excerpts from THE ADOLESCENT by Fyodor Dostoevsky, translated by Andrew MacAndrew. Reprinted by permission of Doubleday, a division of Bantam Doubleday Dell Publishing Group, Inc.

Excerpts from ANNE FRANK: THE DIARY OF A YOUNG GIRL by Anne Frank, translated by B.M. Mooyaart. Reprinted by permission of Doubleday, a division of Bantam Doubleday Dell Publishing Group, Inc.

Excerpts from INSEARCH: PSYCHOLOGY AND RELIGION, LOOSE ENDS, PUER PAPERS, "The Great Mother, Her Son, Her Hero, and the Puer," and "Pink Madness, or, why does Aphrodite Drive Men Crazy with Pornography," all by James Hillman. Reprinted by permission of Spring Publications.

Excerpts from ANNIE JOHN by Jamaica Kincaid. Copyright © 1985 by Jamaica Kincaid. Reprinted by permission of Farrar, Straus & Giroux, Inc.

Excerpt from THE COLLECTED POEMS BY CZESLAW MILOSZ. Copyright © 1988 by Czeslaw Milosz Royalties, Inc. First Published by The Ecco Press in 1988.

Excerpt from THE NOTEBOOKS OF MALTE LAURIDS BRIGGE by Rainer Maria Rilke, translated by M. D. Herter Norton, Translation copyright 1949 by W. W. Norton & Company, Inc., renewed © 1977 by M. D. Herter Norton Crena de Iongh. Reprinted by permission of W. W. Norton & Company, Inc.

Excerpts from DEPRIVATION AND DELINQUENCY and PLAYING AND REALITY, both by D. W. Winnicott. Reprinted by permission of Tavistock Publishers.

Abbreviations

References to C.G. Jung are to the *Collected Works* (*CW*) and by volume and paragraph number, edited by Read, H., Fordham, M., Adler, G. and McGuire, W., translated in the main by Hull R., Routledge and Kegan Paul, London; Princeton University Press.

Introduction

The theory and practice of adolescent psychology form the cornerstone of this book. In bringing the two together in one volume, I am taking heed of their close relationship by demonstrating how contemporary theories of adolescence have obstructed our vision and thus constrained the manner in which we practice. Psychological theories have tremendous influence on the actual practice of psychotherapy. They are like lanterns which help us navigate the dark wilderness of the psyche, regulating how we order and make sense of its complexities. The means by which we are seeing, our theoretical lens, determines which features of a case will emerge in the foreground as the clinical "facts," and which will recede into obscurity. If the source of light is changed, new contours and patterns emerge that previously went unnoticed. My intention is to use the insights of Jungian and Winnicottian theories as potentially new sources of light to illuminate the phenomenon of adolescence. In so doing, I hope to grant a fresh vision to the practice of adolescent psychotherapy so that it does not accede to the pressures of social conformity, becoming primarily a hygienic work. I will provide a theoretical approach to adolescence that is attuned to a practice grounded in the reality of the adolescent psyche, where depth, meaning, and the integrity of one's person can be brought to bear upon the clinical encounter with an adolescent client.

The half-way point of adolescence in the scheme of life-span development suggests three primary directions of orientation for formulating a theoretical understanding of this period of life. The first and most evident direction is to turn to the past as the cause of what is happening in the present. This is exemplified by developmental theory, which understands what happened at an earlier period of development as the cause of later developmental entanglements. A look back toward early childhood becomes the place to search for the origins of the adolescent's current trials and tribulations. While this orientation forms the central foundation of modern psychology since Freud, in Part I, I provide a critique that sets forth its limitations for an understanding of adolescent psychology.

Parents of adolescents also get trapped in causal thinking. When their child reaches adolescence, she may change so dramatically, become so unknowable, that parents are desperate to find out the root of the problem that is upsetting and unsettling to family life.[1] However, instead of looking back to early childhood development, parents instinctively turn toward the adolescent's peer group as causing all the problems. By seeing their children's peers as negative and corrupting influences, they avoid coming to terms with the fact that a transformation is happening within their own child, and that they can no longer rely upon previous familiar patterns of relating and communicating. Blaming the peer group is one of the primary defenses that parents utilize to avoid facing the "otherness" that presents itself in adolescence. Some parents concretize the otherness as a surreptitious virus, meandering through the bloodstream. In that case, adolescence is seen as a disease and parents turn to the medical profession, whisking their children away to doctors, neurologists, and psychiatrists who can root out the biomedical cause and alleviate the symptoms.

In contradistinction, I am seeking to explore the implications of envisioning adolescence outside the domain of developmental psychology. With those adolescent clients who have a history of trauma, our attention is naturally drawn to the past; the client's childhood history announces its relevancy in the course of treatment. But what about those adolescents who experience the transformations of puberty in a stormy and tumultuous manner after having passed through a rather undramatic childhood? Is looking back causally the only direction from which to approach their current state of suffering?

The second direction of orientation is to situate ourselves as much as possible in the actual world of adolescence. This is a realm of being that we, as adults, have long forgotten, but in forgetting that we have forgotten, we are inclined to project our own images of adolescence onto the adolescents we encounter. Projecting one's psychology onto a client is an inherent danger of any therapeutic encounter, but one to which we are especially vulnerable in this type of work. Throughout the book, I articulate the multifarious manifestations of this vulnerability by addressing those situations where such projections are likely to take place. To move past our projections and observe more clearly the realm which an adolescent inhabits involves a willingness to dwell in the indeterminacy between our taken-for-granted, adult ways of perceiving and the world as experienced by the adolescent.

Phenomenology offers a philosophical methodology for making this difficult yet necessary shift in consciousness. Phenomenology is a descriptive and experiential method which requires us to bracket our ontological categories of judgment so that we can be open to how a phenomenon presents itself. For example, one can argue that by focusing on origins or causes to explain adolescent behavior, we are prevented from seeing and hearing what is happening with the adolescent in the context of his own world. By temporarily bracketing our search for causes or any of the other predispositions we bring to bear, including our prescriptive notions of what we think the adolescent should do as well as our intention to fix or cure him, we are in a better position to attune ourselves to the immediacy of his world. By letting go of how we think he should be, the adolescent as other is welcomed into our awareness. Given that the art of concealment plays such a natural role in adolescence, it is perhaps more formidable to enact this kind of "I-thou" encounter with an adolescent than it is with either children or adults. Patience and forbearance are necessary requirements for sustaining a phenomenologically rich vision. The revealing and concealing nature inherent in adolescence is examined in Chapter 7.

One way of illustrating the potency of the phenomenological vision is to reflect upon what happens to us as clinicians when we are told in detail about a "case" before meeting the actual individual. For example, we may sit in on a case conference about a future client, say a fifteen-year-old female adolescent, and listen to the intake clinician's presentation which takes into account the major events and circumstances of our future client's life and connects them to her current presenting problems in the context of a well-integrated psychodynamic formulation. In walking away from such a conference, we are left with a vague sense of who this fifteen-year-old is that over the next two or three days gels into a concrete image of what we can expect when she arrives at our office door. In those first few moments of actually meeting her, sitting down and beginning a conversation, we are startled by the discrepancy between who we imagined this fifteen year old teen-ager to be, based on the case conference, and the living presence of the young woman who has entered our office. That gap points to the phenomenological reality that a living human being manifests in a therapeutic encounter. As the conversation continues, the discrepancy between how we constructed the "case" in our mind versus our growing awareness of this person sitting across from us widens. Letting go of our preconceptions—and we are always filled with them before actually meeting an adolescent client (the reports and phone calls from teachers, parents, probation officers, other clinicians, etc.)—and staying open to the uniqueness of the other grants a phenomenological vision.

Developing a phenomenological eye plays a crucial role in the treatment process as well. What is therapeutic for adolescents is to be granted the opportunity to reveal themselves in the context of a genuine relationship. Adolescents are yearning to be made visible. Thus, they respond to the containment of a therapeutic vessel by giving expression to parts of the self that are typically held in abeyance. When we allow in what has been disowned and give our attention to it, psychic structures loosen and shift. One of the profound transformations that occurs over the course of time in a long-term individual relationship with an adolescent client (and by long-term I mean anywhere from three months to three years) is the movement from concealment to deepening progressive levels of self-revelation.

My approach to adolescent psychotherapy entails the active establishment of connections to the different sides of the adolescent's self so that she can learn to live in a less split-off relationship to them. I will explore the attitudes and stances we inhabit as therapists (often unconsciously) which either promote or interfere with this rather arduous task of welcoming the perplexingly varied facets of the adolescent psyche that show themselves over the course of a treatment. In Chapter 8, I elucidate the effects of this approach on what we typically term adolescent "acting-out." This idea of coming into a therapeutic relationship with the multiplicity of the adolescent self is emphasized in many different places throughout the book. The nomenclature changes depending upon the school of thought being presented. Hence, I interpret the discussion of id impulses in the psychoanalytical school as denoting essential sides of the psyche that must be reckoned with in adolescence. From the perspective of Jungian/ Archetypal psychology, this same phenomenon is thought of in terms of inhibitions, and finally, from the approach of imaginal psychology, exploring one's inmost desires gives access to the richness of the self.

Throughout the book, I refer to the technique of personifying as a method for giving voice and expression to the adolescent psyche. Personifying is a therapeutic tool developed by Jung that facilitates the establishment of a relational dialogue by treating the different sides of the self as "psychic persons." By granting consciousness and autonomy at an imaginal level to the emotions and behaviors of the adolescent, we can enter into the images which are the guiding factors shaping their experience of the world. Personifying thus draws upon the medium of the arts (painting, telling stories, modeling clay, writing poetry, etc.) as a non-discursive means for allowing these images to unfold.

The third direction of orientation we can traverse in order to gain insight into adolescence is to look ahead, asking where a particular symptom or pattern of behavior may be leading. Here, I draw upon Jung's pioneering method of inquiry into the teleological function of the psyche (from the Greek word *telos* which means "goal" or "end"), where symptoms are read not only causally, but as intending an aim or goal. The feelings and fantasies contained within a particular symptom may symbolize a possible future emerging into being; thus, we ask, what a particular symptom is for, where it may be leading and that for the sake of which it is happening (Samuels 1991, p. 17). Jung's view of human nature as well as his notion of the psyche as a self-regulating system points to the necessity of looking at psychological phenomenon from a teleological perspective which complements and extends the psychocausal perspective of psychoanalysis and modern psychology (Rychlak 1991). This is crucial for approaching adolescence because it is an extremely paradoxical and dialectical time of life. Caught between the pulls of dependency and responsibility, no longer a child, but not yet an adult, the adolescent bears the tension of the opposites in a dramatic way. For Jung, synthesizing the dialectics of the opposites gives rise to a teleological approach (ibid., p. 43), and as we shall see, therapeutic engagement with adolescents involves feeling into, dialectically, the differing pulls on their being. Thus, the teleological, or what is also referred to as the prospective function of adolescence is an overriding theme of the book.

One of the inevitable struggles in adolescence is between a regressive pull back to what is known, familiar and safe, and a forward movement out into the world. Indications of this struggle can be found in the clinical symptomatology of adolescents in crisis. An examination of early history only reveals one side of the conflict, whereas the teleological view completes the picture, granting a perspective on the forward progression of energy. Thus, I want to open up the conceptualization of the clinical picture, which tends to look back, to include a prospective reading of a case where consideration is given to the goals toward which the perplexing and disturbing behaviors of adolescents are pointing . Symptoms can be read prospectively with an eye toward how they are subtly leading the adolescent in one direction rather than another. Tracing the telos in the symptom requires imagination and an artful rendering of a case where we are willing to consider the clinical "facts" in light of their possible symbolic meanings. In this regard, the particular item an adolescent may be stealing from a store is as revealing to the case as the fact that he is engaged in shoplifting. Or the messages and images expressed in his graffiti are as important to the case as the fact that he breaks the law by spray-painting the sides of public buildings. The particular details hint at the underlying order of meaning. The prospective view insures that we take into account the individuality and idiosyncrasy of each case, and it protects us from reading the clinical picture of the adolescent as just another case report, hearing it as a repetition of the same old story.

Looking at a case teleologically allows us to maintain a certain equanimity in response to the feelings of despair that frequently arise in a depth-oriented encounter with a troubled adolescent. It is difficult to avoid getting wrapped up in the tragic view of life that certain adolescents embody during the course of treatment. From their perspective, nothing is ever going to work out, there is no hope for the future, and any attempt to try and do something is a waste of time. In the face of such anguish, we lose our objectivity and feel that if we do not intercede, something terrible will happen; it is up to us to rescue the adolescent from her inevitable doom; only our good-intentioned interventions can prevent the tragedy, whether it be a car crash, drug overdose, or the adolescent being kicked out of her home and forced to live on the streets. The therapy shifts into a salvational mode. The teleological view serves as an antidote to getting trapped in the literalism of such fatalism, reminding us that there are larger, imperceptible forces at work that may, in the end, serve progressive development. Without sensing that the painful and complicated experiences our adolescent clients live through are aiming toward something, we unwittingly become overinvolved and rob them of their ability to draw upon their own internal resources for survival during these difficult years. Our natural tendency to want to step in and take charge ultimately becomes disempowering.

By overidentifying with the adolescent's tragic view of himself, we lose sight of a broader vision of life, a perspective granted by age, experience, and status in the world. Having passed through this stage of development ourselves, we are not caught in quite the same way by the obstacles that create so much trouble for the adolescent. The awareness that arises from having suffered through our own adolescence as well as some familiarity with our own shadow bespeaks the "authority" which I allude to throughout the book. Such authority grants perspective and thus increases our ability to withstand the volatile affects that arise as an adolescent works to untangle himself from the pitfalls and snares that can possibly lead to such disastrous endings. I will examine the phenomenon of an adolescent challenging our authority by looking at what it unconsciously sets off in us and by inquiring into what the adolescent is searching for in provoking such a challenge. Another central recurring theme that runs throughout the book is how one uses authority with adolescents in a life-enhancing versus a life-denying way.

It is terrifying to be around adolescents who are truly on the edge, no matter what the circumstances. Their potential for self-destruction is palpable, and during those times, if they are in our care, we lean on whatever resources we have available to help them survive. In offering a theory which asks that we honor and respect the unwieldy spirit (which I refer to as the "puer") that arises during this period of development, it has been essential for me to keep in mind the reality of the immense suffering and pain that manifests during adolescence. Thus, in making the claim that there is something inherently meaningful and potentially life-vitalizing in giving that spirit a place, I am well aware of what havoc it can wreak, of its explosive potentiality. The preponderance of psychological theories of adolescence adopts a removed, distant, and overly-objective approach that seems to be a means of guarding against its volatility. The abstractions of theory are used defensively to build barricades against the destructive potential inherent in adolescence. The result, however, is that the pressing images and feelings on the inside edge of the adolescent experience do not inform the theory. By attuning myself to adolescence as a phenomenological reality, where theory takes into account the volatile spirit and difficult emotions of the time, I am attempting to fill in a gap, presenting a side of adolescence that is for the most part omitted from the psychological literature. In this regard, I draw upon literature and film to supply images that viscerally capture the subjective experience of being an adolescent.

In historicizing the occurrence of adolescence in late twentieth century America, I am seeking to uncover the particular ways the adolescent psyche is manifested in our current cultural milieu. This approach of looking at psyche from a cultural perspective assumes an inseparable conjunction between the individual and the world. Psyche is not inside one's skin or limited to what happens in the therapy office, but can be found in the design of our buildings, the organization of our schools, and the planning of our communities. Although this concern pervades the entire book, I critically address the question of the interplay between adolescence and the culture in Chapter 11 and the Epilogue. In trying to capture the spirit of adolescence, attempting to grasp it as a whole, I see my work as preparatory, clearing the ground for further investigations into our current concern for the influences of gender, race, class, and sexual orientation on development. Although I have tried to be sensitive to these distinctions where I could, my work does not adequately reflect the important differences in the experience of being an adolescent based upon these factors. My hope is that in allowing the phenomenon of adolescence to unfold phenomenologically, we will be in a better position to think through its particularizations based upon these categories of difference.

I am intending to mend the split between reflectively engaging adolescence as a purposive phenomenon that carries significant meaning and the day-to-day clinical realities facing us as therapists whose practices include adolescent clients. A theory of adolescence that does not in some way connect with the "spirit" of the time is dry and academic, whereas one that overspiritualizes adolescence, transfixed by its symbology and numinosity, leaves nothing to hold onto when it comes to facing the enormously complex set of problems that are encountered by the adolescent therapist. The question for me has always been how to bring the two together: an imaginative, non-pathologizing approach to the transformational nature of adolescence which, at the same time, has direct and relevant implications for practice. The charge often leveled at James Hillman's archetypal psychology is that his ideas are too heady, too conceptual, and they have no import for the actual fare of daily therapy. I hope to prove false these charges by illustrating the relevance of his insights for working with adolescent clients (very likely, not a population he had in mind). Hillman's ideas come alive in the therapy hour, not necessarily as practical interventions, but as spurs that cause us to notably shift how we listen, attending to a different order of meaning in the clinical material than what is generally accessible vis-à-vis the traditional theories of adolescence.

In contrast to the developmental perspective which underlies so much of the psychology written about adolescence, Hillman's thinking offers us a non-linear approach to the question of youth. For example, his essays on the puer posit it as a self-originating archetypal phenomenon, having its own phenomenology; it is not the result of anything that came earlier. Freeing ourselves, even momentarily, from the constraints of developmentalism offers new ways of thinking and understanding. Remarkably enough, Winnicott's writings on adolescence similarly do not accord with a strictly developmental perspective. Although firmly allied with the psychoanalytical tradition, Winnicott does not theorize about adolescence as recapitulation in the manner of his psychoanalytical colleagues. In contrast to his other work, which strongly emphasizes the connection between adult functioning and early childhood experience, something breaks open for Winnicott when he comes to reflect upon adolescence. He evocatively captures adolescence as a world unto itself, with its own unique and originary dynamics. On that account, his main emphasis is upon acknowledging the authenticity of the troubling and distressing psychological states that emerge during this period of life.

A main objective of this book is to draw off some of the energy and focus from childhood and bring it to adolescence. Adolescence as a psychological phenomenon is crying out for renewed attention. Perhaps our psychology has kept itself too distant, safely locked up in the fantasy of childhood, to hear its cry. There is something intrinsically embarrassing and shameful in evoking the adolescent as either an inner figure or an outer reality. We can speak circles around our childhood, endlessly analyzing and probing. We are comfortable with its language and mode of discourse. Something shifts, however, when we are asked to reflect on adolescence. Such reminiscences inevitably evoke shameful memories, painful feelings,

shy and withdrawn attitudes. No one yearns to return to adolescence. It is not so sweet. It does not hold and contain us like the
fantasy of childhood innocence. There are no workshops devoted to
loving and nurturing our inner adolescent. It is a turbulent time
whose mode of reflection does not so easily engage us. It is too
other, painful, and distant. We are far removed.

Interestingly enough, though, we meet the adolescent, in a more
immediate manner than the child, while dreaming. The dream
adolescent is a character close to our heart—her feelings of
embarrassment, exposure, and isolation are near enough at hand
that we can easily make the transit and identify with that element of
self. The awareness of ourselves as children in dreams, in contrast,
is more diffuse, further removed, less accessible, a dim memory. As
an imaginal reality, the adolescent is nearer than we think.

The dream adolescent beckons us to remember. In Jung's sense, it
may serve as a compensation for our grandiose thoughts of how far
we have developed, who we have become, and what we have left
behind. We are abruptly reminded of our weakness, timidity,
introversion, and failures. The dream adolescent may appear as the
unsure one, not knowing where to go, where next to turn. We are
forced to remember our forgotten vulnerability, the feeling of being
exposed and at the mercy of the world. This figure also beckons us
to return to our high-flying thoughts, forgotten dreams, repressed
ambitions, and desire for a different kind of future. It reminds us of
an earlier state of potency and fulfillment.

It is as precarious to encounter this inner adolescent, in both its
vulnerability and grandiose dreams, as it is to tolerate these
emotions in our experiences with actual adolescents. Their failures
reminds us of our own. Their weakness and vulnerability echo
distant memories of those places inside ourselves. And their infinite
potential (Winnicott's term) makes us cringe at our own loss of
potency and possibility, how over the course of years, without even
realizing it, our world has narrowed. What we refer to as a mid-life
crisis represents a return to those youthful energies. But like
everything associated with adolescence, there is a taint of shame.
One is judged to be pathetic, awkwardly trying to reclaim one's
youthful fancies. Thus, this book is more than anything else an
attempt to reawaken the emotions that stir in adolescence so that in
reacquainting ourselves with them as adults, we are less afraid and
more willing to listen.

Part I

Theoretical perspectives on adolescence

Chapter 1

Psychoanalytic approaches

The cosmos in which we place youth and through which we insight youth will influence its pattern of becoming.

James Hillman

INTRODUCTION

Kaplan (1986) traces the invention of adolescence as a distinct phase of life back to two sources: Jean-Jacques Rousseau's allegorical novel, *Emile*, written in the mid-eighteenth century, and G. Stanley Hall (the American psychologist responsible for bringing Freud and Jung to America), who, for the first time, in 1904, made the biological process of maturation, puberty, the basis of the social definition of an entire age group (Kett 1977). In exploring psychological theory which attempts to explain and understand the adolescent state of mind, it is important to remember that our contemporary concept of adolescence as a discrete developmental period is a relatively recent phenomena, "conditioned by social forces . . . reflecting the demographic and industrial conditions of the late nineteenth and early twentieth centuries" (ibid., p. 6).

Our theoretical ideas about the psychology of adolescence dramatically influence what we attend to and value as significant during this period of development. The differing theoretical perspectives rest upon a set of implicit assumptions concerning the course and direction of human development, the nature of the psyche, and the psychological implications of a biological process.

I have chosen to review psychoanalytical perspectives in this chapter and Jungian developmental theory in the next for they offer two of the most well-articulated systems of thought on the psychology of adolescence in the depth-psychological tradition. These perspectives are particularly powerful in disclosing key elements of the adolescent maturational process. In examining them, I will show what remains concealed by the theoretical lenses used to explicate this process, and will provide alternative ways of theorizing that brings to light this veiled material.

THE TRANSFORMATIONS OF PUBERTY: SIGMUND FREUD

It is inevitable that a book attempting to revision our understanding of adolescent psychology must begin by reckoning with Freud. Much of what we currently say and think about adolescent develop-ment originates in Freud's ideas on this subject developed early in the twentieth century. Freud only wrote one major essay exclusively devoted to this topic, "The Transformations of Puberty," as the final part of his *Three Essays On The Theory Of Sexuality* (1905). Most of the other references to adolescence throughout his collected writings assert a negative definition of puberty; Freud repeatedly makes the point that puberty is not, as naively supposed, the first awakening of the sexual instinct in human life. The onset of sexual growth is diphasic: its origin is in childhood, and after a resting period during latency, it re-emerges in puberty. Thus, adoles-cence is evoked by Freud as a signpost on the road to his real destination—his theory of childhood sexuality. The negative defini-tion clearly asserted by Freud tells us that puberty is not originary in terms of the awakening of the sexual instinct; however, as I will show, Freud does not offer any substantive definition of what puberty is, in and of itself, outside of its relationship to childhood.

Consequently, the deeper we look into the vicissitudes of the sexual instinct in puberty, the more is revealed about early child-hood, thus creating a structure of investigation that rests upon a theory of recapitulation that pervades the essence of Freud's analy-sis of adolescence and is taken up, in different ways, by the major psychoanalytical writers on adolescence after Freud. The theory of recapitulation states that some portion of one's early infantile and childhood development gets played out again in a repetitive manner during adolescence. A closer analysis reveals how intimately wed is Freud's theory of adolescence to this notion of recapitulation.

Freud begins his essay on adolescence with the following words: "With the arrival of puberty, changes set in which are destined to give infantile sexual life its final, normal shape" (1905, p. 207). The psychological processes of puberty are rooted in the maturation of the sexual instinct. In describing the nature of transformation in puberty, Freud states:

The sexual instinct has hitherto been predominantly auto-erotic; it now finds a sexual object. Its activity has hitherto been derived from a number of separate instincts and erotogenic zones, which independently of one another, have pursued a certain sort of pleasure as their sole sexual aim. Now, however, a new sexual aim appears, and all the component instincts combine to attain it, while the erotogenic zones become subordinated to the primacy of the genital zone.

(ibid.)

A child's sexual life, vis-à-vis the Oedipus or Electra complex, reaches a first climax in the third to fifth year. Freud describes this as a pre-genital organization of libido, where each separate instinct pursues its own acquisition of pleasure, independent of all the rest. The theoretical conundrum plaguing Freud went something like this: How does the polymorphously perverse child transform into an adult with a fixed and stable sexual identity where the genitals now have primacy among all other zones as the source of pleasure, thus insuring that the sexual instinct is in the service of reproduction? Adolescence becomes very crucial in this scheme, for one of its main goals as a discrete developmental period is to bring about the realization of this new sexual aim, which Freud describes as

the appropriate stimulation of an erotogenic zone (the genital zone itself, in the glans penis) by the appropriate object (the mucous membrane of the vagina); and from the pleasure yielded by this excitation the motor energy is obtained, this time by a reflex path, which brings about the discharge of the sexual substance. This last pleasure is the highest in intensity and its mechanism differs from that of the earlier phase.

(ibid., p. 210)

This high intensity pleasure, which we call orgasm, Freud objectively terms "end-pleasure." It results in a phase in which the tension of libido is extinguished. He distinguishes this from "fore-pleasure," which occurs in infancy and latency and comes about through the stimulation of an erotogenic zone (for example, mother caressing an infant's skin). He states:

If at any point in the sexual process, the fore-pleasure turns out to be too great and the element of the tension too small, the motive for proceeding with the sexual act is abandoned.

(ibid., p. 211)

He goes on to say:

Experience has shown that the precondition for this damaging event is that the erotogenic zone concerned or the corresponding component instinct shall already during childhood have contributed an unusual amount of pleasure.

(ibid.)

On account of this logic, when the transformations of puberty get stuck or fixated, one looks to the cause of that fixation in childhood. The most conspicuous example of this mode of thought can be found in Freud's description of the pubertal processes of young women. There are many powerful and compelling critiques by a host of feminist writers of the grave misconceptions Freud perpetuates in his understanding of women's sexual and emotional development during puberty.[1] In light of these critiques, I review the theory here with the sole purpose of showing how completely Freud was gripped by the idea of adolescence as recapitulation.

According to Freud, little girls experience fore-pleasure through the discharge of sexual excitement in the spasms of the clitoris. During puberty, this sexual excitement is severely repressed. A young woman goes through a period when she is anesthetic, that is, she holds back and denies her sexuality; the excitability of the clitoris, what Freud refers to as her "childish masculinity," is extinguished. This period of dormancy allows the leading erotogenic zone to transfer from the clitoris to the vagina. The transfer culminates when a young woman's sexuality locates itself in the passivity of the vaginal orifice; it is only then that Freud considers her to be sexually mature. He goes on to state:

This anaesthesia may become permanent if the clitoridal zone refuses to abandon its excitability, an event for which the way is prepared precisely by an extensive activity of that zone in childhood.

(ibid., p. 221)

In both cases, for boys and for girls, too much stimulation and pleasure from an erotogenic zone during childhood results in a fixity of development during puberty. Childish pleasures refusing to release their hold on the developing adolescent cause a failure in the maturation of the sexual instinct. That sexual maturation in puberty is determined by early childhood sexuality is reiterated by Freud when he states: "It is only at puberty that the sexual instincts develop to their full intensity; but the direction of the development, as well as all the predispositions for it, have already been determined by the early efflorescence of sexuality during childhood which preceded it" (1923, p. 246).

After eroticism is brought into the service of reproduction, Freud views the second major transformation of puberty, on the psychological side, as the process of finding an appropriate sexual object to fulfill the aim of genital maturity. Freud links sexual satisfaction in an infant with the taking of nourishment. In this schema, the infant's sexual instinct has an object outside of herself, that is, the mother's breast. As the infant begins to recognize that she is separate from mother, the search for an object turns inward and becomes auto-erotic. At puberty, this originary search for an object outside oneself takes its shape in the adolescent's striving for a heterosexual love relationship. A child nursing at its mother's breast is Freud's prototype for every subsequent love relationship.

Although in latency a barrier is erected against incest, the immensely powerful physical and psychological transformations of puberty re-animate the incestuous strivings of the individual, although now in the form of fantasy ideas. In these unconscious fantasies, infantile tendencies emerge in combination with the sexually maturing body and the adolescent is attracted to the opposite-sex parent in accord with their oedipal strivings. Although they are mitigated by the incest taboo, these fantasies now become the basis of the "affectionate current" of sexual life in adolescence.

Here recapitulation bears itself out again. The fantasies of the pubertal period originate in the infantile sexual researches that were abandoned in childhood, that is, those initial attempts of children to discover the nature of sexuality and their own sexual constitution. Freud states:

Some among the sexual phantasies of the pubertal period are especially prominent, and are distinguished by their very general occurrence and by being to a great extent independent of individual experience. Such are the adolescent's phantasies of overhearing his parents in sexual intercourse, of having been seduced at an early age by someone he loves and of having been threatened with castration; such, too, are his phantasies of being in the womb, and even of experiences there, and the so-called "Family Romance," in which he reacts to the difference between his attitude towards his parents now and in his childhood.

(1905, p. 226)

Although the Oedipus complex peaks in infantile sexuality, it nonetheless exercises a decisive role on the sexuality of adults through its after-effects. The origin of these after-effects occurs in the intensity with which the Oedipus complex penetrates the heart of puberty. For Freud, the repudiation of incestuous phantasies is the most significant, painful and difficult psychological achievement of this time of life. It is the essence of the pubertal process.

A child's affection for its parents is the most important infantile trace that gets revived in puberty. A young man or woman falling in love for the first time chooses a person who re-animates the image of mother or father. Object choice in puberty is then ultimately based on these childhood prototypes. Freud states this unequivocally:

The innumerable peculiarities of the erotic life of human beings as well as the compulsive character of the process of falling in love itself are quite unintelligible except by reference back to childhood and as being residual effects of childhood.

(ibid., p. 229)

Freud's seed ideas of the nature of adolescence as recapitulation sprouted in the theories of four major psychoanalysts.

ONTOGENY RECAPITULATES PHYLOGENY: ERNEST JONES' CONTRIBUTION TO THE PSYCHOANALYTIC UNDERSTANDING OF ADOLESCENCE

Jones (1922), in his paper, "Some Problems of Adolescence," takes up themes that directly touch upon Freud's theory of recapitulation. He begins by looking at the differences between children and adults and ponders the remarkable changes that happen between these two developmental periods. He then turns his attention toward adolescence to give his account of this transitional period of life. He states:

Before these important changes can be brought about, the transitional stage of adolescence has to be passed through, and this is effected in a highly interesting manner. At puberty, a regression takes place in the direction of infancy, of the first period of all, and the person lives over again, though on another plane, the development he passed through in the first five years of life . . . . Put it another way, it signifies that the individual recapitulates and expands in the second decennium of life the development he passed through during the first five years of life, just as he recapitulates during these first five years the experiences of thousands of years in his ancestry and during the pre-natal period those of million of years.

(ibid., pp. 39–40)

For Jones, then, there is something astonishingly similar between the first five years of life (which he is here referring to as infancy) and the adolescent years. Overwhelming emotional experiences distinguish both periods, which leads Jones to characterize them as the most passionate ages of human being. He then goes on to outline with great specificity what he sees as the analogies between these two periods of development.

Both infancy and adolescence depend on a heightened capacity for tolerating stimulation and inhibiting response. For example, a central task of infancy is the acquirement of control over the acts of excretion. Analogously, a central task of adolescence is the acquirement of self-control. Repression is also crucial in both periods. In infancy, the psyche is being readied for the eventual forgetting of the important events of these first five years. For adolescents, ideas tolerable before puberty—for example, the desire for the pleasure of parental caresses—now becomes repressed.

For both small children and adolescents, altruism and an interest in the outer world come about as libidinal attachments extend away from the self toward outside objects. Both infancy and adolescence have this quality of an initial pre-occupation with the self that later is transformed to an interest in and engagement with the world.

Finally, adolescent dependency is analogous to the need for love characteristic of the oedipal phase of infancy. For example, a young man's feeling of rivalry with his father in adolescence is explained by a regression to a prior oedipal relationship. The defensive nature of his constant rejection of the caresses and intimacies of his mother is explained in terms of fighting off a regressive pull to an earlier period of closeness.

What does Jones mean when he asserts that an adolescent lives over again on another plane the development he passed through in the first five years of life? How is he thinking of the nature of recapitulation? Here, we witness a literal rendering of Freud's idea that an individual going through puberty gets fixated at a certain psychosexual stage both in terms of object choice and physiological development, depending on how he passed through this stage as a child.

Jones states:

> That the autoerotic phases belong to the earlier stage of adolescence rather than the later is familiar enough knowledge. With it goes the tendency to introversion and a richer life of secret phantasy, together with the greater preoccupation with the self and the varying degrees of shyness and self-consciousness, which are so often prominent features during adolescence. The anal-sadistic phases varies in intensity, but it is characteristic enough for the nice gentle lad of ten to change into the rough and untidy boy of thirteen, to the great distress of his female relatives; extravagance, procrastination, obstinacy, passion for collecting, and other traits of anal-erotic origin often become especially prominent at this age. The narcissism may be shown in either a positive or negative way: the bumptiousness, conceit and cock-sureness of youth are as well-recognized characteristics of this stage in development as the opposite ones of self-deprecation, uncertainty and lack of confidence . . . . The homosexual phase is often more positive than negative and is far commoner during adolescence than at any later age . . . . The heterosexual impulse . . . most often breaks through the barriers of prohibition and reaches a directly sexual goal.
>
> (ibid., pp. 41–2)

Along these lines, Jones contends that the five stages of psychosexual development leading up to the resolution of the Oedipus complex in infancy (that is, from auto-erotic to anal-erotic to narcissistic to homosexual to heterosexual) are repeated in adolescence. Thus, if a person had difficulty passing through the masturbatory phase of adolescence, one can ascertain that there was significant difficulty in this respect during childhood. If homosexuality is a problem in adolescence, one finds a similar fixation during childhood.

In summary, Jones' rendering of recapitulation is highly deterministic. He states that:

adolescence recapitulates infancy and that the precise way in which a given person will pass through the necessary stages of development in adolescence is to a very great extent determined by the form of his infantile development.

(ibid., p. 41)

ADOLESCENCE AND THE DEFENSE AGAINST THE ID: ANNA FREUD

Anna Freud (1966) faults academic psychology for assuming that adolescence is of utmost importance in the development of the individual, serving as the beginning and root of sexual life, character formation, and the capacity to love. Psychoanalysis has corrected this view, she writes, by showing that sexual life actually begins in the first years of life. The individual's capacity to love has its origins not in puberty, but rather in the early infantile sexual period during which important pre-genital phases of sexual organization are passed through (outlined by Sigmund Freud). Following Sigmund Freud and Jones, Anna Freud sees adolescence as the first recapitulation of the infantile sexual period. A second recapitulation takes place during the climacteric, commonly referred to as the "change of life."

From a structural point of view, Anna Freud denotes the similarities and differences between infancy, adolescence, and the climacteric. In each case, a relatively strong id confronts a relatively weak ego. The sexual wishes, object cathexes, and fantasies that comprise the id remain basically consistent throughout each of these periods of development. The ego's capacity for transformation accounts for the differences. For example, the ego in early childhood and the ego at puberty are distinct in their direction, content, and in their knowledge and capabilities. Different defense mechanisms are employed as well. Anna Freud's contribution to the psychoanalytical understanding of adolescence is her articulation of the specific ways the ego transforms at puberty as distinct from any other phase of life.

Since later ego development can only be understood in terms of what came earlier, Anna Freud describes the early development of the ego in infancy and latency in order to illuminate the disturbances to which the ego is vulnerable during puberty. For little children, the demands for instinctual gratification arising from the wishes characteristic of the oral, anal, and phallic phases are immensely urgent. The ego that confronts these demands is still being formed and is therefore very weak; however, the child is not overwhelmed by unbridled instinct. The promises and threats of other people (for example, parents and teachers) manifest themselves in the child as hopes for love and expectations for punishment and thereby inhibit the gratification of instinctual wishes. The outside world soon establishes a representative in the child's psyche (which Anna Freud calls objective anxiety,) the precursor of the superego. The ego must hold itself in balance between the urges of the instincts and the pressures from without. The infantile period ends when the ego has taken up a solid position in its battle against the id. It is now capable of deciding which instincts can be gratified and which must be renounced.

During latency, the strength of the instincts decline, resulting in a truce in the defensive warfare of the ego against the id. The child now has the leisure to devote herself to other activities in the outside world. The superego, which embodies the demands of those in charge of the child, is now permanently set up within the ego.

The truce, however, does not last long. The physiological changes which accompany the psychical changes at puberty bring about an influx of libido. The balance between ego and id achieved in latency is destroyed and inner conflicts arise anew. With puberty, increased quantities of libido are at the id's disposal, thus potentially enabling the ego to cathect any id impulse that arises. During this period the id is conceived of as being identical to the id at infancy. Its latent wishes and desires remain unchanged. The following description of id impulses at puberty brings this point home and reveals the place in Anna Freud's theory where recapitulation has the greatest import. She states:

> Aggressive impulses are intensified to the point of complete unruliness, hunger becomes voracity, and the naughtiness of the latency period turns into the criminal behavior of adolescence. Oral and anal interests, long submerged, come to the surface again. Habits of cleanliness, laboriously acquired during the latency period, give place to pleasure in dirt and disorder, and instead of modesty and sympathy we find exhibitionistic tenden-

cies, brutality and cruelty to animals. The reaction formations, which seemed to be firmly established in the structure of the ego, threaten to fall to pieces. At the same time, old tendencies which had disappeared come into consciousness. The oedipal wishes are fulfilled in the form of fantasies and daydreams, in which they have undergone but little distortion; in boys ideas of castration and in girls penis envy once more become the center of interest. *There are very few new elements in the invading forces.* Their onslaught merely brings once more to the surface the familiar content of the early infantile sexuality of children.

(1966, p. 146) (Italics mine)

In this quote, Anna Freud is working out her understanding of how recapitulation happens in adolescence, as distinct from Sigmund Freud and Ernest Jones, who located the source of recapitulation in the resolution of intrapsychic conflicts as one passes through the psychosexual stages of childhood. For Anna Freud, the source of recapitulation is the unchanging nature of the id's wishes and fantasies from infancy onward. Nothing new or originary is occurring except for the ego's capacity for modifying its responses to these powerful instinctual forces.

During puberty, infantile sexuality, now resuscitated, encounters new conditions. The infantile ego was capable of revolting against the pressures of the outside world and allying with the id to obtain instinctual gratification (Sigmund Freud's notion of fore-pleasure). If the ego of the adolescent makes a similar move, it comes into conflict with the superego. The ego at this period desires to preserve the balance achieved during latency. To do so it must defend itself against instinctual demands in a redoubled effort, utilizing defense mechanisms such as regression, displacement, and denial.

Danger, for the adolescent, is located not only in the id's impulses and fantasies, but also in the very existence of libidinal cathexes to love objects from the individual's oedipal and pre-oedipal past. Although in latency these attachments were depotentiated or completely inhibited, adolescence brings them once again to the fore. Pregenital urges or newly acquired genital ones are in danger of making contact with these fantasies. The adolescent experiences tremendous anxiety in trying to eliminate his ties to infantile objects.

In her paper "Adolescence" (1958), Anna Freud enumerates the four types of defenses that the adolescent employs against the anxiety that is aroused in response to infantile object ties. They are as follows:

1 *Defense by displacement of libido*: In this case, libido is suddenly withdrawn from the parents and transferred to either parent substitutes, leaders, or peers. This is often successful. Parents are stripped of their importance and pre-genital and genital drives cease to be threatening. Guilt and anxiety decrease and repressed sexual and aggressive wishes find expression in the wider environment.

2 *Defense by reversal of affect*: Here, adolescents defend against incestuous emotions felt toward the parents by changing them into their opposite. Love, dependence, and respect are changed into their opposites, namely hate, fierce independence, and contempt. This reversal frees one from parental ties. According to Anna Freud, this defense is less successful than the others because it does not reach past the conscious layer of the mind and the adolescent still remains firmly rooted within the family.

3 *Defense by withdrawal of libido to the self*: If an adolescent withdraws libido from the parents and it does not extend toward a new object outside the family, it remains trapped within the self. Thus, the ego and superego have a tendency to become over-inflated. Clinically, the predilection of adolescents for ideas of grandeur, fantasies of unlimited power, and fierce idealism are explained as an enactment of this defense.

4 *Defense by regression*: If the anxiety aroused by infantile object ties is too strong, the most primitive defense employed by adolescents is "primary identification," in which the ego is in a one-to-one state of identification with the objects of infancy. This state of being implies regressive changes in all parts of the personality, including a lapse in ego functioning and blurred distinctions between the internal and external world.

Because the id impulses are so strong and unwavering, old defenses are employed and new ones created in order to protect the adolescent from the onslaught of overwhelming instinctual force. Adolescence is characterized in this orientation as an essentially defensive period of development. Such an approach provides a powerful hermeneutic for understanding much of what gets played out in adolescence as a defense against the regressive pull to the past.

ADOLESCENCE AS THE SECOND INDIVIDUATION PROCESS: PETER BLOS

As has been shown, Anna Freud explained the emotional upsets and structural upheavals of adolescence in terms of the ego's struggle to master the tensions and pressures arising from the drives. For her, danger to ego integrity derived from both the strength of the pubertal drives and the regressive pull toward the objects of infancy and childhood. Anna Freud's theory turns on her notion of the adolescent defenses which protect the ego from being overwhelmed by the anxiety caused by the id impulses and love objects of the individual's oedipal and pre-oedipal past.

Peter Blos (1962, 1967) also tries to explain the meaning of the perplexing behaviors of adolescents and the unique emotional turbulence of this age. The primary difference between his and Anna Freud's psychoanalytical explication turns upon his notion of ego regression, which Anna Freud calls a primary defense. In contrast, Blos views ego regression in adolescence as an essential component in the progressive development of the human being. In exploring the dynamics of this view, it quickly becomes apparent once again that Blos, like Sigmund Freud, Jones, and Anna Freud before him, uses the lens of recapitulation to focus his under-standing of adolescence.

Blos refers to adolescence as the second individuation process. His use of the term individuation to describe adolescence has its origins in Margaret Mahler's (1963) theory of the separation–individuation process in which the infant progressively emerges from a state of symbiosis with the mother during the first three years of life to become an individuated toddler. In a parallel fashion, the adolescent sheds family dependencies and loosens infantile object ties in order to become an individuated adult member of society. Both processes encompass an alternating series of progressive and regressive moves.

Blos (1967, p. 159) amplifies a theme of Anna Freud's by empha-sizing the way in which the adolescent disengages from the internalized love and hate objects of childhood in order to find extrafamilial love and hate objects in the external world. Drive development and ego maturation exert a continuous influence on each other during this process. As infantile object ties loosen and the adolescent ego has the possibility of establishing more mature relationships outside the family, it is confronted with the outmoded and partly abandoned ego states and drive gratifications of childhood. The adolescent longs for the comforts of drive gratification, but fears re-involvement in infantile object relations. This is the paradoxical point upon which Blos bases his concept of adolescence as the second individuation process.

It is only through contact with these inferior ego states that the psychic structures of adolescence have a chance to transform, thereby allowing the adolescent to become an individuated being. Blos contends that what initially appears to be regression actually serves a progressive developmental goal. For example, he views adolescent daydreaming as a regressive phenomenon that, through its ability to try an action out in fantasy, allows an adolescent to assimilate in small doses the affective experience toward which progressive development is moving. Along these lines, Blos quotes Nietzsche's aphorism: "They say he is going backwards, indeed, he is, because he attempts to take a big jump" (Blos 1962, p. 92). Drive regression and ego regression at this time of life constitute an obligatory component of human development. This is best articulated by exploring Blos' conception of ego regression.

Ego regression implies the re-experiencing of abandoned or partly abandoned ego states that once served as places of safety during infancy and childhood in response to stress. This re-experiencing does not, however, affect the whole ego. The reality-bound, self-observing part of the ego is normally kept intact during this regression. Blos identifies the adolescent's idolization and adoration of famous men and women as an example of a regressed ego state. It is analogous to the idealized parent of the child's younger years. Infantile ego states are also recognizable in emotional states akin to merger. This is frequently seen in an adolescent's fascination with abstract philosophical ideas and passionate political or religious involvement. Blos believes that such ego states of quasi-merger through the realm of symbolic representations are sought as a temporary respite from the pain and chaos of ego regression. In other words, mature ideas and ideologies are accessed by the adolescent as a safeguard against total merger with infantile, internalized objects. The functioning of the critical and observing ego prevents ego regression from deteriorating into a total state of merger. Blos goes on to say:

Limited ego regression, typical as well as obligatory in

adolescence, can occur only within a relatively intact ego. There is no doubt that adolescent ego regression puts the ego to a severe test. It has been pointed out earlier that, up to adolescence, the parental ego makes itself available to the child and lends structure and organization to its ego as a functional entity. Adolescence disrupts this alliance, and ego regression lays bare the intactness and defectiveness of the early ego organization, which derived decisive positive and negative qualities from the passage through the first separation–individuation phase in the second and third year of life.

(Blos 1967, p. 167)

Undoubtedly the idea of recapitulation serves as an underpinning for Blos' theory. Early ego organization, from infancy onward, determines how well an adolescent is able to negotiate the developmental crisis of ego regression. In a manner similar to Sigmund Freud and Jones, who interpreted individual impasses in adolescence as fixations in the early psychosexual stages of infancy, Blos indicates that ego regression during adolescence is an actual re-experiencing of traumatic states from infancy and childhood. Adolescent play acting and experimentation, as well as much of what is considered "delinquent" pathology, are seen by Blos as miniature editions of early traumatic states that the adolescent contrives in order to work through the dangerous situations that survived the periods of infancy and childhood. Here, adolescence offers a second chance for correcting the traumatic response of a child who did not have control. Now, as an adolescent, the reality-bound and self-observing part of the ego is brought to bear upon the residues of infantile trauma, conflict, or fixation. They are modified by the ego's extended resources as it grows and matures.

The adolescent emotionally encounters the passions of infancy and early childhood. The manner in which he confronts these early experiences and forces the memory of these events to surrender their original cathexes is what Blos considers to be the essence of the individuation process. Internal changes accompanying this process cause a psychic restructuring. The decathexes from parental object representations brings about a general instability in the ego. Blos states:

In the effort to protect the integrity of the ego organization, a familiar variety of defensive, restitutive, adaptive and maladaptive maneuvers are set into motion before a new psychic equilibrium is established.

(ibid., p. 173)

Blos emphasizes the restitutive and adaptive nature of these maneuvers, whereas Anna Freud only spoke of their defensive capacity. Concerning the adolescent's encounter with early childhood emotions and the resulting psychic restructuring, Blos' thinking is dialectical. He moves between Anna Freud's notion of defense as a displacement of libido, where the adolescent fights against regression, and defense by regression, where the adolescent is in a one-to-one state of identification with the infantile objects. For Blos, some regression must occur so that the disengagement from early object relations and infantile ego states can take place, thereby allowing for the reorganization of psychic structures. He is looking for a half-way point in which he can say the regression is no longer defensive, but progressive and essential to the task of psychic restructuring central to the adolescent individuation process.

Psychoanalytically, primitive defenses are commonly understood as major obstacles to normal development. Generally, regression is thought of as a psychic process in opposition to progressive development, drive maturation, and ego differentiation. Blos is re-thinking a traditional psychoanalytical principle in light of adolescent individuation.

However, Blos is cautious in these remarks and certainly does not overvalue or idealize the regressive states that lead to adolescent individuation. He is quick to show when they can lead the adolescent down the wrong path, to what Laufer and Laufer, in the next section, describe as a developmental breakdown. Blos states:

Adolescent ego regression within a defective ego structure engulfs the regressed ego in its early abnormal condition. The distinction between the pathognomic and normal nature of ego regression lies precisely in the alternative whether ego regression to the undifferentiated state is approximated or consummated. This distinction is comparable to that between a dream and a hallucination. The regression to a seriously defective ego of early childhood will turn a developmental impasse, so typical of adolescence, into a temporary or permanent psychotic illness. The degree of early ego inadequacy often does not become apparent until adolescence, when regression fails to serve progressive development, precludes individuation, and closes the door to drive and ego maturation.

(ibid., p. 167)

ADOLESCENCE AND DEVELOPMENTAL BREAKDOWN: LAUFER AND LAUFER

In the introduction of their book, *Adolescence and Developmental Breakdown: A Psychoanalytic View* (1984), Moses Laufer and M. Egle' Laufer claim that they will not turn to a person's early development in order to understand the psychopathology in adolescence. They purport at the outset to "confine ourselves to an examination of the period of adolescence itself" (1984, p. xi), and view it as a progressive phenomenon, that is, they assume the development during adolescence makes a major contribution to adult normality or abnormality.

Laufer and Laufer base their theory of adolescent development on Sigmund Freud's proclamation that the pubertal processes give infantile sexual life its final normal shape. Unlike Anna Freud, who views adolescence in terms of the anxiety created by the ego's struggle against id impulses, or Blos, who defines adolescence as the second individuation process involving ego regression, Laufer and Laufer follow very closely Freud's original statement about puberty. They echo Freud when they say that the developmental function of adolescence is "the establishment of the final sexual organization, which from the point of view of the body must now include the physically mature genitals" (ibid., p. 5).

Laufer and Laufer's theorizing attends to the ways in which adolescents come to terms psychologically with having physically mature genitals. During this period, the content of the sexual wishes and the oedipal identifications become integrated into an irreversible sexual identity. Oedipal wishes are tested in the context of a sexually mature adolescent who must achieve a compromise between what is wished for and what can be allowed. This compromise defines the person's sexual identity. Most importantly, for Laufer and Laufer the establishment of the final sexual organization is the essential task of adolescence. This final organization is the lens through which one must view all other adolescent processes, including changes in relation to oedipal objects, one's peer group, and one's body.

A key to understanding the value and importance that Laufer

and Laufer place on this task can be found by looking at their concept of the central masturbation fantasy. In accord with Freudian theory, they assume that as a part of normal development from infancy, a person gratifies instinctual demands by using either his own body or an object. The pre-oedipal child has a wide range of autoerotic activities, games, and fantasies that help recreate the relationship to the gratifying mother. After resolution of the oedipal complex, the superego arrives on the scene to judge whether a regressive satisfaction is acceptable or not. Laufer and Laufer define the central masturbation fantasy as that fantasy which contains the various regressive satisfactions and the main sexual identifications that are allowable to the ego at the time of the resolution of the oedipal complex.

During childhood and latency, this fantasy is unconscious. With adolescence and the physical maturation of the genitals, this fantasy takes on new meaning and makes demands on the ego which put its defensive structure under great stress. One remembers similar observations by Anna Freud, who saw the danger in newly acquired genital urges making contact with the infantile fantasies which were repressed during latency. The danger lies in the fact that the adolescent can literally act upon these fantasies with their newly matured genitals. Laufer and Laufer contend that there is a central fantasy that gets enacted during masturbation which the adolescent now yearns to live out in her object relations and sexual life. This fantasy is frightening to the adolescent because of its power and potential for destructiveness.

The adolescent attempts to integrate the central masturbation fantasy through experimentation and trial-action. Normal development proceeds when the masturbation fantasy includes the active seeking out of a love object. This results in adolescents' feeling in control of their sexuality and having an ability to make choices. Pathological development occurs when the defensive organization cannot ward off the regressive pull of pre-genital wishes. Laufer and Laufer point to the fantasies of a group of adolescents who were hospitalized after either their first emission or soon after the beginning of menstruation. These adolescents stated that certain fantasies drove them mad. "Sometimes, more specifically, they said that they either wished for intercourse with parents of the opposite sex or became terrified by the thought that they would kill one of their parents" (ibid., p. 39). Thus, Laufer and Laufer define developmental breakdown in adolescence as

... the unconscious rejection of the sexual body and an accompanying feeling of being passive in the face of demands coming from one's own body, with the result that one's genitals are ignored or disowned or different than what one wanted them to be. ... [A] breakdown [occurs] in the process of integrating the physically mature body image into the representation of oneself.

(ibid., p. 22)

Freud considers the body and the first relation to the body via the mother to be the foundation of future psychic structures—body ego as precursor of ego organization. Laufer and Laufer pick up on this notion that the relationship to one's own body is central throughout life. They state:

We believe that from puberty to the end of adolescence, that is, to about age twenty-one, this relationship to one's own sexually mature body encompasses one's past history and reactivates conflicts and anxiety that repeats solutions of the past but within a new and much more dangerous context.

(ibid., p. xiv)

They go on to state that adolescence is

a process of experiencing, reorganizing and integrating one's past psychological development within a new context of physical sexual maturity.

(ibid., p. 4)

From these passages, one can see how recapitulation plays a central role in their theorizing. It is implicit in Laufer and Laufer's theoretical position that an adolescent's sexual life and object relations are best understood in the context of his infantile sexuality, autoeroticism, early relationships to gratifying objects, and pre-oedipal fantasies.

The form and content of the central masturbation fantasy is solidified by the resolution of the Oedipus complex. This occurs from the ages of three to five years, during the phallic-oedipal period. Resolution of the Oedipus complex implies an unconscious compromise that satisfies the id and external reality and is consistent with the awareness of one's own helplessness in the face of the oedipal parents. At this time, a child realizes his or her own body is separate from the parent's body. Laufer and Laufer go on to say:

But "oedipal resolution" also implies the ultimate narcissistic cathexis of the sexual body image, which means that the preoedipal relationships and internalizations are now emotionally experienced as love or hatred for one's own phallic or castrated body. In other words, the earlier feelings of love and hatred from the parents become part of the love and hatred by the child of his own body, now experienced as phallic or castrated.

(ibid., p. 28)

The central masturbation fantasy renews contact with pre-genital incestuous wishes and strivings. Laufer and Laufer posit that this provides the adolescent with access to experiencing a reaction to being sexually male or female in terms of his or her original reaction to experiencing the body as being either phallic or castrated. Thus, the establishment of the final sexual organization in adolescence, the image of oneself as either male or female, is a recapitulation of an experience that occurred at the end of the phallic-oedipal period. Fixation in adolescence, according to this theory, necessarily implies an earlier oedipal fixation.

REVIEW OF THE PSYCHOANALYTIC THEORISTS

As we have seen, each of the five psychoanalytical theorists hold fast to some form or other of recapitulation theory in their analysis of adolescence. It is my contention that the idea of adolescence as recapitulation nullifies a phenomenological viewing of the adolescent process. Underlying the idea of recapitulation is an assumption that what is happening during this time can best be grasped by looking back on an earlier period of development. If theory compels us to look toward early childhood to explain an adolescent's mood, behavior, and comportment, is it not all the more difficult for us, as clinicians, to stay with, perceive and comprehend the adolescent before us in the present moment?

Kegan, in his book *The Evolving Self*, provides an insightful critique of the psychoanalytical investment in viewing adolescence as recapitulation. Basing his work on a constructive-developmental approach growing out of the Piagetian tradition, Kegan views infancy as being characterized by the beginning of meaning-making activity for an infant, what he calls the "psychological" meaning of evolution: a lifetime activity of differentiating and integrating what is taken as self and what is taken as other. "While infancy has great

importance for a neo-Piagetian view, it is not, in its most fundamental respect, qualitatively different from any other moment in the
lifespan" (1982, p. 77).

Thus, when distinctive features of this differentiating and integrating process of infancy recur in new forms at a period later in
development, they are not seen as later manifestations of what
happens in infancy, but "contemporary manifestations of meaning-
making" (ibid., p. 78). On this account, Kegan points out that the
psychoanalytical notion of recapitulation in adolescence—for
example, viewing the difficulties that an adolescent experiences in
separating from family in light of what went on during the separa-
tion-individuation phase of early childhood—is misleading. The
connection between the two is categorical, that is, both evoke
similar themes and developmental struggles, thus revealing the
continuity of life themes, but not causal. He states:

> While constructive-developmental theory is less inclined to
> perceive an identity between childhood and later lived
> phenomena, it is more inclined than psychoanalytic theory to see
> the unity and continuity of such phenomena. The evolutionary
> model permits one to observe recurring phenomena of similar
> color and tone throughout the lifespan without having at the
> same time to regard such similarities as regression or recapitula-
> tion . . . these later phenomena, while similar on the surface, are
> also far more complex and importantly different than their
> earlier cousins.
>
> (ibid., p. 188)

In this regard, Kegan faults the psychoanalytical position for
missing the importance of the latency stage where a great deal of
development and change is occurring, especially in terms of the
impulses. "Lacking a modern evolutionary model it fails to consider
the possibility that the intellectual development and self-sufficiency
of middle childhood (which it recognizes) are actually in part those
same impulses integrated into a more complex organization" (ibid.).
Hence, for Kegan, there is a world of difference between the oedipal
child's newly acquired ability to resist striking out at someone in
rage and the adolescent's increasing ability for self-direction in the
absence of another's expectations. In contrast to Anna Freud's
conception of the id remaining essentially the same from childhood
to adolescence, Kegan states, "From a constructive-developmental
view, impulse is not an unchanged phenomenon throughout life

which is merely differently managed by more complex defenses as the person develops" (ibid., p. 189).

Cognitive changes contribute to the kind of differences Kegan is evoking. Abstract reasoning, which Piaget calls formal operations, emerges at adolescence from the stage of concrete operations. Now, an adolescent has the ability to "unhinge the concrete world as 'what is' is seen merely as an instance of 'what might be.' The actual becomes but one instance (and often one not very interesting instance) of the infinite array of the possible" (ibid., p. 38). This cognitive shift ushers in a whole new mode of meaning making.

Therapeutically, it has considerable consequences, for once we free ourselves from the idea of recapitulation which fails to take into account these important differences between children and adolescents, we can see that what Kegan calls the emergence of abstract reasoning and what I prefer to call a developing capacity for fantasy and imagination, are natural modes in which adolescents can be engaged therapeutically. For example, an adolescent's ability to imagine what could be in terms of future possibilities allows them to use the imagination as a vehicle for containing and giving expression to the bodily impulses that exuberantly burst forth into consciousness urging the sudden transformation of thought and feeling into action.

The quiet reflective space of a journal becomes important in this regard. We need only to remember the incredible gift Anne Frank left to the world with her diary. There, through daily journal writing, she found containment for her deepest capacity for imagining and playing with life's possibilities in conjunction with her emerging sexuality and bodily transformations. The plastic and literary arts—painting, drawing, sculpting, writing, and poetry writing—become important tools the therapist can utilize to help an adolescent contain the newly emerging emotions deeply rooted in the body.[2] The protected space of the therapeutic relationship can become a vessel where this kind of self-expression is given value and credence.

The idea of recapitulation, by contrast, assumes that the essence of the adolescent process is sexual, given the nature of infantile and childhood sexuality of which it is a repetition. Think back to Freud's theoretical maneuverings which intended to insure that adolescence brings about a permanent, stable heterosexual identity. With this kind of narrow focus on sexuality as a fixed, heterosexual instinctual drive, the deeper implications of one's emerging sexuality, as well as other aspects of the adolescent process which are non-sexual in nature, are missed. Jung's revisioning of Freud's libido theory, which I address in Chapter 5, will offer a contrasting vision. In this light, we will examine how psychic energy in adolescence moves between instinctual impulses and expressions of the spirit such as religious inclinations and the capacity for reflection and self-awareness.

Another theme that permeates all of the psychoanalytical theorists, but is most explicitly stated by Anna Freud, is the defensive nature of adolescence. She points to the paradoxical nature of the adolescent ego trapped between powerful id and superego forces. From this perspective, the crises and upheavals of adolescence can be interpreted as defenses against the overwhelming internal forces that plague the adolescent mind. This way of thinking casts a shadow on the unique and revelatory nature of the adolescent's thoughts, feelings, and behaviors.

Winnicott (1963b) offers a compelling alternative. He speaks of the adolescent's need to hide and conceal from others the moods and feelings that are stirred up during puberty. Here, the defenses are seen as offering a protective cocoon, shielding an internal process from impingement by the external world: defense as a kind of brooding. Along these lines, Winnicott warns of the danger, therapeutically, of prematurely analyzing an adolescent when the process of self-formation is in need of concealment.

Both of these themes, recapitulation and defense, imply that nothing new is going on in adolescence. Recall Anna Freud's quotation, cited earlier, that the id's wishes and fantasies do not transform from the time of infancy. This leads her to say of the emergence of id impulses in adolescence, "There are very few new elements in the invading force" (1966, p. 146). Nothing originary is occurring. This kind of determinism, although conceptually convincing and illuminating, has a tendency to blind one to the prospective function of adolescence as an originary and unique time of human development. Certainly childhood forces are active and present in adolescence; however, isn't there something else going on? That "something else" is the main theme of this work.

Another way to grasp the originary nature of this time is to think back from an adult standpoint on what happened to us during our own adolescence. The crises that marked this period often had significant implications for where one's life was headed and what direction one ended up embarking on. As adults, our dreams still take us back to high school and those nascent feelings touched off by early romances and passionate friendships. Why does the psyche continually return us to this period of development? What was borne there that needs to be recalled and remembered?

Chapter 2

Developmental analytical psychology

INTRODUCTION

One branch of analytical psychology, which Andrew Samuels (1985) terms the "Developmental School" employs a Jungian approach to the theory and practice of adolescent psychotherapy. This is outlined in a recent book of essays edited by Mara Sidoli and Gustav Bovensiepen (1995), *Incest Fantasies and Self-Destructive Acts*. Sidoli and Bovensiepen refer to their approach as "developmental analytical psychology." The most dramatic difference in this approach from the psychoanalytical theorizing we have reviewed thus far is a conceptual shift away from an emphasis on the ego and its mechanisms of defense during adolescence toward an analysis of the transformations of what Jung terms the "self" (the totality of conscious and unconscious personality in which the ego is contained). Jung's self is viewed as the force that holds together the adolescent's inner world during the upheavals of adolescence; it has its own set of defenses in contradistinction to the defenses of the ego.

I find this to be a very welcome move, for it allows a broader range of interpretative possibility, as the realm of the self is far greater than that of the ego. When adolescent symptoms are understood in terms of their implications for the viability of the ego–self axis, affects and behaviors that have the tendency to be viewed as pathologies evoke new significances. In Part III, which focuses upon Jung's notion of individuation, I will draw together Jung's concepts of the self and the self-regulating nature of the psyche in order to show how this combination of ideas alters our view of the clinician's role in the therapeutic process with adolescents.

Developmental analytical psychology draws upon the work of Michael Fordham, who operationalized Jung's theoretical model of the self as a developmental construct. Fordham hypothesizes an original or primary self, existing at the beginning of life and containing the whole range of innate archetypal potentials that can be given expression in a lifetime. The primary self of the infant

> is radically disrupted by birth in which the psychosoma is flooded by stimuli both internal and external which give rise to prototypic anxiety. Following this, a steady state re-establishes itself and the first clear sequences of disturbances followed by resting or steady states has been completed. The sequence repeats again and again during maturation and the motive forces behind them are called deintegrative and integrative. At first the sequences are rapid, but as psychic organisation proceeds, they become spread over longer periods till relative stability is attained for most of the time.

> (1994, p. 75)

The deintegrative/integrative process corresponds to the opening-up and closing-down system of the self that allows for psychological maturation.

In a compelling manner, the Developmental Analytical School applies Fordham's process of integration and deintegration to adolescence in order to provide a theoretical understanding of the fragmentary nature of the adolescent state of mind. Puberty is seen as triggering the deintegration of the self so that the adolescent is open to both internal and external experience. The state of being deintegrated causes confusion and upset to the adolescent, but, analogous to Blos' idea of ego regression, it is necessary for progressive development.

Fordham clearly distinguishes between deintegration and disintegration, a state of being where the ego is completely overwhelmed and things fall apart beyond repair. The boundary between deintegrative and disintegrative states has significant therapeutic implications. Sensing where a series of events are headed and whether or not to intervene based on the adolescent's ability to recover and reintegrate is one of the main discriminations an adolescent therapist must make. One common mistake in many treatments is premature panic at a natural process of deintegration. Such panic can block the natural recovery from a state of deintegration, thus preventing further maturation. This is an extremely important matter that I will take up again in Part II, as I explore Robert Jay Lifton's work on life and death imagery in adolescence. Sidoli provides an apt description of the deintegrative processes that occur in adolescence. She states:

> ... with the upsurge of sexuality the young person has to undergo a major deintegration in order to be able to integrate all the major changes which are occurring both in his body and in his or her new experiences of life. This deintegration will reactivate those archetypal motifs in the unconscious related to the difficult task of acquiring sexual and intellectual capacities, compounded with the urge to live these out—moving away from home and severing childhood ties to the parents. It is a stage of renegotiating one's lifestyle and identity, and brings about conflicts and powerful emotional and anxiety states. Unconscious fantasies and primitive collective archetypal motifs become activated, and a regression–progression dichotomy sets in, usually acted out in relation to parents, teachers and society.
>
> (Sidoli 1989, p. 163)

The regression that Sidoli refers to (the upsurge of sexuality triggering the deintegration of the self) is understood in terms of the adolescent ego being catapulted into relationship with early infantile objects. Thus, developmental analytical psychology rests upon as strong a notion of recapitulation as we saw with the psychoanalytical theorists. The regression of libido, however, is not to the oedipal past, but to the pre-oedipal period of development. Here, the move is made to integrate the work of Melanie Klein in her description of pre-oedipal states with Jung. Kleinian part-objects in the pre-oedipal state between mother and child are amplified using Jung's archetypal imagery.

The Developmental Analytical School draws upon much of Jung's early theory about the progression and regression of the libido, especially in his book *Symbols of Transformation* (*CW* 5), as a means of providing amplificatory material for this process. Jung's regression of the libido is taken in this context to mean a regression to pre-genital parental imagoes in the unconscious. From the perspective of developmental analytical psychology, separation in adolescence presupposes an emotional and affective revival of the infant's early relationship to mother, especially to the body of mother. And, following closely along the lines of Blos' work, adolescence as a phase of the individuation process offers a second chance for integration of those infantile parts that could not be integrated during early development. Infantile conflicts are reactivated and a second chance is given for personality reorganization.

CRITIQUE OF THE DEVELOPMENTAL ANALYTICAL APPROACH

As an augmentation of my general critique of the theory of recapitulation, which I have discussed in relation to the psychoanalytical theorists, I will now offer further comment on the Developmental Analytical School's position on the reactivation of pre-oedipal states of mind in adolescence. Samuels outlines the current debate in post-Jungian psychology around the validity of describing and theorizing about early childhood, asking if it " . . . is un-Jungian because, for Jung, the 'whence' is less essential than the 'whither' " (1985, p. 140). In addition, he notes the debate among post-Jungians within the Developmental School about "the relative merits of a model of infancy derived from empirical observation of real mother and babies and a model involving empathic explorations from material obtained in adult and child analysis" (ibid., p. 144).

The Developmental Analytical School, following Fordham, supports the idea that the archetypal images that arise in adolescence hark back to what was actually experienced and felt in infancy. I am in full agreement that archetypal motifs are activated in adolescence (which Sidoli, in the above quote, eloquently expresses); however, the Developmental Analytical School places these archetypal motifs squarely in the pre-oedipal past as a result of one's actual relationship with mother. This leads to the question concerning Jung's view of incest, which he envisions as the regression of libido to a new encounter with the internal world and one's ground of being. Jung noted that this process was personified by the figure of a parent; however, was he always referring to a literal parent? What role one's actual relationship with one's personal mother played in the dynamics of this regression is what I am calling into question. Or, put another way, how does this correspond with a symbolic understanding of the nature of incest where the incest fantasy is a metaphor for a path of psychological growth and development?[1]

When an adolescent regresses in an incestuous manner and merges with a great parent figure, what bearing does this have on his literal pre-oedipal experience with parents, and how does that cohere with our understanding of incest as an attempt at spiritual and psychological regeneration? For example, a seventeen-year-old male high-school student refusing to go to school but staying home all day smoking marijuana, living in a tranquil, dreamy state, could be described as having identified with the great mother archetype, and we could speak of a regression of the libido that appears to be stuck. What are the implications, though, of interpreting this state as a reactivation of the difficulties in early attachment? Do the "unconscious fantasies and primitive collective archetypal motifs" that become activated in adolescence have a source independent of one's personal experience (Sidoli 1989, p. 163) ?

If we take the pre-oedipal encounter between mother and child as the literal basis for an archetypal explication of adolescent states of being, we become trapped by a psychic determinism which relies upon a reductive notion of causality. Take, as another example, the Developmental Analytical School's way of explaining heroic behavior in adolescence. As we have noted, successful separation in adolescence presupposes an emotional and affective revival of the infant's early relationship to mother. When there is a disturbance in the mother–infant bond, a negative mother imago is formed in the child's inner world. At adolescence, this early trauma is reawakened and the hero appears on the scene to protect the adolescent from his or her "larger-than-life enemies" (Sidoli and Bovensiepen 1995, p. 46). Heroic deeds are seen as "a manic defense against severe early split-off infantile depression derived from faulty mother– infant attachment" (ibid., p. 67). The heroic stance defends against the impotence, helplessness, and dependency of this earlier period. The adolescent-as-hero tries to separate from the regressive pull of mother and the overcoming of parental imagoes.

This notion of the adolescent needing to heroically separate from mother to form a separate identity is sharply critiqued by theorists from The Stone Center. These theorists have illustrated how relational development, that is, the ability to think in terms of and relate to others, has been disregarded by current developmental and psychoanalytical paradigms that emphasize the achievement of independence, self-sufficiency, and personal autonomy. In response, they have constructed a new model of feminine development that they term "self-in-relation."[2] Surrey proposes that a female adolescent "does not necessarily want to 'separate' from parents, but to change the form and content of the relationship in a way that affirms her own developmental changes and allows new relationships to develop and take priority" (1984 p. 7). The notion of self-in-relation implies that for adolescent girls (whether this is true for boys is not addressed), a separate relational pathway is primary. Self-development can occur in the context of relationship, and thus the connection between mother and daughter remains strong during adolescence.

Hillman (1990), in his essay, "The Great Mother, Her Son, Her Hero, and the Puer," can be read as offering yet another look at the relationship between the adolescent and the struggle to separate from parents. Hillman evokes the archetype of the puer aeternus, or eternal youth, an important figure in Jungian psychology. Von Franz (1970), who wrote exhaustively on the subject, saw the puer as reflecting a general immaturity characterized by an inability to ground oneself in a committed way. The source of the puer's problem, for Von Franz, derives from an attachment to mother and an inability to separate from her. Hillman offers a strikingly different vision.

Before we turn to it, I want to point out that I will be using the term "puer" in a slightly different fashion from the established Jungian literature. For the purposes of my argument, I am identifying the puer with the spiritual yearnings of the adolescent, even though the puer aeternus is an archetypal figure that presents itself at any stage of development, and an adolescent is certainly not an archetypal figure (although, as we will see, adolescents in our culture are often the container for the puer). My aim here in interweaving the two is to see what light puer psychology sheds on our study of adolescence. The puer aeternus is a male figure—the puella was designated to connote his female counterpart—and much of Hillman's writings on the puer can be construed as pertaining to male psychology. Although it is impossible to draw gendered conclusions from the biological sex of an archetypal figure, I evoke the gender question at this point to keep in mind that this discussion pertains equally to young women and to young men. Given the scope of this book, I will not address the question of how to understand the important difference in the manifestation of the puer spirit in female and male adolescents. Currently, in America, the topic of female adolescence is receiving significant attention both in psychological research, as well as in literature and film.[3] There is an emerging receptivity to hearing her story and feeling into her experience, and it is possible to hear these stories with an ear toward the manifestation of the puer/puella spirit.

The Developmental Analytical School keeps puer psychology bound to mother, not the Freudian mother of Oedipus, but the Jungian pre-oedipal archetypal mother, in her terrible and frightening manifestations as well as in her positive, life-affirming wonders. The puer and his high-flying antics are seen as a defense against the early encounter with mother and the resulting failures of that relationship.

Hillman, on the other hand, distinguishes between the puer and the hero by noting that the hero is always trapped in mother's psychology, whether he is giving into her or rebelling against her. Mother as victor keeps the hero bound to her in a compensatory way. In contrast, Hillman's view on the puer deviates from the classical Jungian position which connects the spiritual phenomenology of the puer aeternus motif with the mother archetype. He states:

> Rather, as we are working out, these puer events pertain to the phenomenology of spirit. By not grasping this fact as it appears in young men and women today, and in the puer eternus figures in our dreams and fantasies, we miss the epiphanies of the spirit archetype, judging them as something "too young," too weak, sick or wounded, or not yet grown up. Thus does the perspective of the mother archetype prevent the possibilities of spirit as it emerges in our lives.
>
> (1975a, p. 51)

I am making an analogous critique of the Developmental Analytical School's theory of adolescence. Their insistence that adolescence is ultimately distinguishable by the revival of pre-oedipal states of being keeps our perception of what is happening in adolescence tied to the mother archetype. Does it constrict our perception of what else might be going on?

Again, Hillman:

> One can attribute a crucial event of any life wrongly to an inappropriate archetypal constellation. Then genius is not viewed authentically in terms of the spirit and its early call but is rather attributed to peculiarities in the fate of the mother.
>
> (1990, p. 184)

Hillman's notion of calling is the kind of phenomenon that remains concealed when adolescence is filtered through the lens of the mother archetype. It presents an alternative way of envisioning a young person's life. The past is important, but equally important is the future: adolescence as becoming. To what future is an adolescent being called? Following Jung, a prospective analysis of symptoms and behaviors fits this model, thus inquiring into where a symptom is leading, toward what ends, rather than looking for its origins in the parental complex, or in mother. This perspective gives a novel twist to how we comprehend an adolescent's action in the world.

Hillman's notion of youth as puer is not in tension with mother so much as with its opposite, old age. Old age is personified as the senex—the ordering principle of consciousness that draws limits and sets up barriers around the puer. Thus Hillman's puer phenomenology brings the puer in contact with a fathering principle which is equally relevant for female and male adolescents.[4] We can now listen with another ear to the shibboleth of those who are in responsible positions with adolescents: What an adolescent needs is firm limit-setting. Or 1996 Republican presidential candidate Bob Dole's exhortation in response to the rising use of drugs and alcohol by American youth: "Just Don't Do It." Could this be an element of the puer–senex encounter? Is it a matter of setting limits or allowing an adolescent the painful experience of coming to face his or her own sense of limitation?

YOUTH IS THE EMERGENCE OF SPIRIT WITHIN THE PSYCHE

I want to conclude this section of the book by amplifying a quotation from Hillman on the emerging spirit in youth. This will set the stage for how my work departs from the theories and ideas thus far presented by both the psychoanalytical theorists and the developmental analytical school. Yet to depart is not to abandon; as I develop alternative ways of reflecting on the psychology of adolescence, the tension between the differing perspectives will unfold.

In his essay, "The Great Mother, Her Son, Her Hero, and the Puer," Hillman states:

Youth carries the significance of becoming, of self-correcting growth, of being beyond itself (ideals) since its reals are in status nascendi . . . . Youth is the emergence of spirit within the psyche.

(ibid., pp. 189–90)

... of self-correcting growth

Fordham's rhythmic waves of deintegration–integration can well be imagined as the adolescent's ability to be wounded by experience and recover from it. Allan (1988) comments on the symbolic themes of children and adolescent's drawings by noticing how art images change over time reflecting a "movement from damage and violation to repair and healthy functioning" (p. 22). The notion of self-correcting growth implicit in each of these examples has crucial implications for how we approach adolescent psychotherapy.

Winnicott's ground breaking ideas about the time-limited nature of child and adolescent psychotherapy are relevant here.[5] For Winnicott, therapy is initiated when a child or adolescent has, for whatever reason, been knocked off the path of development. Psychotherapy then is seen as gently nudging a child back into a state of self-correcting growth where the reality of the child's world can reassert itself as the proper holding environment to nurture further emotional development. When life once again can minister to progressive development, the therapist is no longer needed.

It is narcissistically wounding to us as therapists to make a close connection with an adolescent client and then be abruptly abandoned. One young man whom I saw for approximately one year on a weekly basis began interrupting his consistent weekly attendance by being tardy for appointments and eventually missing them completely. When I questioned him on this, he said: "In the beginning I liked coming here and talking to you. It was very important to me. But now my life is busy and full of other things and I have my friends." He was telling me, in essence, that life had taken over and his own process of self-correcting growth in the world had resumed. The phenomenon of needing to break off the therapy when life reasserts itself is especially relevant for adolescents given the social nature of this period of development.

It is essential for us as therapists to be sensitive to this dynamic and not hang on for our own sake when an adolescent is emotionally ready to sever the tie. We need to become conscious of what Racker (1968) terms "complementary countertransference," that is, where we start to perceive the adolescent client in a way parallel to how she is perceived by her parents. In other words, we identify with the inner image of the client's parents by responding to the client as if we were a parental introject. For example, we may unconsciously identify with the image of an overly-protective parent. This manifests in our pressuring the client to stay in the safe and protected space of therapy because she is not "really" ready to go back into the dangerous world without our guidance. Such a phenomenon forces us to re-think our tendency to explain all non-compliance to therapeutic treatment as resistance. What I am pointing to here is the possibility that an adolescent's insistence upon ending treatment can originate from a healthy instinct to move back out into the world.

This also evokes Jung's notion that therapy is not about a once-for-all cure. "In the last resort it is highly improbable that there could ever be a therapy that got rid of all difficulties. Man needs difficulties; they are necessary for health" (*CW* 8, para. 143). This idea is especially meaningful for adolescent therapists. We must recognize that therapy does not bring to an end all of an adolescent's suffering. There is a collective expectation that creeps in which imagines that an adolescent will straighten up and have it all together so that by the end, therapy has transformed the adolescent client into a well-functioning "young adult" who can smoothly negotiate life's difficulties. On the contrary, it is in the on-going struggle with these very difficulties that allow an adolescent to continue to grow and mature.

Self-correcting growth implies that the adolescent psyche itself can be relied upon to guide the therapeutic process. The psyche knows how to heal itself. This idea is rooted in Jung's notion of the compensatory nature of the psyche which struggles to keep itself in balance. The clinical techniques I describe in Part IV are based upon this idea that the psyche itself can lead an individual into a process of growth and transformation.

... of being beyond itself

Youth is beyond itself because it can feel a calling and it has an urge to respond to that calling in a profound, vital way and yet, in the process, overestimates its current abilities. Adolescents have the capacity to deeply imagine where they are headed in the world, conjuring up powerful insights into the meaning of their lives. What they are missing is the life experience or skills to enact what feels so alive on an ideational plane. In the past, an apprenticeship often served to teach a young person the skills needed to fill out at a practical level what was contained in a life's vision. A mentor rousing a youth to a unique and particular set of talents and potentialities would be another example.

Therapeutically there are many wrong moves to make in response to the "grandiosity" of the vision or calling. A therapist is genuinely challenged by the accidents, failures, crashes, and let-downs which express the disparity between what a youth longs for and his actual abilities in the world. Does a fundamentally "reality-oriented" psychotherapy betray the vision in the name of keeping the adolescent functioning and safe? Or is there a way to try and incorporate both, where the vision or calling is given space for expression in the therapy hour while at the same time practical concerns and concrete realities are addressed?

Can adolescent psychotherapy be re-imagined as a place where different kinds of calls can be heard? The one-on-one nature of individual therapy creates a stillness which can aid an adolescent in sorting through the differing claims on her being—what parents, teachers, and peers expect and demand in contrast to the fledgling expression of her own psyche. Group psychotherapy allows for intensification of this expression amidst the competing din of other peers' voices. Family therapy can help initiate the practice of differentiating the demands and expectations and fantasies that a family has for an adolescent from her own sense of where things are headed; this is negotiated in terms of the boundaries and understandings that are generated as part of family life.

Along these lines, the adolescent's ability to deeply imagine the "infinite array of the possible" (Kegan 1982, p. 38) comes into play. A therapist's questions can stimulate that kind of imagining. For example: What kind of person are you likely to become? In what ways would you like to see yourself change? How do you imagine yourself five years down the road? and ten? and fifteen? Questions about vocation can enter into this sense of calling and identity. The artfulness here is in allowing for a nascent expression of fantasy and imagination to develop simultaneously with the willingness to suspend our cynical disbelief in terms of its actuality in fact. At adolescence, the imagination needs to be stirred. This approach is therapeutically effective because it allows adolescents an imaginal connection to their own life-affirming possibilities.

For example, one young man I worked with who was severely physically and emotionally abused by his father, found his way during one session to talking about what it was going to be like when he had a son. I asked him to imagine himself as a father in contrast to how he experienced his own father. In other words, how would he, as father, treat his son when he failed a class in school? Or how would he react if his son came home late at night after curfew? (Both of these questions referred to actual situations where his father reacted by losing his temper and raging at my client.) After a long moment of reflection, my client, in a quiet, subdued voice, with a mournful expression on his face, evoked the image of a gentle and tolerating, yet firm father, who displayed a strong ability for empathic connection. In this moment, my client was able to connect to the image of a positive "archetypal" father whose life-affirming ways were a great support to him. As he went through the anguishing period of physically moving out of his father's house and emotionally separating from him, this intrapsychic figure served as an important source of strength and forbearance.

. . . (ideals)

What I find extremely dispiriting in the psychoanalytical theories is how adolescent idealism is reduced to something inferior, such as the lost remnants of one's childish past. Recall how Blos interprets an adolescent's idealism about a political figure, for example, the way an African-American youth might idealize Malcolm X, as a regressed ego state analogous to early infantile idealization of parents. Does that kind of interpretation, although conceptually compelling, block us as therapists from hearing the other side of the ideal—in other words, how a political figure carries something for the adolescent psyche in terms of future development? Isn't it equally valid to ask: What is it about the figure of Malcolm X that can evoke such a passionate response that an adolescent might be pulled into the world of political action?

Ideals engage the passionate moral, political, and social imagination. Destroy the ideals of the youth and society stagnates. We as educators, parents, and therapists have difficulty tolerating the all-or-nothing vision contained in adolescent idealism. We are disrupted by it, alienated and disturbed; it touches off those places inside us where our own idealism was shattered at some critical juncture. We arm ourselves with a "I know better" kind of cynicism in the name of protecting an adolescent from getting too carried away. Does this very attitude contribute to the political apathy and despairing nihilism found in the current generation? For whose sake are we rushing in to crush an adolescent's fervent idealism?

. . . its reals are in status nascendi [state of being born]

Here the nascent, tender and fragile side of the adolescent spirit is evoked. By its reals being in a state of becoming, I want to emphasize the broody and moody quality of this time and the necessity at some level to let it be by leaving it alone. Winnicott (1963a) states it clearly in the following dictum: "The process cannot be hurried up, though indeed it can be broken into and destroyed by clumsy handling" (p. 145).

It is taxing to patiently foster what is unformed. The immediate response, especially for someone trained in Western therapeutic techniques, is to fix it or change it or transform it. This is the opposite of nurturing it, being moved by it or truly seeing it. It is extraordinarily difficult to stay present with an adolescent because they are in a state of becoming. No longer a child but not yet an adult means that in essence something is unformed. Does the theory of recapitulation capitulate to our desire to get away from the unsettling movements of becoming by promising the discovery of fixed origins in the adolescent's past?

Tolerating a sense of incompleteness and not yet being formed, without treating the adolescent like a child or prematurely forcing upon him the burdens of adult responsibilities is one of the most demanding aspects of both parenting an adolescent and trying to engage him therapeutically. It requires an ability to tolerate a borderline state. Culturally we do not do well with the unformed. We prematurely force children into adult patterns of being, and harbor the crazy expectation that an adolescent will have his life all figured out and ordered by the time high school begins. The theory of recapitulation contributes to this intolerance of the unformed in the sense that the mystery of becoming is eradicated with certain knowledge of what has been.

. . . the emergence of spirit within the psyche

Following Hillman, I am intimating that something is born or awakened in adolescence that was not generated in childhood. Hillman refers to it as a kind of spirit. This spirit in adolescence is hungry for experience and seeks extreme states of being, whether they be emotional, bodily or ideational. To comprehend this, we must attend to how the adolescent's imagination is fed through the music, movies, television, literature, and poetry that adolescents are attracted to and actively seek out. From an archetypal perspective we might ask: How do the songs, poems, dances and stories resonate with pre-existing patterns in the adolescent psyche that actively demand expression? Another important question to consider is: What kind of world does the spirit awaken to in adolescence? This question compels us to consider the cultural and collective responses to the adolescent spirit: how the emerging spirit in youth is received by the culture has significant impact on the process of becoming, an impact that has lasting consequences throughout the rest of one's life.

In our developmental thinking, we have trouble contemplating the birth of anything that does not coincide with biological birth or early childhood experiences. In some way something unique and originary is given at adolescence which directly informs the experience of being an adolescent. This is the peculiar quality that I will trace by staying close and witnessing the phenomenology of the adolescent spirit as revealed through the intimacies of psychotherapy.

Part II

Adolescence, initiation, and the dying process

Chapter 3

The archetype of initiation

Without a ritual to contain and inform the wounds of life, pain and suffering increase, yet meaningful change doesn't occur. Where drops of blood once symbolized life trying to change, pools of blood stain street after street without renewing the spirit of life. Instead of ritual descent and emotional resurrection, complete death occurs; actual corpses pile up. Instead of the hum of bullroarers twirled by unpredictable elders, the wail of sirens, the crack of bullets, and the whirl of flashing lights bring the "underworld" to life each night. Instead of participating in a prepared rite for leaving childhood games through ordeals of emotional struggle and spiritual alertness, gangs of blindly wounded youth hurl their woundedness at the darkness and spit angry bullets at groups that are their mirror image, attacking masks of themselves. The sacrificial blood once offered by those trying to glimpse mysteries at the thresholds of the stages of life has become bloody "street sacrifices" of entire generations. An unconscious, chaotic amassing of death gathers where the terms of passage instead required some honest suffering, a scar to mark the event, and a community to accept and acknowledge the change. Denying that each individual must struggle at the thresholds of spiritual and emotional self-discovery eventually destroys any shared awareness of the sanctity of life.

Michael Meade

To discuss adolescent initiation in traditional societies, in the context of its applicability for late twentieth century adolescents growing up in a post-industrial society, opens the floodgates to a myriad of opposing responses and reactions. For example, there may be a murky intuition that there is something important to be learned in the study of these rites. On the other hand, one could argue that there is nothing to be learned from these rites, since they are essentially homophobic, sexist and misogynistic, especially given what we now know about the role of clitoridectomies in African rites of passage ceremonies. Moreover, thinking in terms of initiation forces us to assess the vision of a meaningful life we are unwittingly passing down to adolescents. In doing so, we may be confronted with remorse and shame as we consider the portrait of the world and models of humanity which we offer to them.

Amidst this murkiness, anger, and discord, two features of initiation rites stand out clearly. First, there is an abundance of anthropological literature detailing accounts of ceremonials, rites, and rituals in traditional societies for both boys and girls, cross-culturally, at or near the time of puberty. Van Gennep (1960) characterizes these rites as a symbolic, psychological, and social transition, in essence, a transition from a non-sexual to a sexual existence. Eliade emphasizes the personal transformation that characterizes this symbolic transition. He defines initiation as a

> body of rites and oral teachings whose purpose is to produce a decisive alteration in religious and social status of the person to be initiated. In philosophical terms, initiation is equivalent to a basic change in existential condition; the novice emerges from his ordeal endowed with a totally different being from that which he possessed before his initiation; he has become another.
>
> (Eliade 1958, p. x)

Among the varied practices of different cultures all over the world, there are a set of common themes that characterize initiation rites for adolescents. We shall be examining these themes in the context of their applicability for today's youth.

Second, it is abundantly clear that outside of certain religious practices (for example, Catholic confirmation and Jewish Bar and Bar Mitzvah) and certain secular rituals (for example, high school graduation, obtaining a driver's license and voting) no such formal, proscribed rites exist today in our current culture.

By exploring the common elements of initiation rites in traditional societies, I am not attempting to devise ways of creating rites of passage for today's youth. There is a growing body of literature to date which examines this dimension of using traditional societies as models for recreating these rites in modern practice.[1] My aim in investigating the anthropological literature on adolescent initiation is to put us in a frame of mind that allows us to imagine into the extremes of behavior and emotion that get enacted by adolescents today against the background of traditional initiation rites, where even more extreme and complicated patterns of action were enacted, primordially bearing upon issues of sexuality, death, and the sacred.

As myths allow us to analyze psychological phenomena by holding them up to the light of archetypal figures whose attributes and behaviors are more complicated than what we are examining, (Hillman, 1975b), so too, with the varied practices and rites from other cultures in relation to the initiation of youth. These rites are often mythic in nature, re-enacting the creation of the world by divine beings. The ritual intensity and complexity of such practices offer us rich images for reflection. Thus, this and the next two chapters draw upon these accounts not in an attempt to literally re-enact them today, but as psychological prods which can stimulate us to think more profoundly and less reductively about the significance of the experiences that we are confronted with in today's adolescent culture.

Many writers and theorists from various fields including psychology, sociology, and anthropology have tried to make sense of the fact that initiation rites have virtually disappeared in modern culture. Although the literal practice of these rites has for the most part ceased, it is not a far stretch to wonder if they are still influencing the psychology of adolescence. In other words, is the need for formal markers to acknowledge the passage from childhood to adulthood still alive, albeit unconsciously, in the psyche of modern man? Is the need for initiation archetypal? If the archetype of initiation is a structural component of the psyche, then it is going to occur whether or not a given culture formally invests in such rites. The following examples support the idea of adolescent initiation being an archetypal necessity.

Bruno Bettelheim (1962) begins his work, *Symbolic Wounds: Puberty Rites and the Envious Male* by telling a story about four adolescents, two boys and two girls, each around the age of twelve, who were in residential treatment at the now-famous Orthogenic School in Chicago. During a series of meetings, all four conspired together to enact a ritual in response to the first menstruation of one of the girls in the group. It was decided that a secret society should be formed where all the members of the group, boys and girls, would cut themselves once a month and mix their blood. Further discussions, at the time of the second girl's menarche, led to a revised plan whereby only the boys would cut their index fingers on a monthly basis and mix their blood with the girl's menses.

In trying to make sense of this incident, Bettelheim studied the anthropological literature on puberty rites which formed the basis for his book. Although a prominent psychoanalyst, Bettelheim

outrightly rejected the psychoanalytical explanation which understood circumcision (a central feature in many male initiation rites)
as deriving from the father's jealousy toward his sons and the need
to create castration anxiety in them to insure the inviolability of the
incest taboo. Bettelheim sought an alternative understanding of the
psychological motives behind these rites, inquiring into the nature
of the emotional needs which they were meant to satisfy, and
assuming that each generation must grapple with the gratification of
these primary emotional needs, with or without rites. What had
been linked narrowly and pessimistically with castration, a destruction of life, Bettelheim links to constructive desires, progeny and
new life. He alludes to the archetypal necessity of these rites by
stating: " . . . many of the customs that are part of initiation rites
among preliterate societies also take place spontaneously and
sporadically among normal adolescents in Western society" (1962,
p. 34).

Edith Sullwold recounts the story of a nine-year-old boy, Peter,
with whom she was working in a children's clinic in the inner city of
Los Angeles, who had the spontaneous desire to build a fire in the
concrete courtyard of the clinic. Sullwold observed that "Peter's
interest was not so much in the fire itself but in his ability to control
it—ignite it, fan and feed it, check its boundaries, and eventually
put it out" (1987, pp. 111–12). Soon two others boys arrive on the
scene as Peter re-ignites the fire. One of the boys uses an empty
coffee can as a drum by turning it upside down upon his leg and
begins thumping a steady beat. Sullwold describes what happens
next:

> Again without a word, the other new boy went to one side of the
> courtyard and made a stunning leap over the fire. Invited, Peter
> also went to the beginning place, hesitated a moment, and leapt
> over. For almost an hour, the three took turns beating the drum,
> tending the fire, and jumping over it.
>
> (ibid., p. 112)

Analogously to Bettelheim, Sullwold concludes that, "these events
point to the reality of the spontaneous emergence of ritual action in
puberty and adolescence" (ibid.).

In their work, *The Gang: A Study in Adolescent Behavior* (1958),
Herbert Bloch and Arthur Niederhoffer, respectively a sociologist
and a New York City police officer with fifteen years' experience
working with gang youth, take note of the similarities between

puberty rites in traditional societies and the informal practices of city street gangs. They interpret certain aspects of gang practice as spontaneous, informal rituals which arise because the culture refuses to meet the initiatory needs of adolescents.

> When a society does not make adequate preparation, formal or otherwise, for the induction of its adolescents to the adult status, equivalent forms of behavior arise spontaneously among adolescents themselves, reinforced by their own group structure, which seemingly provides the same psychological content and function as the more formalized rituals found in other societies. This the gang structure appears to do in American society, apparently satisfying the deep-seated needs experienced by adolescents in all cultures.
>
> (ibid., p. 17)

Another example of a contemporary initiatory process is portrayed in the 1996 film *Girls Town*, which chronicles the response of three adolescent girls, seniors in high school, to their friend having committed suicide. Even though they were a close group of friends and had known each other for many years, Emma, Angela and Patty were completely caught off guard when they found out that Nikki had taken her own life.

After Emma steals Nikki's journal during a condolence call at her home, the three girls gather together at their basement hang-out, and amidst candlelight and the jolting pain of Nikki's loss, begin reading aloud from her journal and soon discover that she was raped. Since Nikki never told anyone about the rape, the three girls question one another as to what in their own lives has remained secreted. In a heated conversation, Emma reveals her own undisclosed rape while Angela and Emma confront Patti about the abusive relationship she is in with the father of her child. Strictures are being broken through in this dialogue as the girls open themselves up to each other and to the reality of what becoming a woman in our culture means. The impact of this dialogue, as they are being called to face these truths, summons them to carry out a series of actions that from an outsider's perspective appear as typical teen-age delinquency, although when seen from the inside, it is evident how the breaking through of silence sets the stage for a series of initiatory ordeals where what is spoken and felt between them takes on concrete meaning in the world.

While the rest of the school is at a pep rally, the three girls come across the car of the boy who raped Emma and in which she was raped. Without forethought, Patty begins to scratch a long line in the side of his car with her key. Emma watches, dumbfounded at first, but as the rage over what happened moves into her body, she takes the key and makes her own mark on the car. Meanwhile Angela is spray-painting the word rapist on the car's hood in red letters and the scene concludes with Emma, now clearly feeling the violation of the rape, throwing a concrete brick at the car, smashing out a window.

What is so striking about this scene, and a subsequent one in which the girls confront and then rough up the boy who raped Nikki, is the combination of fierce intentionality and measured bounds within which these acts are committed. There is nothing gratuitous about the expression of the girl's rage and this gives it the quality of a ritual gesture that sets down and contains aggressive energies that, if remained locked up inside, would slowly poison the self—as evidenced by what happened to Nikki. This is demonstrative in Emma's response to her boyfriend's judgment that the car attack was an expression of meaningless violence. She states, "It looked like someone was trying to make a point," and later acknowledges, "I'm proud of what I did."

The other ordeals that the girls go through in the film, including robbing the apartment of the father of Patti's child and getting into a fight with classmates in the school bathroom, are all means of expressing and containing the rageful energies that are stirred up in the wake of Nikki's death. The relationship between the three girls intensifies as they share a mutual awakening that is foreign and incomprehensible to those outside of it. Emma expresses this to her boyfriend in the process of breaking up with him when she says, "You don't have to take it and you don't understand it—why don't you just go." What was important in the past fades away as this evolving awareness creates a momentum for re-evaluating one's life and one's future possibilities.

As a final example, Eliade concludes his study of initiation rites by stating:

> ... initiatory themes remain alive chiefly in modern man's unconscious ... in the depth of his being modern man is still capable of being affected by initiatory scenarios or messages.
>
> (1958, p. 134)

If we accept the claim that the initiatory impulse is archetypal and becomes activated during adolescence, where does that leave us today living in a culture where formal rites of passage no longer exist? As the above examples illustrate, adolescents end up unconsciously creating their own ritual structures. The adolescent psyche seeks experiences that will radically alter its perception of the world and enable it to move to another level of existence. If society does not sanction a way for this to happen, what we find are adolescents attempting to do it for themselves. I now want to explore this idea that certain behaviors that we judge negatively and to which we respond punitively may indeed be covert attempts on the part of adolescents for self-initiation.

ATTEMPTS AT SELF-INITIATION

There is a growing body of literature (Henderson 1967; Mahdi *et al.* 1987, 1996; Zoja 1989) commenting on the lack of meaningful rites of initiation in modern American culture that enacts a separation from the state of childhood and the parental home. A strong argument can be made for the connection between the "prolonged" adolescence of American youth and the lack of rites to mark the transition into adulthood. Gentry comments on this connection:

Adolescence as we've come to know it is a modern phenomenon. In previous societies and tribal cultures, the adult usually merges quickly out of childhood through participation in puberty rites. Now however, for ten years or more, modern adolescents must make attempts to say farewell to childhood without the benefit of such socially sanctioned rights of passage. Puberty rites of passage have not disappeared. They've taken on newer and disguised forms of expression. Today our youth reach out to grasp adulthood in rather dangerous ways. By participating in religious cults, by the abuse of increasingly more harmful substances, by running away from home, by their symptoms of self-starvation, self-mutilation, self-destructive suicidal attempts. The affirmation of self, once the aim of the so-called search for identity, has become for some adolescents a search for self-negation.

(1989, audio tape)

Drug and alcohol experimentation is one way of creating

experiences that have the potential to fundamentally alter one's perception of the world. Marin asserts that adolescents use drugs to

provide for themselves what we deny them: a confrontation with some kind of power within an unfamiliar landscape involving sensation and risk. It is there, I suppose, that they hope to find, by some hurried magic, a new way of seeing, a new relation to things, to discard one identity and assume another.

(1974, p. 45)

Marin's description of adolescent drug use contains within it the essential elements of an initiation ritual. An unfamiliar, risky experience that puts one in touch with a potentially transformative power granting a new vision of the world and the assumption of a new identity. When looked at from this perspective, it is no wonder that drug and alcohol usage is so prevalent in adolescence; it offers itself as a compelling possibility for psychological transformation.

Marin goes on to speak about the ritual elements in drug use in its capacity to create connection and a shared sense of identity among adolescents:

Theirs is a world totally alien to the one we discuss in schools; it is dramatic, it enchants them; its existence forms a strange brotherhood among them and they cling to it—as though they alone had been to a fierce land and back. It is that which draws them together and makes of them a loose tribe. It is, after all, some sort of shared experience, some kind of foray into the risky dark; it is the best that they can do.

(ibid.)

One of the essential differences between formalized initiation in traditional societies and modern youth's attempts at self-initiation in the absence of those rituals, is the presence of tribal elders who were on hand to guarantee containment for the powerful energies unleashed through the ritual process. In other words, someone older, more experienced, already initiated, is overseeing the whole enterprise and maintaining the boundaries so that the initiate can wholly partake of the experience in relative "safety." This is one of the reasons attempts at self-initiation result in what Gentry was calling "self-negation." If the telos of initiation is discovery of one's adult identity and status in the world, self-initiation that gets enacted in a vacuum has the potential for disaster as witnessed by the increasingly self-destructive ways adolescents are turning upon themselves.

One of the most unnerving aspects of Larry Clark's 1995 film *Kids* that portrayed the life of teen-agers in New York City was the fact that there were so few adults shown in the film. A vast amount of self-destructive, frenzied activity takes place: criminality, indiscriminate sexual activity with the threat of AIDS, unrestrained substance use, and gratuitous violence. As all of this goes on, out in the open, it seems as if nobody is paying attention. The portrayal of these activities, in their uncontrolled and uncontained nature, is all the more disquieting to watch given the absence of anyone on the scene who might know better. One gets the feeling that the parents, teachers, police officers, and community leaders have completely washed their hands of any responsibility for what is occurring. The abdication of responsibility is negatively correlated with how zealously out of control these activities are undertaken.

Without guidance, left on their own, adolescents' attempts at initiation take on an extreme character. Think for a moment of the difference between a seventeen-year-old native American youth using peyote as part of a vision quest structured by tribal elders and an American teen-ager's weekend "partying" ritual which involves tripping on heavy doses of L.S.D. This extremity of behavior may lead an adolescent to the threshold of an initiatory door. However, without the proper structures in place, he cannot pass through it. A need then arises to constantly repeat the experience because there is an unconscious wish to be transformed by it. Like the repetition of a symptom after the experience of trauma, the compulsion to repeat these events, be it drug and alcohol use, acts of violence, or indiscriminate sex, may be better understood not under the rubric of the psychology of addiction, but as failed attempts at initiation that leaves one in a state of yearning for a kind of deliverance that never seems to quite manifest itself.

In my practice with substance-abusing adolescents, I point out to them the fact that the use of mind-altering substances in other cultures around the time of puberty is often only a one time event. The substance grants to the initiate a vision that one spends the next twenty years integrating into their life. To keep relying on the substance to create the vision is to miss the point. This way of articulating the dynamics of drug use validates the initiatory telos in the drug usage as well as pointing to the addictive pattern that ensues when one is not able to cross over an initiatory threshold.

Adolescents then feel acknowledged in their yearning for something beyond themselves, and at the same time can begin to deconstruct the belief that it is the substance itself that provides this experience. In other words, they learn to see and feel how what they are wanting in these kinds of experiences is already a potentiality of the self.

THE INITIATORY WOUND

In discussing the initiatory impulse in the context of the psychology of the puer, Hillman makes a connection between the bodily wound incurred in traditional initiation ceremonies, be it through circumcision, knocking out a tooth, or scarring the skin and its contemporary counterpart.

> The wound that is so necessary to initiation ceremonies ends the state of innocence as it opens one in a new way at another place, making one suffer from openness, bringing to a close the world as wonder. Now it hurts, and I must protect myself. I am no longer innocent. So, the puer impulse will force a car-crash or a ski-spill, not merely for the risk or the penchant for destruction, but as well because these adolescent accidents may move the soul into a harmed and initiated body. It is as if the soul can find no path out of innocence other than physical hurt.
>
> (1977, p. 113)

Thus, the wounding which was enacted ceremonially in traditional societies as a way of insuring passage out of childhood still exists today, albeit with a different emphasis and form of expression. The accidents, psychosomatic illnesses, fights, sports injuries, etc., can be understood as the adolescent psyche's susceptibility to suffer wounds to the physical body, thus bringing to an end the attachment to childhood innocence. In addition to physical calamities, powerful emotional upsets seem to serve a similar wounding function. In this regard, I think of the crises that emerge in families when one of the children enters puberty. The ensuing conflicts, fights and confrontations between parents and an adolescent child cause a loss of innocence for both parties. Parents are no longer able to see their sons or daughters quite so angelically—"She's always been such a good girl"—and must come to terms with the fact that their once compliant, loving, tender child is now capable of acting in ways that cause major disruptions to family life. Similarly,

the adolescent can no longer simply remain in the role of a dependent, carefree child who always has mother and father around for protection.

It seems that in many cases, underlying the battles between parent and child, is a force attempting to separate the adolescent and his family. In family therapy, where these domestic parent-child conflicts dominate the sessions, it is never completely clear who is pushing whom away, but the end result is that many adolescents end up being removed or removing themselves from the family home. Whether they run away and live on the streets, get placed in a foster home or institutionalized, move in with relatives in another state, or end up getting pregnant and raising a child on their own, increasing numbers of adolescents in our culture find themselves separated from their family before the age of eighteen. Clearly, economic and social forces play a major role, but I am wondering if the psyche's need for initiation contributes to what is becoming a social epidemic.

As therapists, we meet these cases in our practice every day. The first words uttered, in the form of the presenting problem, echo this sense of separation from family. "I couldn't live with my mothe anymore—I had to get out of there," or "My father threw me out the house and told me never to come back." Is there an initiat process occurring here? To leave one's home, even under intole circumstances, for example, in cases of abuse and neglect, cal dramatic psychological reorientation. To find oneself on th or in an institution or part of the foster care system, ca turning point in one's life.

One function of the initiatory wound is to move a from a state of psychological ignorance to psycholog means that one can stand on one's own two feet by be into a situation and know what is going on witho someone else for guidance. Today we call that " listening to the stories adolescents tell after being familiarity of their home, one recognizes an i psychological reflection, the ability to think f people up, and make sound judgments.

Therapeutically, we can listen to these bespeaking initiation and reflect back th of psychological wisdom is manifest. F therapists respond when we hear stat look at the world in the same way ag

like I once did"? There is a tendency to reply to such utterances in a sentimental manner, as if an innocent perception of the world can be magically restored by psychotherapy. I am proposing another approach where what is heard, felt, and reflected back and explored in such stories is the awful experience of having the rug pulled out from under oneself, the wounding that comes with the shattering of innocence and the move into a more self-protective and enclosed place. Can we stay attuned in hearing these stories to the emerging awareness of the indifference and cruelty of life?

Adolescents need reassurance that such experiences, although horrible and earth shattering, can be suffered and lived through. The tendency to make it more bearable by sugarcoating it robs the adolescent of the ability to contain and bear such tragedies. The whole enterprise of projective identification that plays such a central role in adolescent psychotherapy, in this context, is a way in which the therapist is being asked to carry the experience, feel the burden of its raw intensity and pain, and eventually offer it back to the adolescent after it has been metabolized by the therapist.

The ability to endure the kinds of losses we are talking about here, of family, childhood, and one's innocence about the world, is a major task in adolescence, magnified for those adolescents who, for economic and social reasons, have suffered at the hands of larger systems (foster care, residential treatment, juvenile justice) which are notorious for repeating the abuse or abandonment that was suffered in the family. As a culture, in response to overwhelming pain and suffering, we often go for the quick fix. This means that we have a greater tendency to work with loss and depression through a medical approach (psychiatric evaluation and medication) rather than a therapeutic one where learning to bear the pain and suffering of loss is a developmental necessity.

This approach to therapy allows for the recognition and integration of the awareness that one has passed through an initiatory threshold and is now on the other side. Hillman characterizes this transition: "Initiation refers to the transition from only-puer consciousness, wounded and bleeding, to puer-et-senex consciousness, open and scarred" (1977, p. 122).

Therapy can play an important role in this process. Being wounded at a core level in adolescence can call forth two responses as impediments to further development. One can become self-protective, isolated and withdrawn; here the need to protect this wounded place from getting hurt again is at the center of one's

consciousness and results in never allowing oneself to fully engage in life. Or, one repetitively enters relationships and situations that recreate the trauma, reopening the wound in an unconscious attempt to feel it more fully. In both cases, consciousness remains wounded and bleeding.

As therapists, we are forced to consider what type of dialogical encounter is fitting to an individual who is caught in one of these patterns. The ability to bear witness to the pain and suffering of an initiatory-like wounding experience means one is attending to a bleeding wound in the hope that it may scar over leaving the individual open to new experiences. This is done with great sensitivity and care, helping an individual feel at the level of affect what has happened to her and how it has changed her outlook on the world. The psyche wants to feel deeply into the nuances of the experience so that a release can occur and this wounded place can become integrated into a person's character. The danger for an adolescent is that if the wound is left unattended it can easily become split off from consciousness so that unconsciously one seeks outlets for anesthetizing the pain of which one is no longer aware. This dynamic of woundedness is a way of re-imagining and re-narratizing the psychology of addiction which is currently the prominent mode of discourse for understanding many of the self-destructive behaviors which occur in adolescence.

Chapter 4

Life and death imagery in adolescence

In the year I turned fifteen, I felt more unhappy than I had ever imagined anyone could be. It wasn't the unhappiness of wanting a new dress, or the unhappiness of wanting to go to cinema on a Sunday afternoon and not being allowed to do so, or the unhappiness of being unable to solve some mystery in geometry, or the unhappiness at causing my dearest friend, Gwen, some pain. My unhappiness was something deep inside me, and when I closed my eyes I could even see it. It sat somewhere—maybe in my belly, maybe in my heart; I could not exactly tell—and it took the shape of a small black ball, all wrapped up in cobwebs. I would look at it and look at it until I had burned the cobwebs away, and then I would see that the ball was no bigger than a thimble, even though it weighed worlds. At that moment, just when I saw its size and felt its weight, I was beyond feeling sorry for myself, which is to say I was beyond tears. I could only just sit and look at myself, feeling like the oldest person who had ever lived and who had not learned a single thing.

Jamaica Kincaid

INTRODUCTION

I will now turn to the work of Robert Jay Lifton who, in his book, *The Broken Connection* (1979), analyzes the prospective meaning of one's individual imagination surrounding awareness of death and the continuity of life. Lifton's work is germane to our study of adolescence in that he focuses upon imagery that arises during life-cycle transitions. In sharp contrast to the psychoanalytical view of adolescence as recapitulation, Lifton views adolescence as its own event. Adolescents are viscerally affected by an awareness of mortality and struggle to make sense of the resulting life and death imagery that pervades consciousness during this time.

According to Lifton, life-cycle transitions are experienced at an imaginal level through the symbolization of what has occurred in the past and what will continue on in the future. This symbolizing process is replete with images of death and contingency. Lifton faults the life-cycle psychology of Erickson and Freud's model of instinct and defense for leaving out the imagery of death and life-continuity that accompanies these transitions.

Lifton's work is in dialogue with Freud's view of sex and death as the great instinctual adversaries (Eros versus Thanatos), where aggression, destructiveness and even guilt are seen as deriving from the death instinct. One consequence of this dichotomy in Freud's theorizing is that the death instinct is left vague and unembodied so that our everyday experience of death imagery is given no place. It is only in relation to the other adversary, sexuality, that Freud dramatically portrays its texture and imagery as being an integral part of individual psychological development.

Lifton's interest in images parallels Jung's. In inquiring into the ways in which human beings symbolically come to terms with their mortality, he explores the imagery that pertains not only to an awareness of one's own death, but also to an individual's experience of participating in a sense of life-continuity at a collective level. Lifton argues that the psychological awareness of life-continuity is not a denial of death, but rather a corollary to death. Indeed, without the sense that one's life goes on in a significant manner after one dies, in what Lifton calls "symbolic immortality" (an imaginative form of transcending death), one cannot genuinely confront the fact of death.

For Lifton, images of death begin forming at birth and continue throughout the life cycle. Much of this imagery consists of what he calls "death equivalents," that is, psychic precursors and models for later feelings about one's actual death. He enumerates three that are especially relevant in understanding the adolescent psyche: separation, disintegration, and stasis.

> Each of these death equivalents has a counterpart with vitality and affirmation: connection is the counterpart of separation, integrity of disintegration, and movement of stasis . . . . The parameters operate at both proximate and ultimate levels of experience and reveal the connection between the two.
>
> (1979, p. 53)

Ultimate levels, for Lifton, symbolize one's connection to history and biology, those aspects of existence which lie outside the realm of immediate experience. Proximate levels concern more immediate feelings and images. "The two combine in the human struggle not merely to remain alive but to feel alive" (ibid., p. 5).

Images, feelings, and experiences of separation, disintegration, and stasis are an important part of initiation ceremonies in traditional societies. In his examination of their imagery, Lifton summarizes the characteristic sequence of initiation ceremonies in the following manner: separation from the community, transformation (usually physical as well as psychological), and a return to the community in a new role. These three death equivalents (separation, disintegration and stasis) always play a prominent role although the specific details of each ceremony vary from culture to culture.

> For boys that means "separation from the world of women and children," and then subjection to a terrifying ordeal—mutilation, confrontation with sacred objects, or exposure to what appears to be monsters, ghosts, or grotesque corpses. All this the boy not only endures but actively accepts, invites, conquers. For girls the stress is on extreme seclusion following the first menses, including a great variety of taboos—about eating, exposure to the sun, touching the earth, being seen, and sometimes physical restraint to the extent of living in tiny rooms or cages for weeks, months or even years.
>
> (ibid., p. 74)

Traditional rites of initiation are compelling illustrations of how primordial imagery is harnessed and utilized in the initiation of youth. Lifton is assuming that life and death psychic imagery surrounding the transition from childhood to adulthood is continuous for both the pre-modern and modern adolescent and is not created by the ceremonies and rituals that were part of the initiation process. "Rather, the initiation process expresses, embellishes, and orders universal psychobiological struggles specific to puberty and adolescence around life and death imagery" (ibid., p. 77).

Thus, in this view, tribal rituals are set forth to meet images and forces that already exist within the adolescent psyche, that originate on their own accord. What we can learn from examining such rites is how traditional societies used ritual to engage and contain the turbulent energy and profound imagery that bursts forth at puberty. Michael Ventura describes the wisdom of their approach. He states:

> Unlike us, tribal people met with the extremism of their young

(and I'm using "extremism" as a catchall word for the intense psychic cacophony of adolescence) with an equal but focused extremism from adults. Tribal adults didn't run from this moment in their children as we do: they celebrated it. They would assault their adolescents with, quite literally, holy terror: rituals that had been kept secret from the young till that moment—rituals that focused upon the young all the light and darkness of their tribe's collective psyche, all its sense of mystery, all its questions, and all the stories told both to contain and answer those questions.

(1993, p. 30)

In this chapter and the next, I want to stay with the idea that these states of mind are given as part of adolescence itself and thus inquire into the life–death struggles that serve as a background for this profound shift in personal identity as one departs from childhood. Following Lifton, this line of inquiry allows us to approach adolescence as an intense testing time for both life and death imagery; the struggle not merely to remain alive but to feel alive is ever-present and can be discerned in the behavior, emotionality, and spirituality that we find in adolescence. We will compare and contrast how the death equivalents of separation, disintegration, and stasis occur in traditional rites of passage and in contemporary experiences of adolescence, with attention toward the significance of their role in psychotherapy.

SEPARATION

In describing traditional initiation rites, Lifton states:

> . . . separation for both sexes is stark and absolute—separation from parental nurturers, and, more generally, from the childhood state of dependent privilege and protection. The initiate must psychically experience a new dimension of separation imagery that not only lends intensity to his subsequent reintegration but deepens his knowledge of isolation, abandonment and death.

(1979, p. 74)

There are marked gender differences in the enactment of this first stage of separating from the community. With boys, greater emphasis is placed upon the breaking of emotional ties to mother. For example, in nearly all the Australian tribes, the mothers of initiates are convinced that their sons will be eaten by a hostile and mysterious divinity, and although this same divinity will subsequently resuscitate the novices, the mothers are well aware that their boys will return to the tribe as men. Among some tribes, mothers mourn over the initiates as the dead are mourned (Eliade, 1958).

Jung stresses this aspect of male initiation:

The first bearer of the soul-image is always the mother; later it is borne by those women who arouse the man's feelings, whether in a positive or a negative sense. Because the mother is the first bearer of the soul-image, separation from her is a delicate and important matter of the greatest educational significance. Accordingly among primitives we find a large number of rites designed to organize this separation. The mere fact of becoming adult, and of outward separation, is not enough; impressive initiations into the "men's house" and ceremonies of rebirth are still needed in order to make the separation from the mother (and hence from childhood) entirely effective.

(*CW* 7, para. 314)

For Jung, separation from mother and separation from childhood are synonymous for a man. Separation and its counterpart connection is a central focus of much of the current writing on female adolescent development. Gilligan (1982) critiques the developmental theorists (Freud, Erickson, Piaget, Kohlberg) for adopting male psychology as being normative for developmental theory. For example, she points out how, for Erickson, autonomy, initiation, and industry are highly valued in the stages of development preceding adolescence when it is thought to be necessary to create a strong enough sense of self to withstand the diffusion of identity that occurs during puberty. This need for boys to prepare themselves for the inevitable separation from mother, in the development of an autonomous self, is not true for girls, according to Gilligan, where identity formation takes place in the context of on-going relationships. For girls, the experience of attachment and connection coalesces with the formation of identity; a woman comes to know herself through her relationship with others. Due to the differences between male and female psychology, female development must be charted along a different path. The Stone Center's work on female development that emphasizes growth through connection explicitly calls into question the assumption of a female adolescent needing to experience a radical separation from mother as a developmental necessity.

Gilligan's critique touches on the fact that developmental psychology, filled with images of striving for autonomy and separation from parents, has neglected the importance of attachment and connection for identity development. However, this critique centers on the experience of female adolescents and does not challenge, say, Jung's perspective that for males a decisive break with mother is a psychological necessity. This problematic expresses the current state of turmoil as the deconstruction of gender roles and the question of essential differences in the psychology of males and females clash, leaving open the controversy as to whether the psychology of separation, as a psychological necessity at adolescence, is culturally relative, and if so, for whom? In a certain respect, Lifton is offering us an integrative perspective by stressing that all three death equivalents (separation, disintegration, and stasis) are intimately bound up with their vital and affirmative counterparts. Thus separation and connection form two sides of the same coin and adolescence is filled with imagery that encompasses both.

This separation–connection spectrum also plays an important role in the psychoanalytical literature on adolescence. Blos' writings on adolescence are permeated with the theme of separation from parental nurturers. Blos is not making a statement as to whether or not this need for separation is normative. Rather, he is interested in examining the latent content that is revealed by these attempts to separate. In this schema, typical adolescent phenomena such as delinquency, promiscuity, and friendship loyalty (among others) are interpreted as fledgling attempts to separate from early love objects. Blos characterizes these attempts as defensive, a way of avoiding the emergence of oedipal strivings that reoccur during adolescence. The phenomenology of separation imagery is not seen for itself but in the light of struggling to avoid the taint of its opposite, that is, the desire for newly awakened oedipal connections to parents.

On the other side of the spectrum, Anna Freud interprets moments of connection, such as close peer friendships, adolescent love relationships, or a strong teacher–student relationship, as a defensive displacement of libido from parents onto parent substitutes. New attachments take the place of repressed fixations to the love objects of childhood. She states:

While they last, these love relations are passionate and exclusive, but they are of short duration. Persons are selected as objects and abandoned without any consideration for their feelings and others are chosen in their place. The abandoned objects are quickly and completely forgotten, but the form of the relation to them is preserved down to the minutest detail and is generally reproduced, with an exactness which almost suggests obsession, in the relation to the new object.

(1966, p. 118)

Anna Freud argues that essentially these passionate relationships in adolescence are best understood through the lens of recapitulation, that is, the adolescent is repeating his or her primary relationships to early love objects. Her tone is derisive, and at one point she even states, "These passionate and evanescent love fixations are not object relations at all" (ibid., p. 119). She goes on to describe them as merely primitive identifications which have no real bearing on the inner life of the adolescent. In other words, we cannot trust the authenticity of adolescent connections because there is an unconscious dynamic in play that distorts their true value.

In contrast to their basic mistrust of the phenomena, I propose that we can better understand the drama of adolescent relationships as experiential enactments of separateness and connectedness which involve images of life-affirmation, loss and death. Gentry comments on how the dialectical interplay between separateness and connectedness expresses moments of rich psychological experience. He states:

. . . this period of life [adolescence] can be characterized as an intensely psychological time. And the most psychologically illuminating ties are those liminal moments where the world becomes fragmented, relationships are severed, things fall apart. Psychological moments also occur when the world becomes unified, where relationships take hold and where things fall together. Adolescence must be filled to capacity with such moments. Intense connections and equally intense separations seem to take place daily. Moment by moment. The despair and breakup of a steady relationship can be followed by the delight of a new seemingly eternal love. Violent, murderous rage directed toward an anxious parent is often replaced by rapid hugs and affection which confuse a parent further.

(1989, audio tape)

The experiential enactment of separateness and connectedness appears in the drama that ensues when an adolescent comes to see a therapist for the first time and offers no resistance. She will tell it all and the hour is filled with an outpouring of highly personal, affectively charged material. In the immediacy of the interaction, one feels proud of one's therapeutic skills; the client is sharing a great deal, unburdening herself, and it is very satisfying to have made such a strong connection so quickly. As she gets ready to leave, an appointment is set for the next week. The next week arrives and she does not show up. After repeated attempts, she cannot be coaxed into returning.

The raw intensity of the connection scared the client away. She went too deep, too quickly, and since there was no time for a container to be built, it was too threatening to once again sit in the same room with the object of her self-revelations. For adolescents, it is common for feelings of distance and separation to follow upon the heels of an intense, all-encompassing connection. Thus, it is incumbent for the adolescent therapist in these situations to avoid getting caught up in the intensity of the adolescent's narrative and seek out opportunities to slow the process down and offer containment for what is being shared. For example, one can pause in the middle of the process, take a few deep breaths and ask the client what it is like to be here together talking about this material. This pause allows for reflection upon the process itself rather than the content being shared and reminds the client that even though she is doing most of the talking, a two-way exchange is going on. Or, one may gently interrupt the client's narrative by saying: "It seems like you have told me a lot of really important things about yourself today . . . I just want you to know that what we talk about stays between us." Then to go on and, in a general way, review the main points that were shared and say, "O.K. why don't we make a time for next week and talk some more." This reassures the client that what has been revealed is safe and it may be a good time to stop and get some distance on the conversation. It is also helpful to predict for the client that she may feel frightened or confused about the conversation and may not want to come back. Letting her know that this is a normal reaction can be reassuring and helps set the stage for another meeting.

Lifton, in discussing modern equivalents of separation imagery in traditional rites, asserts that the modern adolescent can be seen as "gravitating from feelings of absolute separateness and isolation from everyone and everything to a sense of merging totally with a group of peers—or with a single chum—in something approaching total connection" (1979 p. 83).

In a move that goes directly against the psychoanalytical tendency to evaluate these states as inferior and unreal, Winnicott (1963b) describes the adolescent as being essentially an isolate. It is from the position of isolation that he or she launches out into a relationship. With this in mind, we can then value states of isolation and merging as more than just ways of keeping instinctual anxiety at bay. They are also profound experiences of the world falling apart and coming together, moments that have their analogue in religious experience and may have their strongest valence in adolescence.

This way of viewing the fervor and upheaval of adolescent relationships stays closer to the lived experience of the adolescent. We are better able to attend phenomenologically to the powerful, life-affirming feelings that emerge as involvements with others deepen in love relationships and friendships, as well as attending to the image-feelings of separation, sorrow, loss (as if a small death has occurred), that subsumes one when falling out of a relationship. My concern here is that we do not simply pathologize these states. By recognizing their necessity, which grows out of the nature of adolescence as a central life-cycle transition, we can value their importance for the adolescent psyche.

Winnicott's idea has important clinical implications. Feelings of being isolated and separate are often compensated by an intense desire to be part of a group. I have witnessed this in high school freshman, at the beginning of the school year, struggling to fit themselves into one of the various groups at school. The desperate quality of this search to belong, which is a way of escaping feelings of isolation, can cause a kind of splitting for an adolescent who is trying to join a group which does not really jibe with who he is. There is an important psychological moment in that struggle to move out of a state of isolation and begin defining oneself through connection to a group.

It is also important to keep this dynamic in mind when someone is forced out of a group. For example, one of the greatest difficulties for an adolescent trying to make changes in her relationship to drugs and alcohol is the threat that comes in losing her peer group. It is critical in a clinical situation to explore the ensuing sense of isolation and loneliness that can result when she stops using and can no longer hang out with old friends who are still involved. This dynamic is mistakenly overlooked in the zeal to keep the adolescent sober; it is often the draw of comradeship and belonging that entices her back to using rather than a desire for the substance itself. Adolescents who are ostracized by others for being different experience an added layer of isolation that comes from being marginalized. For example, a serious danger for a young person negotiating a homosexual identity is the sense of isolation and despair that comes when he does not have a peer group with which to identify. The remarkable transformation in psychological functioning that occurs when such an individual finds membership in a supportive and caring group demonstrates the necessity of group life as a central part of identity formation in adolescence.

Winnicott's idea of the adolescent as isolate bespeaks an existential condition. With the onset of adolescence, the familiar taken-for-granted feeling of belonging shifts, and for the first time in life one encounters, at an existential level, what it means to be alone. In this sense, during a moment of feeling separated, an adolescent is thrown back on herself, forced to confront who she is as an individual on her own. There are not many containers in our culture for developing a capacity to be alone and this may account, in part, for the incessant push toward extroversion and group life that we find in adolescence. This period of development is especially hard for an individual with a more introverted nature, where finding one's identity in groups is already a troublesome task.

States of isolation and separateness in adolescence can be beneficial. In our culture, given the collective push toward extroversion, this is very difficult to divine. But consider for a moment the Native American vision quest in which a young person spends four or five days out in the wilderness, alone, in search of a guiding image for his life. The separation from family, friends and the village has a positive connotation in that one is provided a space in which to turn inward and discover a sense of his own uniqueness.

Hall eloquently describes this in the following passage:

> Initiation into manhood requires this temporary disavowal of the biological mother. It is comparable, in a general way, to a girl's initiation into the bear cub pack of the Goddess Artemis. During their pubescent years in the wilderness between the ages of nine and fourteen, Artemis' saffron-robed cubs see not boys or men. For youths of any gender this protected time of indeterminacy

between childhood and adulthood is needed for finding the God, or the myth, or the power that claims them. This lineage claims their soul alongside the earthly rights of physical parentage.[1]

(1989, p. 21)

As children are pushed into adult roles at younger ages, there is little time left in a culture like ours for a period of indeterminacy. Collective pressures are strong and adolescents must strain to find their own voice or their own images for what life is about. I believe this speaks to the special importance of individual psychotherapy with adolescents, which is often downplayed in managed care thinking where group and family work is favored. Can the solitude and containment of a one-on-one session be envisioned as creating a place quiet enough for some initial recovery of this indeterminate space?

DISINTEGRATION

The actual experience of ritual mutilation in traditional initiation rites expresses for Lifton the theme of disintegration. He states:

Mutilation in males can take forms we would judge to be extremely brutal—not only circumcision but subincision (the slitting of the length of the urethra from below, via the underside of the penis), the knocking out of teeth, scarifications, removal of a testicle, bitings, burnings, and the cutting off of a portion of a finger. There are analogous female mutilations—deformation of the labia minora, excision of portions of the clitoris, perforation of the hymen, and section of the perineum, though they tend to be a little less extreme and perhaps less central to the ceremonies.

(1979, pp. 74–5)

No doubt such practices strike our contemporary sensibility as extremely brutal, and it is valid to examine their meaning from political, sociological and economic points of view. I, however, want to stay within the realm of analyzing the psychological significance of these practices of mutilation. Are they responses to a psychological reality, in the context of life and death imagery, in the transforming body of the adolescent?

For example, the cutting of the skin in both male and female rites can be understood metaphorically as perforating the boundary one had around oneself as a child and thereby allowing in a new awareness of one's mortality. Intense pain brings forth a new relationship to the body; mutilation may serve to awaken the initiate to the singular reality of their embodiment and a deep-rooted connection to the natural world.

Adolescence is replete with bodily changes that evoke feelings of disintegration and fragmentation. Boys experience this when their voice cracks mid-sentence and all of a sudden they find themselves speaking in a falsetto tone, or the first time they take a sharp razor to their previously smooth faces. Both boys and girls are subject to bouts with acne, where it feels as if one's skin is virtually disintegrating before one's eyes and it is nearly impossible to conceal this from others. Powerful sexual urges and impulses arise that can feel as if an alien force has entered one's body. Growth spurts in both sexes also bring about a sense of disorientation, not being accustomed to the emerging contours of one's body. For girls, with the development of breasts and hips, their bodily definition as well as self-image transforms leaving them feeling frightened and confused. Lifton (ibid.) points out how menstruation, the bleeding and exfoliation of bodily tissue which signifies the beginning of puberty for girls, was thought to be a natural form of bodily disintegration in traditional societies. It radically alters a young woman's relationship to her body. Anne Frank expresses how it brought forth an awakening to the mystery of her body in the following passage from her diary:

> Each time I have a period—and that has only been three times— I have the feeling that in spite of all the pain, unpleasantness, and nastiness, I have a sweet secret, and that is why, although it is a nuisance to me in a way, I always long for the time that I shall feel that secret within me again.
>
> (1952, p. 117)

Discussing the disintegration–integrity spectrum in modern adolescence, Lifton says, "The American adolescent may fluctuate from disintegrative feelings of being 'wiped out,' reduced to 'absolutely nothing' and euphoric feelings of 'having everything together,' of things being 'just right' " (1979, p. 83).

While leading adolescent psychotherapy groups, I have witnessed adolescents fluctuate between experiencing the overwhelming feelings of being reduced to absolutely nothing one moment and then suddenly feeling energetic and connected the next. These disintegrative feelings are most ripe during the first few minutes of a group, when the resistance to settling down and talking things over with each other is at its highest. There is a cacophony of loose associations that fill in the quiet moments before a topic is arrived at: "I'm hungry"; "This sucks"; "I'm so bored"; "I'd rather be doing anything else right now." These utterances, spoken in anguish, echo disintegrative feelings akin to a fragmentation of the self. It is infecting to be so close to them. As a group leader, one is thrown into this cesspool of unrelenting emotion and asked to bear the tension. Its source is not any particular adolescent group member; it is a suffering that has a truly collective dimension. Over the years of trying to figure out how best to diminish it, I discovered that the most meaningful adolescent groups I ever ran were those in which this fragmentation reached a peak in the beginning and I did not, out of the unbearable feelings it stirred up in me, rush in to fill it up with structure.

"More structure" is always the recommended antidote for the kind of anxieties that adolescents in groups stir up in us. The alternative to increased structure is to know that a space needs to be given in the beginning of the group for these difficult affects in order to increase the chance that things can move to another level once the group process sets in and takes hold. It is as if the ground is being churned up in order that something new can take root. The trick is to resist personalizing those rough moments at the beginning, to resist seeing them as resulting from a failure in oneself as a group leader, and to resist collapsing the tension by rushing in too quickly to fill the void.

It is during adolescence that one is highly susceptible to the disintegrative feeling of being "wiped out." To recognize this state of disintegration as a death equivalent, an experience of primordial imagery, provides one with a keener appreciation for the depressive moments that run through adolescence. Crying, loneliness, self-pity, thoughts of death, exile, and long, lugubrious sadnesses are part and parcel of the adolescent experience. Attuning oneself to the prevalence of this kind of emotion and finding ways to engage it clinically diminishes our tendency to overpathologize these states of mind.

STASIS

Lifton describes the experience of stasis in traditional initiations in the following manner:

> In male initiations, the frenzied activities are frequently interrupted by a "long night of silence" often in the forest or wilderness, usually in the presence of sacred objects before whom elders perform gentle rites . . . . In female ceremonies stasis is more marked and prolonged, and, in fact, tends to characterize the predominant theme of seclusion. A sense of cessation of all life-powers suggested by the taboos on contact with earth and sun, which are respectively the source of and energy for that power . . . . While in these rites all three death equivalents are closely associated with death itself, patterns of stasis provide the most literal rendition of lifelessness.
>
> (1979, p. 76)

In terms of contemporary adolescence, Lifton describes stasis as "the feeling of being 'stuck' or 'dead' inside [which] can alternate with a sense of brimming over with energy and vitality" (ibid., p. 83).

The imagery pertaining to the state of stasis is brilliantly evoked by Winnicott (1963a) in his classic essay on adolescence, "Struggling Through the Doldrums." He describes as an essential part of adolescent maturation the need to go through a doldrum phase, a time in which one feels futile, where nothing is moving or going anywhere. This is a particularly painful experience to bear and resonates with the more explicit imagery of lifelessness in traditional rites of passage. Winnicott accounts for these states by recognizing that adolescents are in a fluctuating process of establishing their identity where things are not yet fixed, and one cannot rely upon a core of self-representations for feelings of self-worth as one does as an adult. Adolescence as a process involving a depth transformation of identity evokes feelings of futility, numbness, and inferiority. The result is a kind of psychological down time, which I earlier characterized as a state of becoming.

It is typical for adolescents to respond to the doldrums, feeling dead or numb inside, by sleeping a lot, watching hours upon hours of television, holing up in their room for days on end. Some experience periods of weakness and passivity in the face of an overwhelming world. Figure 4.1 provides us with an apt image for this state of being.

Figure 4.1 Doldrums

The spectrum between stasis, the cessation of all activity, and its counterpart, movement and vitality, plays an integral role in adolescent psychotherapy. Adolescent therapists frequently feel that the treatment is stuck, nothing is happening, and there is no sign of change. The difficulty of treating adolescents is magnified when our therapeutic expectations fail to take into account the inherent periods of stasis in the adolescent psyche. Winnicott (1964) evokes this sense of stasis when he asserts that there is no cure for adolescence except time and maturation, and that the process cannot be hurried along. An excellent question to ask when we are feeling stuck is: are we trying to cure the adolescent of their own adolescence?

In this respect, I worked with a seventeen-year-old girl who came in weekly complaining about her boyfriend who was mistreating her. We worked closely together exploring the feelings that his emotional neglect brought up for her and discussing other times in her life when she felt equally mistreated. I had expectations, each week, that through the therapy something concrete was going to change in her relationship with her boyfriend. For example, I imagined she was going to stand up for herself and demand to be treated with respect and if things did not change, she would leave him. My hopes were thwarted week after week. It seemed that no matter how much we talked about it the situation between them remained the same.

I felt like a failure. I was not getting through to her and the therapy was useless. However, as time went on, I made a decision to lower my expectations and accept that she was really stuck and not ready to make a change. This shift in attitude on my part opened up something new between us. It was as if she could feel my acceptance of her stuckness and this allowed her to be more genuine with me.

Rather than fight the lack of movement, it is more effective to ask adolescents to articulate where they feel stuck and what aspects of their lives feel futile. A statement by an adolescent such as "Nothing in my life is ever going to change," threatens our view of ourselves as agents of change. How difficult it is then to hear such a statement. If we are able to let go of our need to fix it or make it better and bear the sense of futility it stirs up in us, we communicate to an adolescent that such moments can be tolerated and survived.

Jung's model of the regression and the progression of the libido is another way of characterizing the spectrum of stasis and movement in adolescence. For Jung (*CW* 8, paras 60–76), regression of the libido occurs when a change in the environment has created the need for a new way of interacting with the world; one's habitual attitude can no longer satisfy the demands of adaptation. In the case of adolescents, childish patterns of relating are suddenly no longer valid, something else is needed. As psychic energy changes direction, searching for a new channel in which to flow, adaptation to the demands of everyday life are compromised. The regression of libido activates unconscious contents in the form of symbols and images which hint at new directions for forward movement. It may seem to an outside observer like the person is never going to move from where he is, never going to change.

For Jung, this kind of regression has an incestuous quality to it. One way of understanding why Jung calls it incestuous is to hear his description as a metaphor for a call back to the past, to an earlier state of dependence and passivity. As we noted in Chapter 2, both the psychoanalytical school and the developmental analytical school understand the incestuous quality of adolescent regression as a recapitulation of what actually occurred in one's oedipal or pre-oedipal past and this focus on the revival of these incestuous states forms a main locus of their work. I believe it is possible to be cognizant of the incestuous forces that arise in adolescence and work with them in terms of their pull back to an earlier state of protection and dependence without having to reify them into a theory of recapitulation.

It is also necessary to differentiate when the doldrums seem to be part of the natural course of adolescence and when states of stasis become pathological. In the former case, one must help parents in becoming conscious of the imaginings that such moments of stasis bring forth. I have heard fantasies such as "He is going to be a bum, just like his father," or "She'll never make it to college. I'll have to take care of her the rest of my life." It is helpful to reassure parents that these moments of immobility are a natural part of growing up. Therapeutically, we must help them negotiate the difficult middle ground between relinquishing some control by accepting the inevitable moments of stasis and still maintaining certain expectations around the responsibilities of everyday life.

I have seen this period of stasis reach pathological dimensions in adolescents who, over a long stretch of time, are unable to get out of bed in the morning, go to school, and carry on in any way with their lives. Although there is frequently a flurry of commotion after the morning alarm goes off, parents screaming and yelling, urging their son or daughter to get out of bed and get ready for school, a typical case consists of the adolescent remaining in bed till noon, spending the rest of the day at home watching television and then going out with friends until late at night. Very often there is a tacit agreement between the adolescent and one of the parents that this kind of regression will be tolerated and, at the most basic level, left unchallenged. In my experience, parental attitudes can exaggerate the doldrum period and may serve their unconscious need to have their adolescent son or daughter remain dependent and never develop the skills they need to leave home.

METAPHORIC DEATH VERSUS LITERAL DEATH

As we have now seen, separation, disintegration, and stasis each in their own way evoke images and feelings related to the presence of death in life and are an integral part of adolescent initiation rituals. The overall initiation ceremony itself is commonly conceived of as a ritualized death experience followed by a symbolic rebirth, representing the dying of one's childhood and rebirth as an adult.

> The majority of initiatory ordeals more or less clearly imply a ritual death followed by resurrection or a new birth. The central moment of every initiation is represented by the ceremony symbolizing the death of the novice and his return to the fellowship of living.
>
> (Eliade 1958, p. xii)

> The novice is considered dead, and he remains dead for the duration of his novitiate.
>
> (ibid., p. 76)

According to Scott, images of death and loss accompany all fundamental transitions in human life: "During such transitions, there are times of unusual suspension, loneliness, senses of being vaguely out of joint, heightened sensitivity to pain and loss, symptoms of grief" (1982, p. 97). The importance of this type of death imagery for an understanding of adolescent development should not be overlooked. Scott describes the extreme nature of adolescent transformation:

> What is close and important to the child grows more and more distant to the emerging youth. The child, as a place of experience, dies away. What cannot be forgotten by the child cannot be remembered by the youth.
>
> (ibid.)

This framework places us in a better position to understand the pervasiveness of suicidal imagery in adolescence. Hillman (1964), in his book, *Suicide and the Soul*, speaks of the impulse toward suicide as a transformative urge: metaphorically, a part of the self must die in order to make room for a new way of being. In this regard, the suicidal impulse contains within itself an urge for new life. It is very important to hold in one's mind the literal and metaphorical levels when assessing suicidal ideation. The problem of suicide forces us to reckon with our susceptibility to confound these two levels, for what may be an authentic wish for a part of the self to metaphorically die can become literalized in the actual act of taking one's life. Understanding the symbolic nature of the suicide impulse is especially relevant in the work with adolescents. While traditional societies recognized the need of the adolescent psyche for this kind of transformation and provided a ritualized experience of death and rebirth, the modern adolescent may be unconsciously drawn to the imagery of suicide as the only means available to express the urge for radical transformation.

This brings us back to Fordham's distinction between deintegration and disintegration that I touched upon in Chapter 2. Fordham uses the term disintegration differently than Lifton. For Fordham (1957, p. 118), a disintegratory process represents the destruction or splitting of the ego. He contrasts this with the self's dynamic ability to deintegrate—the spontaneous division of the self in its readiness for new experience. Deintegration involves a sense of dislocation, being knocked off balance, but is followed by the self's ability to reintegrate, incorporating what is new. This is a useful way of distinguishing between different types of suicidal ideation that an adolescent client may present. When a client is at risk and feels at the mercy of suicidal impulses, one could say that this is a disintegrative process. A downward spiral is occurring as there is real threat to the integrity of the ego. In such a case, an individual would require an outside intervention, such as hospitalization, for safety and protection.

We can now bring together Fordham's notion of deintegration and Lifton's sense of death imagery as being part of the fabric of adolescence such that it is possible to work therapeutically with suicidal fantasies in adolescence as legitimate psychological processes that may be part of the deintegration of the self. Traditional rites of passage teach us of the psychic necessity of metaphoric death during adolescence. In contrast, in our culture, the appalling rate of adolescent suicide is in part a result of our lack of imagination about the very possibility of metaphoric death so that it has to be literally enacted. As a result, we frequently miss what is metaphorically being reckoned with in the urge to take one's life.

As an example, I worked with a thirteen-year-old male junior high school student who was incredibly gifted academically but was constantly teased and made fun of by his classmates. He responded to his classmate's jeers by acting clownish and goofy, which only served to alienate his teachers and worsen his standing in the class. As a client in therapy, I found him to be highly controlled in his emotional output, depending upon his well-developed intellect to defend against feeling.

As trust between us developed, he opened up to the fact that he frequently felt like killing himself and had never shared these feelings with anyone else. In contradistinction to his usual non-demonstrative, emotionless presentation, the letting forth of these fantasies brought forward a flood of tears and grief. Through my questions, I got the sense that he did not feel in danger of acting on these feelings and being able to sit with him and listen and discuss them became a central part of the therapy. At one point, I said, "Sometimes feeling like you want to kill yourself is about wanting a part of yourself to change very badly. Can you think of a part of yourself you'd really like to be different?" This type of question is one way of getting at the urge for transformation in the suicidal impulse. My client responded by talking about the clownish one, desperate for attention, who does all the stupid things in class. As the therapy progressed, we worked on helping him find other ways of expressing himself and connecting with his classmates. What is striking in this case is how releasing the suicidal feelings, having them be heard and felt, allowed for a dramatic shift in my client's psychological orientation and behavior.

An important aspect of therapy with adolescents is learning how to work with such unsettling imagery. Consider the following two statements from therapy:

A fourteen-year-old girl tells me: "Late at night when everyone is asleep, I think to myself, 'Am I going to die and float around up there?' Then I get scared and turn on the light and read."

A sixteen-year-old boy challenges, "What does it matter? We are going to die. You're going to die. You're nothing."

Provocative and disturbing images abound when we allow ourselves to truly listen and observe what is going on with adolescents. We must carefully watch which fantasies get set off in us before making an intervention that may be premature. In fantasy, it feels like our client is falling apart but we must remember that we felt this last week, and that today, she came back, whole.

THE PARADOXICAL NATURE OF ADOLESCENCE

Lifton remarks on the fact that after an initiation ceremony, the death equivalents are "transmuted into their vital components on behalf of reunion with the group: the initiate is reconnected, reinte-grated, and reactivated as an adult in a sacred community" (1979,

p. 77). In other words, one undergoes an experience of mutilation, loss of vitality, lifelessness, but in the last stage of the ceremony, is revitalized by their counterparts as one returns to the community in a new role. American adolescents, according to Lifton, seem to have an unsteady relationship with the death equivalents and their counterparts, flip flopping very rapidly from one extreme to the other.

This also evidences the contradictions and paradoxes in adolescence. In the following quotation, Anna Freud captures the essence of adolescence as a paradoxical state of being—the polarities that manifest in the thoughts, feelings, and behaviors of one who is no longer a child but not yet an adult. She states:

> Adolescents are excessively egoistic, regarding themselves as the center of the universe and the sole object of interest, and yet at no time in later life are they capable of so much self-sacrifice and devotion. They form the most passionate love relations, only to break them off as abruptly as they began them. On the one hand, they throw themselves enthusiastically into the life of the community and, on the other, they have an overpowering need for solitude. They oscillate between blind submission to some self-chosen leader and defiant rebellion against any and every authority. They are selfish and materially minded and at the same time full of lofty idealism.
>
> (1966, pp. 137–8)

One significant aspect of working with adolescents is being able to bear these essential paradoxes that are at the heart of the adolescent process. Scott comments on the arduousness of bearing the tension of these contradictions in psychotherapy. He states:

> Therapeutic eros, true to the classical heritage of eros, includes profound contradictions, and allowing these contradictions, which are basic in human being for character formation, is one of the most difficult and overlooked aspects of what in fact ordinarily goes on in psychotherapy.
>
> (1982, p. 95)

As therapists, we find ourselves constantly maneuvering between these polarized states of being. One encounters difference and contradiction at every turn. For example, an adolescent will appear to be one way in a group situation with other adolescents, but sit with him alone and it is as if another person has entered his body. Another alteration occurs in the contrast between how adolescents act when they are alone and how they act when they are together with their families. Within an individual session, an adolescent may abruptly alternate between acting like a young child and behaving in a more mature manner. It takes a great deal of flexibility on the part of the therapist to move with these shifts in identity.

Changes occur rapidly, week to week, hour to hour. In my work in schools, an adolescent could be sitting in my office crying one minute and laughing and joking out in the hall with friends the next. Or what seemed horrible and unbearable one session was shrugged off as no big deal the next week. We have to be careful and deliberate in how we maneuver, making sure we do not intervene before we have gotten a consistent picture of what is going on in a situation.

It is also important to be conscious of the countertransferential response Hillman refers to as "disintegrative anxiety" (1977, p. 117). This is the feeling that things are coming apart, decaying, and falling away. It is a process that accompanies change. Nowhere is this more noticeable than in work with adolescents. Hillman proposes that we respond to the disintegrative process by engaging the client from our own state of wounded consciousness. The concept of a "wounded healer," being able to heal through one's wounds, is itself paradoxical. But I understand it to mean that unless we can bear the disintegrative process within ourselves, that sense of turmoil and loss that comes with change, we cannot be open to it with our clients. When we resist the dislocation and fragmentation that an adolescent may be living through, we may unconsciously compensate by emphasizing ideals of wholeness and order. In this sense, we deny the fundamental paradoxes that form the basis of the adolescent psyche and prematurely close off the possibility of an adolescent finding her own sense of order and integration that arises out of these contradictions.

Chapter 5

Bodily, idealistic, and ideational awakenings

"Your ideas about people are still pretty naive," the thirteen-year-old chief said coldly. "No adult is going to be able to do something we couldn't do. There's a huge seal called 'impossibility' pasted all over this world. And don't forget that we're the only ones who can tear it off once and for all." Awe-stricken, the others fell silent.

Yukio Mishima

INTRODUCTION

Concomitant with the imagery of death and dying that manifests itself during adolescence, another set of image-feelings evolve that symbolize the adolescent's relation to power and powerlessness. Lifton uses the term power not in the sense of control over others, but rather as basic life-power, "the experience of vitality, competence and control, as opposed to the powerlessness of feeling inundated by death imagery and reduced to deadness" (Lifton 1979, p. 82). As the adolescent departs from the world of childhood and begins to acquire adult status, new modes of world engagement emerge: adult sexuality, employment, higher education, a new level of sociopolitical responsibility heralded by the right to vote and increased participation in cultural life. In tackling these new roles, there is a struggle to feel and act in a competent and self-assured way. Thus, vitality and life-power as visceral image-feelings are intimately entwined with new dimensions of bodily experience (adolescent sexuality), involvements beyond the self (idealistic yearnings), and the attainment of knowledge (ideational processes). The psychoanalytical literature recognizes these three modes of engaging in the world as essential aspects of the adolescent experience. Given their importance as primary developmental undertakings, it is crucial to arrive at a perspective that allows us to see in a clear way what is at stake for the adolescent in the emerging relationships to these tasks. In examining these dimensions of the adolescent experience, I will contrast psychoanalytical and phenomenological approaches, thinking through the implications of each orientation's understanding of what it means to achieve adult status.

ADOLESCENT SEXUALITY

Blos contends that the essence of adolescence is the transition from a non-sexual to a sexual existence.

> The decisive progress in emotional development during adolescence proper lies in the progress toward heterosexuality. This stage can only be reached after the pre-genital drives have been relegated to an initiatory and subordinate role in favor of genital sexuality or orgiastic potency.
>
> (Blos 1962, p. 123)

> What is the instinctual modality specific for adolescence along-side of which the ego develops its own corollary characteristics? The novelty lies in the subordination—only gradually, and most often only partially, achieved—of the erogenous zones to genital primacy.
>
> (ibid., p. 174)

Blos' theoretical system rests upon the implications of the above two passages. He deems the goal of adolescent development to be the adolescent's new desire for a heterosexual love relationship. The genesis of this desire, rooted in pre-adolescence and finding its ultimate expression in late adolescence, is a biologically based, instinctually determined transformation which forms the core developmental issue of adolescence. Indeed, emotional development and ego development are seen as secondary to the attainment of an irreversible heterosexual identity.

To unfold the dynamics of this process, it is necessary to take one step back and look closely at Blos' characterization of pre-adolescence. During the pre-adolescent phase, there is a quantitative increase of instinctual pressure. At this stage, one does not discover a new love object or experience a shift in instinctual aim. Instead, the libidinal and aggressive modes of gratification which were relied upon at an earlier period of development are re-cathexted—a resurgence of pre-genitality takes place (ibid., p. 57). Any experience has the potential of becoming sexually stimulating. For example, Blos notes that pre-adolescent boys often have spontaneous erections; a boy's genitals serve as non-specific discharge organs of tension. Through a gradual transformation the male adolescent's genitals acquire exclusive sensitivity to heterosexual stimuli. For pre-adolescent girls, play-acting and tomboyishness, what Blos calls a "thrust of activity," are prevalent. He conceives of these as phallic activities, stemming from an unresolved childhood conflict of penis envy. Through a developmental transformation occurring with the onset of female adolescence, a strong assertion of femininity takes the place of phallic play and tomboyishness.

What differentiates pre-adolescence from adolescence proper is not just a quantitative drive increase, but the emergence of a new drive quality. Blos states:

> Pregenitality loses increasingly the role of a satiatory function, by becoming relegated to an initiatory activity—mentally and physically—it gives rise to a new drive component, namely forepleasure. This shift in drive organization eventually gives genitality a place of prime order.
>
> (ibid., p. 71)

Thus, the pre-adolescent obsession with filth, oral greed, sadistic, and anal activities (all examples of the upsurgence of pre-genitality which played a satiatory function) transform in adolescence to a concern entirely with specifically sexual matters. One moves out of a "perverse" mode of polymorphous existence into a focused, mature, "natural" mode of searching for a heterosexual love object.

The other essential shift concerns object choice. After pre-adolescence, one makes repeated attempts to separate from primary love objects. The crowning achievement of this is a complete renunciation of the incestuous object and a final and irreversible turn toward heterosexual object choice.

For Blos, this turn toward heterosexuality is the driving force in adolescent development. He states, "The various defensive measures employed during adolescence proper are under normal circumstances temporary emergency measures. They are dispensed with as soon as the ego gains strength by joining forces with the forward movement of the libido toward heterosexuality" (ibid., p. 123). Blos goes on to compare the movement of instinctual energy in adolescence to a classical drama:

> The phase of adolescence which we are now about to explore corresponds to the second act of the classical drama: the dramatis personae have all become intricately and irrevocably entangled; the spectator has come to realize that there can be no return to the expectancies and propitious events of the opening scene; and he recognizes that the conflicts will relentlessly drive forward to a climactic final settlement.
>
> (ibid., p. 88)

Here, Blos is describing the psychodynamic mechanisms, occurring between latency and late adolescence, that allow for a basic change in existential condition: one enters this period a child and emerges from it a young adult. It is not a far stretch of the imagination to read Blos as describing a kind of extended initiation process, the essence of which is the transformation of instinctual (sexual) energy. For Blos, as well as in traditional cultures, the essence of adolescence is the transition from non-sexual or pre-genital existence to sexual existence. Sexuality moves things forward. It is the engine driving the transformational processes of adolescence.

What is in contention, though, is how we are to understand the nature of this sexual energy. For example, Lifton concurs that sexuality is central to all initiation imagery. "Sexuality, from the beginning, provides the imagery and energy that keeps life going" (1979, p. 30). However, he does not conceive of it as a literal dynamism that fixes sexual orientation, but rather as a vital force that provides much of the content for the drama of death and rebirth. Whereas for Blos, the call of adult sexual life sets the whole process in motion, Lifton describes it as "the essence of the new adult power held out before the initiate, a form of vitality that must be earned . . . One must know death in order to become a powerful and responsible sexual adult" (ibid., p. 77).

The distinction here between Lifton's and Blos' conception of sexuality accords with the difference between Freud's and Jung's conception of libido. Blos' understanding of sexuality as fueling the adolescent process is based upon Freud's view that libido is primarily sexual in nature. Indeed, the transformation that occurs is a literal transformation of sexual energy from a childish state (forepleasure) to an adult state (striving after heterosexual objects).

Lifton, on the other hand, is closer to Jung in equating libido with psychic energy or life-energy. This distinction, which played a crucial role in the eventual split between psychoanalysis and analytical psychology, impacts our understanding of adolescent sexuality.

The conception of libido as life-energy frees us up to re-imagine and re-mythologize our understanding of adolescent sexuality so that it does not depend upon a vision of a stable heterosexual identity as the universal driving force pushing forward the process of sexual transformation. What is at stake here is a perspective on the sexual transformation itself which includes symbolic and arche-typal dimensions. This deliteralizing move makes it possible for us to expand our frame of reference to include an understanding of adoles-cent sexual development in a wider context that does not exclude or pathologize the formation of a homosexual or bisexual orientation.[1]

Keeping in mind the strong connection between becoming a sexual being and acquiring life-power opens the door to accessing the manifold layers of meaning that accompany the experience of adolescent sexuality. As an illustration, I worked with one young man, seventeen years old, who was born with severe physical and cognitive handicaps including debilitating heart and lung problems and mild mental retardation. Given his extremely tall and thin frame (he was well over six feet) coupled with his physical handi-caps, walking was an arduous task—he could only move his body in a slow and methodical manner. Throughout his life, he was picked on and teased by other children, sometimes brutally and abusively. Adults were generally afraid of him, viewing him as a monstrous figure who would strike out aggressively or sexually if given the opportunity. In actuality, this young man never struck anyone and his sexual expression in the world was limited to being very attracted to older women and asking them out on dates whenever he had a chance to interact with them.

Part of our work together centered on his overwhelming feelings of worthlessness that came about because he was constantly being rejected (no one wanted anything to do with him), along with his strong wish to feel loved and to actively love another person. In describing the flood of sexual feelings that would erupt when he saw a woman to whom he was attracted on television or in real life, he used the metaphor that it was as if a sex werewolf came on the scene and took over for a while. On a hunch, with no awareness of his ability to express himself pictorially or his willingness to do so, I asked him to draw me a picture of this werewolf (see Figure 5.1).

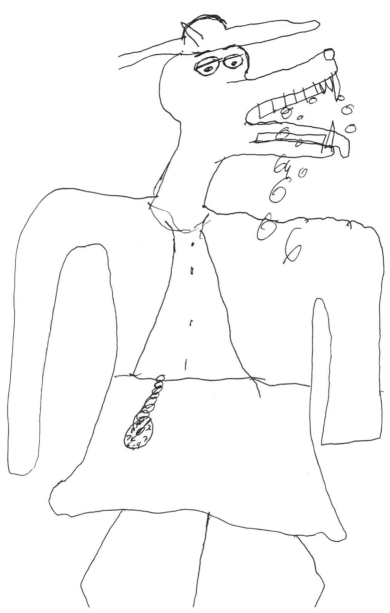

Figure 5.1 Werewolf

The werewolf's clothing was described as a kind of "zoot suit" worn by a man out on the town having a good time. The lack of hands in the picture may symbolize my client's impotence in the face of establishing human contact. He had been repeatedly told not to touch, that touching was bad and wrong, thus the conspicuousness of the absent hands. The sex werewolf can be seen as an illustration of the potential for life-power that is evoked in sexual desire. The watch hanging from his pocket shows how sexuality brings the individual into an embodied sense of time and history (think, for example, of the way in which sexual experiences become life-markers in adolescence). The yearning look in the eyes and the foaming at the mouth express a voracious hunger. However, the sex werewolf was not seeking literal genital sexuality (something of which my client did not even have a clear cognitive conception), but a longing for the vitality, life-energy and connection that was evoked in his imaginings about sexuality. Therapeutically, we explored how to integrate the sex werewolf, how to relate with him in a way where he did not have to completely take over once his concerns were legitimated and given room for expression.

For Lifton, the inquiry into sexuality is not ultimately concerned with infantile sexual development, but rather with delineating how the particular kind of sexuality proper to adolescence forcefully emerges out of the body and connects with a core sense of self. He asks, "How does this powerful bodily impulse, newly experienced in a fullness that encompasses the entire self, relate to the rest of life and death imagery confronting one in immediate and ultimate ways?" (ibid., p. 83).

At personal and immediate levels, sexuality brings with it the struggle for bodily integrity in the face of the unyielding impulses and feelings that are evoked at puberty. There are terrible fears and insecurities about whether one's body can work well, in a coordinated way, such that one can feel competent and integrated while exploring sexuality with another. There is the terrifying possibility of things falling apart, not working, not being in tune. The self is on the line as one submits to these feelings in the context of letting go of control with another person. The expression of physical love touches at the roots of one's identity as the merging of intimacy, closeness and trust transforms the developing personality.

At ultimate levels, sexuality holds out the promise of transcendence:

Immediate sexual pleasure is appreciated and sought after, but in the service of organismic transcendence—one "loses oneself" in order to merge with some form of ultimate life-power. However free or restricted sexuality may be, it is always part of something larger than itself.

(ibid., p. 77)

Music videos tantalize with images of sexual transcendence. The tone of the singer's voice, the lyrics and the beat as well as the seductive images that attend the music all point to the connection between sexuality and the desire for the self's dissolution. Likewise, rock concert theatrics and pyrotechnics evoke moments of experiential transcendence.

This same desire for transcendence is equally expressed in the idealistic and ideational yearnings which mark this age. Lifton states, "For sexual awakening is virtually simultaneous with historical awakening, a leap in awareness concerning cultural forces (whether political movements, athletic traditions, or schools of art) extending beyond the individual life span" (ibid., p. 83). The psychoanalytical theories of adolescence also connect the awakening of sexuality in adolescence with an outpouring of ideation and idealism. However, as illustrated in the next section, I will offer an alternative understanding of this connection.

LIFE-VITALIZING KNOWLEDGE

Blos asserts a psychoanalytical disclaimer against the authenticity of adolescent idealism and ideation:

Such states are frequently experienced, for example, in relation to abstractions such as Truth, Nature, Beauty or in the involvement with ideas or ideals of a political, philosophical, aesthetic, or religious nature. Such ego states of quasi-merger in the realm of symbolic representations are sought as temporary respite and serve as safeguards against total merger with infantile, internalized objects.

(1967, p. 167)

Here, the adolescent's fervent idealism and fascination with ideas is interpreted as an ego defense against regressive merger with dependent childhood states of mind. Along the same line, Blos equates adolescent idolization of famous men and women as examples of regressed ego states. He says:

> In our contemporary world they are, predominantly, chosen from show business and sports. These figures are the collective great ones. We are reminded of the idealized parent of the child's younger years. Their glorified images constituted an indispensable regulator of the child's narcissistic balance. It should not surprise us that the bedroom walls, plastered with the collective idols, become bare as soon as object libido is engaged in genuine relationships. Then, the pictorial flock of transient gods and goddesses is rendered dispensable almost overnight.
>
> (ibid.)

Blos' analysis fails here because he is not looking broadly enough into the teleological developmental function of these phenomena and therefore reduces them to either temporary stop-gap measures on the way to heterosexual object love, or as defensive measures against oedipal strivings and a recapitulation of early infantile development.

Idealization, from a teleological point of view, puts an adolescent in touch with a source of vitalizing possibilities. Idealistic yearnings express an active search for energy and inspiration that connects one to a power lying outside of everyday ego boundaries. One clear way of perceiving the teleological function in action is to simply ask an adolescent to talk about who it is they admire and why. By listening with a metaphorical ear, one hears that what they most admire about the idealized individual (whether it is their intellectual or athletic ability, moral courage, sense of humor, ability to gain power and prestige, etc.) resonates with and gives voice to undisclosed layers of their own personality. In other words, it is not just who they choose to idealize, but, more importantly, the particular way this person is imaginatively taken up that offers us a striking glimpse of the adolescent's psyche.

Furthermore, idealistic yearnings express themselves in the search for a mentor, that is, an older and wiser individual who has the ability, through a commensurate vision of life, to raise one's spirit, usually through instruction and edification. The closest approximation to the idea of a mentor in modern psychological nomenclature is that of a role model. A role model is usually conceived of as a successful member of the community with high moral standards who is worthy of emulation. Here, the emphasis is on the positive moral influence the role model will have on youth. Role models, such as sports stars, movie and television actors and musicians, supposedly inspire adolescents to make positive moral choices, for example, not to take drugs or get involved in crime. This is not the same thing at all as a mentor who uses the relationship to awaken vital life-energy in an adolescent. A different sensibility is involved in discerning when an adult has the potential to mentor an adolescent in comparison to declaring someone with high moral standards to be a role model. What attracts an adolescent to an adult mentor is not always visible; it is not so easy to immediately perceive the nature or source of the connection. The commensurate vision of life uniting the two may remain hidden.

One seventeen-year-old with whom I worked had a history of school avoidance since the third grade. He talked with me about a neighbor of his, a carpenter whom he helped out on weekends and in the summer. About this man, he said, "He, I can learn from. It's not like school where I space out and hate coming. He's got something to teach me." The hunger for mentoring is particularly palpable today, where what little contact adolescents and adults have with each other has an increasingly hostile and antagonistic tone.

I now want to make even more explicit the connection between adolescent idealism and the yearning for knowledge, skills, and ideas. Anna Freud, in keeping with the psychoanalytical tradition, derides the way in which adolescents passionately get involved with ideas. In her paper, "Instinctual Anxiety During Puberty," she proposes that during adolescence the ego is terrified of being submerged by the instincts. She interprets the adolescent's increasing interest in applying intelligence and ideas to matters of the world as a result of the strengthening of ego institutions forged to resist the fierce attacks launched upon them. She states:

> The abstract intellectual discussions and speculations in which young people delight are not genuine attempts at solving the tasks set by reality. Their mental activity is rather an indication of a tense alertness for the instinctual processes and the translation into abstract thought of that which they perceive. The philosophy of life which they construct—it may be their demand for revolution in the outside world—is really their response to the perception of the new instinctual demands of their own id, which threaten to revolutionize their whole life. Their ideals of

friendship and undying loyalty are simply a reflection of the disquietude of the ego when it perceives the evanescence of all its new and passionate object relations.

(1966, p. 115)

Thoughtfulness about the world as well as political and moral responsiveness is read in terms of its "supposed" latent meaning, that is, ideational processes primarily serve as a defensive structure of the ego, protecting it from submersion by the emergence of powerful instincts in the body. She concludes that "the aim of intellectualization is to link up instinctual processes closely with ideational contents and so to render them accessible to consciousness and amenable to control" (ibid., p. 117).

Anna Freud's theory is problematic in that it demeans the integrity of what an adolescent perceives, senses, and thinks in relation to the world. This kind of theorizing too quickly severs the connection between psyche and world, such that what may be a genuine engagement with and responsiveness to the zeitgeist is explained by a series of internal dynamics that reduce the adolescent psyche to a solipsistic mechanism.

Could it not be that the very awakening of instinctual life that is at the center of the psychoanalytical perspective places the adolescent in a unique position of viewing the world? In other words, could we imagine that the instinctual turmoil of adolescence creates a special sensitivity and receptivity to the world and that this can manifest in the pleasure with which ideas are entertained, engaged, and undertaken. Adolescents might not have the life-experience, formal knowledge, or intellectual skill with which to articulate an idea in a measured way, but they do have penetrating visions of the world whose impact has long-lasting effects. What would happen if we engaged adolescents more seriously at an ideational level? Certainly a good teacher is one who is able to tap into these visions, while at the same time providing intellectual tools to help clarify and articulate what is being seen and felt and thought about.

A significant aspect of adolescent psychotherapy involves the back and forth exchange of ideas. The work at an ideational level is at the same time a way of working with emotion. Discussing ideas is an opportunity for an adolescent to fully engage her emotional life in a safe and non-threatening manner. Dialogical engagement with ideas is also a way of working on behavior. As ideas evolve, behavior changes. New ways of thinking about the world open the adolescent up to new modes of being in the world. This is the positive side to the fluid boundary between understanding and action in adolescence.

By placing ideational awakening in the context of the struggle with life and death imagery, Lifton is in dialogue with Anna Freud and Blos' approach. In his view, the quest for knowledge revolves around the adolescent self feeling its way toward adult integration of both newly emerging bodily states as well as mental or spiritual feelings. Examples of this are found in adolescent fascination with religious or spiritual systems, adolescent interest in machines and mechanics (what Lifton calls "adolescent tinkering"), and adolescent devotion to political or environmental causes. However, the pursuit of these types of knowledge is not seen as a mechanism of defense. Lifton comments:

Adolescent tinkering or spirituality are frequently viewed . . . as means of further separating body from mind via a transformation or sublimation of bodily (erotic) impulses. This view holds some truth, but it misses the central point: whatever the valence of one kind of feeling versus another, the adolescent is moving toward an adult style of symbolization and constructing psychic forces for adult use. Even when the tinkering or spirituality seems to be self-enclosed, rote and technicized in the extreme, the knowledge activity now reaches far beyond itself.

(1979, p. 84)

He goes on to say:

The quest for even the most mechanical forms of knowledge as with the most vividly spiritual (or religious) makes manifest the principle that knowledge is mana, and mana is desperately required by the beleaguered adolescent self. Knowledge is not only cognitive and emotional but also (as the Bible makes clear) erotic, and in all spheres it includes competence in performance. To be sure, knowledge from birth is equated with life-power.

(ibid.)

Anna Freud's declaration that the seeking of intellectual knowledge is a sublimation of erotic impulses, a method for keeping them in check, is contested by Lifton's assertion that knowledge itself has an erotic aspect: it grants life-power. It is not a disguised attempt to separate body from mind. In fact, it unites body and mind as it reaches out toward a deeper sense of self that is the source of vitality.

Winnicott (1963a) makes a similar point when he asserts that adolescents "struggle to feel real." It is a struggle because much of the time they experience themselves outside the perimeters of life-vitalizing knowledge. Adolescents often display a fierce and stubborn morality that allows them to accept only what feels real; Winnicott describes this as a refusal of the "false solution." We tend to cast this refusal in a pathological light by labeling it "black and white thinking." What if there needs to be a period in development where seeing the world as a series of starkly contrasted oppositions is necessary and crucial for integrating important life-events in a meaningful way? The strong contrast between right and wrong, good and bad, amplifies experiences and events so that one can discern what feels authentic, what moves the psyche.

Our usual response to this fierce moral sense and unswerving devotion is to interject the pabulum, "But compromise is part of life." Teaching compromise may well ignore what Ventura (1993, p. 28) speaks of as the adolescent's fundamental craving for negatives and their refusal of what we as adults have to offer. Part of this refusal and negativity is the need to discover a mode of authenticity that connects with one's individual take on the world. Intuitively, adolescents sense when they are in the vicinity of this kind of knowledge, and many aspects of problematic adolescent behavior—that is, their defiance, delinquency, anti-authoritarianism —can be understood as their attempt to author their own lives.

I have witnessed this longing for life-vitalizing knowledge in therapy sessions with adolescent clients. It emerges covertly as they begin to speak about the meaninglessness of life, the corruption of the world, the failure of our political system. While this tirade is going on, I have observed a certain look in their eye that intimates they are searching for some kind of response. A part of them is beckoning for an alternative vision. The underlying question seems to be: Given the current state of the world, what I experience in school, through the media, observing the adults in my life, how is it possible, in the face of all of this, to maintain my spirit?

This is also linked to student complaints, particularly in high school, that classes are boring and have nothing to do with real life or the real world. If we respond to the literal level of this grievance by showing, for example, the relevancy of geometry to the workplace, it is impossible to hear what their peeve is more truly expressing, namely, that what is being taught and how it is being taught is not life-vitalizing. The erotic aspect of knowledge, knowledge as mana, is somehow trapped in the overcrowded classrooms, thick, dull text books and standardized multiple choice tests. The lack of vitality in the American classroom is an important dimension of our current educational crisis which finds an increasing number of adolescents deeming public high school a waste of time.

A LARGER CIRCLE OF MEANING

The particular historical and cultural milieu amidst which adolescents develop is mainly left unthematized in psychological accounts of modern adolescence. This is a grave mistake since the cultural climate has a pervasive effect on one's capability during adolescence to make links from what one is experiencing bodily, idealistically, and ideationally to a larger order of meaning. In other words, if the psychobiological struggles specific to puberty and adolescence are in some sense "universal," then the particular way these struggles are lived out in a given society is culturally and historically determined. We need to be cognizant of the cultural context in which these struggles are taking place.

In this regard, we may ask how the culture of late twentieth-century America impacts the passage through adolescence. What obstacles do contemporary adolescents run up against as they try to make connections between the transformations they are experiencing with the onset of puberty and larger orders of meaning that touch upon history and tradition? What does it mean to search for adult ways of symbolizing and containing the dynamism of energy unleashed in adolescence in a culture such as our own?

As part of a traditional initiation ceremony, the initiate is told the sacred stories of their tribe's past and is shown ritual objects that have been kept secret until the moment of the ceremony. The creation myth of the tribe is dramatically re-enacted before the initiate by the tribal elders. Stories are told about how it all began and how it all fits together. Thus, the revelation of the history and tradition of the tribe allows an individual tribal member to make contact with the tribe's ancestral past. An initiate comes to learn about the value and purpose of his life in the context of this larger circle of meaning. A totalizing world view is granted which outlines the relation between self, society, and the universe.

In contrast to the single comprehensive cosmology which exists in traditional societies, American culture as a whole lacks a shared system of belief and meaning. The American adolescent encounters a multiplicity of beliefs and values (political, religious, ethical) which has the advantage of expressing the diversity of our culture. However, it can leave the adolescent vulnerable to a feeling of fragmentation so that he is "less able to find coherent expression for his pressing image-feelings" (Lifton 1979, p. 83).

With no living philosophy to pass on, mass consumerism, which barrages our youth on a daily basis through the media, has become a substitute for a coherent world view. There is no grand vision that speaks to the meaning and purpose of life other than amassing wealth. The Swiss psychiatrist Medard Boss comments on this theme in the context of how the dominance of technology frames our view of the world. He states:

> For the most part, adults themselves do not know what has happened and still is happening to them. They have hardly a clue that they are prisoners of the technological spirit of the times. And so they are even less aware that the way their world view has been blocked out to so extremely narrow a vision follows not from their own dealings and intrigues, but, rather, from this era's destiny. With these blinders they can see, of all the ways to be in relation to the world, only the increase of power over things for the sake of control and for the consequential increment of power for who is in control . . . . But when the elders no longer have much to say that is humanly useful, or humanly meaningful, surely the young cannot be faulted for wanting to have their way and take their part in shaping society and their own lives.
>
> (1983, pp. 287–8)

Boss is referring to the despair that young people experience when the adults fail to provide them with a sense of vitality about life. The acute feelings of hopelessness and meaninglessness with which adolescents are so identified with today may be in part connected to what it means to live in a postmodern culture where the spirit of technology is the dominating force. Boss is also touching upon the myth of the individualistic self which goes hand in hand with today's high-tech society. This myth posits that we are self-contained and isolated subjects surrounded by a world of objects completely at our disposal.

The incessant warnings to adolescents about staying safe, just saying no, and avoiding peer pressure replicate this myth. This line of rhetoric implores youth to stay separate and resist the pull into community. The broader cultural disintegration of sustainable communities coupled with a fierce allegiance to individualism is subtly expressed in the pedagogical instruction given to youth to "stay straight." Community is painted as being corrupting and dangerous. The world at large is to be distrusted and feared. The current resurgence of strict curfews for adolescents being legislated by local governments across the nation drives home this message. As does the lack of funding for community centers, public libraries, and parks which represent a potential way for adolescents to belong to the community by having a sanctioned space in which they can feel at home. With the schools and mass media's promotion of the "saving grace" of computers, adolescents are drawn into an isolated interior space as virtual community takes the place of real community. We will keep them off the streets and out of our lives by locking them into cyberspace. Marin states, "In few other cultures have persons of fifteen or eighteen been so uselessly isolated from participation in the community, or been deemed so unnecessary (in their elder's eyes), or so limited by law" (1974, p. 46).

Ivan Illich (1982) remarks that one reason for the prevalence of drug use in our culture is that it counterbalances the anesthetization of our daily lives, that is, some strong stimuli is needed to provide people with a sense of being alive. This idea resonates well with what I have been saying about the lack of life-vitalizing experience currently available to adolescents. If the culture offers nothing to offset the death imagery in adolescence, where one feels powerless and inundated by pressing image-feelings of lifelessness and stasis, then the turn to drugs and alcohol makes sense. The abusive manner in which these substances are taken up by adolescents may mask a desperate attempt to make themselves feel alive or real and to know that life is worth living.

A similar dynamic plays itself out as inner-city adolescents, and more and more of those living in the suburbs, feel the need to carry a weapon. Hume describes the seductive nature of joining a gang or participating in crime at a young age. In the following passage, he describes an adolescent's first experience of robbing someone at gun point.

"All right, let's do it," John whispered, and they sprang up, raced around the Pontiac, and confronted a middle-aged man as he was opening his car door. John had his revolver out—he didn't even remember drawing it from his waistband—and saw that it was pointed at the man. He saw his victim's eyes grow wide with fear, and for the first time, John understood the truly seductive nature of gangbanging: the genuine power. This guy was about to piss his pants. Because of him.

(1996, p. 92)

For those adolescents growing up in impoverished neighborhoods plagued by unemployment, crime and violence, the image-feelings of loss, numbness, and death, which I have been characterizing as attributes of adolescence as a central life-cycle transition, are not only experienced as internal realities, but as everyday actualities. Geoffrey Canada, in his memoir *Fist Stick Knife Gun* points out how youth coming of age in such communities take advantage of the easy accessibility of guns as emblems of power that hold out the illusion of overcoming feelings of powerlessness. With a gun, one holds in one's hand the power over life and death. However, as Canada points out, this is a premature and highly dangerous way of trying to grasp life-power. He states:

Kids with guns often see no limits on their power. They have never run up against the natural checks that we faced growing up, when for many of us a broken nose or a cracked tooth tempered our reactions to the daily push and shove of street life. Too often today kids with guns experience the limits of their power only when they are dying. Having a gun means that you can adopt a new set of standards of what you will or will not take from others. Where once if someone bigger than you called you a name you might have mumbled under your breath and kept walking, if you have a gun you will probably stop and confront the person then and there . . . . Possessing a gun feels like the ultimate form of protection.

(1995, p. 100)

Since drug and alcohol abuse and teen-age street violence are two of our culture's most tragic and intractable youth-related problems, I have tried to create a context for understanding why adolescents are so willing to put their life at risk by participating in such self-destructive behaviors. What I have been exploring in the past three chapters concerns the profound need of the adolescent psyche to experience affirmation and vitality in response to the moments of separation, disintegration, and stasis that accompany the passage through adolescence. What happens, then, in a culture where there are few vehicles available for contacting the counterparts of these death equivalents: connection, integration, and movement? We see the result all around us today as adolescents are desperate to stimulate a sense of vitality and aliveness in the short-run even though their attempts carry with them a destructive edge. Is there a way to shift the debate about teen-age drug use, violence, the spread of AIDS in the adolescent population, etc., such that greater recognition and value is given to the hunger adolescents have for life-vitalizing experience? Allowing such knowledge to inform our vision, brings us closer to understanding, appreciating, and responding to the disquiet reality of their desperation.

Part III

Jung and adolescence: a new synthesis

Chapter 6

The individuation tasks of adolescence

It was difficult to accept, and it was frightening too, that the most important thing that was ever going to happen to me, the thing that was my life, happened when I was not quite seventeen years old.

Scott Spencer

INTRODUCTION

I now turn to the psychology of C.G. Jung in order to apply his ideas about the development of the personality to my continuing elucidation of a non-reductive psychology that accounts for the unique and revelatory nature of adolescence. Although not much of Jung's writings deal explicitly with the question of adolescence, several of his main ideas and concepts, such as persona and shadow (which I will examine in the next chapter), as well as his teleological approach to psychological phenomena and his notion of the psyche as a self-regulating system, further an understanding of the adolescent psyche. In this chapter, I will explore the pertinence of Jung's concept of individuation for understanding many of the important transformations that occur in adolescence.

As Samuels (1985) points out, Jung repeatedly contradicts himself in his accounts of the psychological development of the child. On the one hand, he emphasizes the unique psychological configuration that is given with each and every child and which maintains its individual character in the face of environmental and social forces. According to this essentialist side of Jung, the child is no tabula rasa, but born into the world as a "sharply defined individual entity" (*CW* 9, para. 151). On the other hand, Jung writes sensitively about the susceptibility a child has to the unconscious life of its parents: "Fathers and mothers deeply impress their children's minds with the stamp of their personalities; the more sensitive and impressionable the child, the deeper the impression" (*CW* 2, para. 1007).

These two perspectives clash and give rise to different schools of psychology and different perpectives on adolescent development. I began the book by engaging the tension between these perspectives in taking an opposing stand to the psychoanalytic school and Jungian Developmental School which emphasize how early interactions with parents are the primary determining factors for what will happen in adolescence. Now, in this first section, I will examine the here-and-now manifestations of the parent–adolescent relationship through an exploration of Jung's idea regarding the effects of the parent's unconscious on the developing child. In the two sections following that, I will develop themes more in accord with the other side of Jung, where the child enters the world as a sharply defined individual, tracking how that individuality manifests itself during adolescence. This follows thematically from my emphasis upon the teleological nature of adolescence; how something new enters that has important implications for the future which can be obscured when the primary focus is upon the past.

THE INFLUENCE OF THE PARENT'S UNCONSCIOUS ON THE ADOLESCENT CHILD

Frances Wickes (1927), a child therapist and early follower of Jung, grounds her therapeutic approach to children and adolescents in the idea that the unconscious life of the parents impinges upon the developmental unfolding of the child's psyche. For Wickes, the child's vulnerability to these impingements takes on unique characteristics during adolescence.

Wickes describes the tremendous changes that take place in family life when a child enters puberty. A shift occurs; comfortable, taken-for-granted ways of being together get shaken up, and for the parents, this moment, which is highly symbolic, marks a significant change in their role and function as head of the household. Some parents welcome this change, others do not. Some parents are terribly threatened by the prospect of their child becoming a teen-ager because it reflects for them a stark reminder of the years passing by and the ever-widening gulf between the present time and their own youth. What can result, then, is an unconscious attempt to keep their adolescent child in a dependent role, restricting her life-activities by keeping her close to home.

I have encountered families where there was no differentiation in curfews, bedtimes, or privileges between the younger children in the family, eight, nine, and ten years old, and the sixteen-year-old. Adolescents are usually aware of the underlying dynamic: one hears statements such as: "My Mom doesn't want me to grow up. She treats me like I'm still a little kid." Under such circumstances, it is beneficial for the therapist to meet with the parents and help them think through how the boundaries in the family might now need to shift with an adolescent living at home. Parents might also benefit from having a place where they can express the sadness that they are carrying around about losing the intimacy and closeness they once felt with their child. When this sadness remains unexpressed, parents interpret the adolescent's increasing differentiation from the family as a personal rejection which only fuels the tension in the household and keeps the adolescent further away than perhaps need be. Pointing out to parents the developmental necessity of such behavior can give them just enough perspective to emotionally release their child and feel for themselves their own sense of loss in regard to the changes that are occurring within the family.

An impingement also occurs when parents use the energy that is engendered by their children's adolescence to stimulate a sense of their own youthfulness. They become overly involved in the friend-ships, romances, and intrigues of their child's peer group, re-living what they might have missed as a youth or unconsciously trying to prolong their own youth. This kind of parent can be seen as feeding off the energy and excitement that an adolescent brings into a family.

Or parents may use a "power play" to keep their child tied to them (ibid., pp. 104–5). For example, they may constantly bring up all the sacrifices they have made for him (one father I knew even went as far as adding up the total amount of money he had spent since infancy on his adolescent son and presented it to him in bill form). Thus, they pressure the adolescent to act properly and conform to their wishes in order to pay them back. Wickes speaks to the growing sense of unconscious resentment this creates in the child. In many cases, once the surface of the facade of a deeply loving child is scratched, tirades of hatred for the parents burst forth, expressing the child's exasperation with this dynamic.

Zinner and Shapiro's (1972) work with families of adolescent children, which focuses on projective identification, offers [another means of conceptualizing the impingement of the parent's unconscious upon the adolescent. In this model, the parent's need to disavow certain aspects of themselves, such as anger, rage or sexuality, is met by projecting it onto the adolescent and then identifying the adolescent as the embodiment of that trait. For example, a parent might say, "This is the family fuck-up" or "She is always so angry." Often a child will collude with the parent by taking on an assigned role because she knows it is calming to the parent and offers the relationship a chance to survive.

Adolescence is a time when behavioral traits that in the past may have been hidden or partially concealed by parents come alive vis-à-vis their adolescent child. If a parent suffers an addictive relationship to a substance, the adolescent's substance abuse problem can become the major focus of the family. If sexual infidelity is occurring in a marriage, the adolescent's own sexual activity can take center stage. Much of Zinner and Shapiro's work with families is about helping the parents to withdraw their projections so that they can see their adolescent child in a less obscured light.

Assessing the quality of the actual relationship between an adolescent and her parents is difficult and confusing for a therapist. Feelings erupt suddenly; there is hatred and enmity one moment, loving devotion and idealization the next. I have listened to an adolescent girl violently protest one week how awful her mother was and how viciously she hated her. The next week, in a family session, I was shocked to witness the devotion and tenderness that existed between them once they were together in the same room.

One is never quite sure of the level of unconsciousness that is expressed in the portrait that adolescents present of their parents. This is why it is a mistake to take as absolute truth an adolescent's communication about his parents early on. Adolescents fearlessly dive into the waters of unconscious resentment and rage toward mother and father, painting a bleak picture of the relationship. I have been tricked into taking this literally many times because it is so full of energy and spoken with such conviction. However, one must learn to listen in a more neutral way in order not to support and reinforce the most monstrous image of a parent that an adolescent can conjure up. After all, this is only one side of a complex and complicated relationship. Indeed, there is a grave danger in empathizing too strongly with the unconscious portrait of the parents. If, as a therapist, one dares to reflect back at a later point to an element of this horrendous picture, an adolescent may feel betrayed and go on the attack: "Who are you to talk about my father that way?"

These dialogues about parents in therapy become even more textured as an adolescent's anger and resentment toward her parents expresses itself in her extreme opposition to whatever it is she perceives her parents would want for her. Such a dynamic becomes clear when talking with adolescents about why they are behaving in certain ways or making certain choices in their lives. One frequently discovers rebellion against parental attitudes and values as the main motivating factor to do or not do something. "Why are you dropping out of school?" "Because the only thing my parents really care about is if I graduate."

It is important here to remember Jung's statement, "The adolescent at first tries to become as separate as possible from his family; he may even estrange himself from them, but inwardly this only binds him the more firmly to this image of his parents" (*CW* 2, para. 1007). It is tricky to communicate this insight to an adolescent: that by his doing exactly opposite what his parents want, he is still trapped and bound to them. In other words, this form of rebellion keeps one as dependent as ever upon parents for determining one's behavior. Thus, it is of great importance to help an adolescent sort out the difference between what he does because he knows his parents would be angry and disapprove and what he does because he really wants to do it. Therapy can be a place for making these discriminations.

Jung remarks: "But the real therapy only begins when the patient sees that it is no longer father and mother who are standing in his way, but himself, that is, an unconscious part of his personality which carries the role of mother and father" (*CW* 7, para. 88). This is written with adults in mind, but is ultimately a central piece of the work with adolescents. The archetypal ramifications of this statement will be explored in Chapter 8 where I take up the dynamic of adolescent projection.

THE TELEOLOGICAL SIGNIFICANCE OF ADOLESCENCE

According to Jung, adolescence is when it is first possible for the child to experience the world outside of the restricting effects of its parents' psychology. In the following passage, he describes the developmental forces that propel the child forward at puberty.

In the childish stage of consciousness there are as yet no problems; nothing depends upon the subject, for the child itself is still wholly dependent on its parents. It is as though it were not yet completely born, but were still enclosed in the psychic atmosphere of its parents. Psychic birth, and with it the conscious differentiation from the parents, normally takes place only at puberty, with the eruption of sexuality. The physiological change is attended by a psychic revolution. For the various bodily manifestations give such an emphasis to the ego that it often asserts itself without stint or moderation. This is sometimes called "the unbearable age".

(*CW* 8, para. 756)

Thus for Jung, what is being birthed at adolescence is the newly developing psychological individual. One's relationship to the psyche is transformed (Jung here refers to it as a psychic revolution) as one begins to differentiate from parents. This idea was illuminated by Jung, early in his career, when he was a participant in the seances led by a fifteen-year-old girl, Miss S.W., who acted in the role of spiritualistic medium. In his doctoral dissertation, "On the Psychology and Pathology of So-Called Occult Phenomena," Jung interprets Miss S.W.'s psychic channeling and contacting of spirits from beyond as an expression of her own split-off unconscious contents which had formed autonomous complexes. According to Jung, Miss S.W. was mistakenly attributing to spirits the contents of her own unconscious. In his description of Miss S.W.'s capacity, at fifteen years of age, for psychic channeling, which he refers to as "double consciousness," Jung reveals something important about adolescence. He states: "It is therefore conceivable that the phenomena of double consciousness are simply new character formations, or attempts of the future personality to break through" (*CW* 1, para. 136).

In other words, a new aspect of one's character attempts to break through at adolescence. This is teleologically significant. Imagine if we considered the most difficult aspects of adolescent development in the context of an imminent source of energy and future way of being that is trying to manifest itself in the adolescent personality. Rather than pathologizing the disruptions that this energy brings, would it not be wiser and therapeutically more meaningful to develop ways of being receptive to it? Imagining adolescence in this way resonates with Jung's notion of the individuation process.

ADOLESCENCE AS INDIVIDUATION

At the end of *Psychological Types* (*CW* 6), Jung offers a compelling definition of individuation, a key concept in his psychology. I have chosen this particular definition in order to further the connection between Jung's characterization of adolescence as a psychic birth and individuation as the emergence of the psychological individual as distinct from collective psychology. Jung defines individuation as follows:

> In general, it is the process by which individual beings are formed and differentiated; in particular, it is the development of the psychological individual as being distinct from the general, collective psychology. Individuation, therefore, is a process of differentiation, having for its goal the development of the individual personality.
>
> (*CW* 6, para. 757)

There is wide divergence among post-Jungian schools of thought in regard to interpreting Jung's concept of individuation which Samuels succinctly renders as "the gradual realization of the self over a lifetime" (1985, p. 101). The debate in understanding individuation as a psychological construct centers around whether or not it is a natural, universal process occurring in all people or one that only applies to socially adapted individuals with well-developed egos. In the latter case, psychological integration is a necessary prerequisite for embarking upon the path of individuation.

The other question open to debate is whether the individuation process originates in the second half of life, as Jung most typically described it. Classically conceived, the first half of life is governed by expansion and adaptation to outer reality. During this time, the ego is maturing and consolidating in its struggle for independence and is split off from the self, the deep center of the personality. The individuation process is initiated during the second half of life, in response to a crisis that forces an individual to redress the one-sidedness of pursuing the ego's expansion in an outwardly attuned direction. As an individual turns inward, making contact with the self, images and symbols are produced which, through the process of conscious engagement, create the grounds for psychological transformation (Jacobi 1965).

The Developmental School offers a contrasting vision of the individuation process. There it is seen as an activity that spans the entire life-cycle. Fordham (1994) was the first Jungian to observe that all of the essential features of the individuation process take place in childhood. He contends that by the age of two the infant is separated and differentiated from the mother. His formulation accords with Jung's notion of individuation as the birth of the psychological individual.

I am following the Developmental School here in understanding individuation as a life-long process. As Fordham's work details the enactment of individuation in infancy and early childhood, I will outline features of the individuation process that take place in adolescence. The upheavals and crises, the wounding to the personality, the images of death and rebirth and initiation and the arduous suffering will be understood as part of the current of individuation that flows through adolescence.

In proposing that adolescents undergo a process of individuation, I am deviating from the Classical School's conception of individuation, where the focus of analysis is on the self's manifestation through interior psychic phenomena rather than the outward events of a person's life, such as interpersonal relationships, or the interactions that occur in psychotherapy. My thinking here is more in line with the Archetypal School, which assumes an ontological unity between self and world and works with a vision of psychic reality as world-related.[1] Since adolescence by its very nature is such a crucial time of testing oneself in the world through action, I am stressing how these worldly encounters significantly affect the adolescent psyche in addition to the images, dreams and fantasies that originate during this time.

Guggenbühl-Craig challenges the linking of individuation to the second half of life. He deconstructs the narrative that outlines the tasks of a young person as first mastering the outside world, becoming professionally established and having a family, before she can, during the second half of life, turn toward the question of meaning. He states:

> In my analytic experience I have found that the individuation process may appear at any stage of life. I have often been able to observe it in young people, many of whom wrestle with the problems of God, death and the Devil. Such young people are completely open to the overall polarity of human existence,

and delineation of the persona, and that despite the exclusive identity of the ego-consciousness with the persona the unconscious s   one's real individuality, is always present and makes itself fel   irectly if not directly. Although the ego-consciousness is at firs   ntical with the persona—that compromise role in which we   le before the community—yet the unconscious self can never   ressed to the point of extinction. Its influence is chiefly ma   in the special nature of the contrasting and compensati   ontents of the unconscious. The purely personal attitude of   conscious mind evokes reactions on the part of the unconsc   s, and these, together with personal repressions, contain the   ds of individual development in the guise of collective fant   s. Through the analysis of the personal unconscious, the c   ious mind becomes suffused with collective ma   al which   gs with it the elements of individuality.

(*CW* 7, para. 247)

Jung's insi   that although the persona is at heart a collective pheno   e choice of which persona one acquires and how it is express   he world is a reflection of a person's individuality. Rather th   ding one's identity, a well functioning persona has the poter   amplify one's own voice (Pollack 1996, p. 58); it is the outwar   he unconscious self.

This is a crucial in   for   king sense of the adolescent's tendency to externalize   rience.   of the best indicators of an adolescent's internal st   s found   oking at how he uses external objects to hold   arry parts o   elf.

These objects freque   have a coll   dimension. For example, an adolescent n   lentify with a co   ve figure in the culture: a musician, a m   or television star, c   sports hero. While on the surface this   ms to be a way of   icking the individuality of another, Ju   pointing out how the se   of one's individuality can be contai   a collective figure, or w   the guise of the fantasies he has   this figure.

For example, I worked wi   venteen-year-old, Thomas, w   was clinically depressed. He   nade two suicide attempts and required hospitalization. Foll   the death of his favorite rock star who had overdosed on   s, Thomas began to wear the clothes, style his hair, and ove   ake on a persona that matched the late performer. Thomas play   uitar and wrote and performed music in a fairly successful ban   at had the same sound as his fallen idol. Near the one-year anniversary of the rock star's death, Thomas' depression worsened and his suicidal fantasies increased. During this time, our therapeutic work centered on engaging Thomas' image of the rock star. Thomas had specific fantasies about why the rock star wrote the sorrowful songs he wrote, and their connection to his drug overdose. It was through the image of this collective figure that Thomas found admission into his own suffering and began disclosing the suicidal thoughts and fantasies that had led to his hospitalization. Thomas' imaginings about the demise of the rock star served as a vehicle for exploring his own wounded nature.

The adolescent struggle to discover individuality converges with the creative expression of persona. In order to discover what is truly unique about themselves, adolescents strain against collective norms of attitude, dress, and comportment. Many assume a persona that unremittingly confronts community standards. Piercings, tattoos, colored hair, ripped and torn clothing, hats that never come off, those ways of stylizing the body that provoke and outrage. The psyche's need in all of this may be to externalize concretely the marginalization that is so acutely felt in adolescence. Enacting it in the style of dress, speech, or manners brings forth a dramatic response. Attention is drawn to the part of the self that wants to appear on the margins, as outcast, as outrageous. While, on the one hand, adolescents are seemingly the most rebellious against the collective standards of the culture, within their own culture, there is pressure to conform.

Fashioning for oneself a darkly textured persona serves the function of allowing an adolescent to disidentify with their family of origin by refusing to be a projective screen for their parents. For example, I worked with one young woman, seventeen, who, when it was time to redecorate her bedroom, insisted upon painting it black. This turned into an enormous conflict in the family and when I asked more about it, I was told that this girl's mother was planning on painting the room pink in order to match the white lace curtains and pink and red bedspread she was purchasing as part of the overall room makeover. Can we look at the desire for black in the context of the mother's need to hold onto the little girl image of her adolescent daughter? Then darkening the childhood bedroom in the most radical way possible communicates to mother: "I have stopped being your little girl. Quit trying to keep me in that place. My needs and wants are no longer so light and pretty."

The formation of a persona during the adolescent years has tremendous importance for shaping the individual personality during adulthood. The more an adolescent can be left to explore the outer edges of identity, the greater the chance for resiliency in their identity as adults. This is another indication of the importance of persona in adolescence as a phenomenon of individuation. As parents, therapists, and educators, we have to contend with our own cruel streak that wants to insult, scorn, mock, or shame a developing persona. Perhaps this irrational urge can be traced back to having been shamed ourselves as adolescents when trying out a new role. If that is the case, we try to dispel the affect caused by the memory by attaching it to the adolescent in a fashion parallel to how adolescents ask us to carry unwanted feelings of humiliation or shame. Or our scorn may have the same primal source as the cruel delight adolescents take in mocking an adult persona. Whatever the reason, adolescents assuming a new persona are extremely vulnerable, and out of respect for the process, we must watch this impulse in ourselves and try to tread lightly.

The rich investment of emotional energy that goes into forming a persona is a hidden and ephemeral process which takes place outside of ordinary awareness. To glimpse this in the adolescent, we must listen and observe in an oblique way, not taking the presentation of self too literally, but instead feeling into its nature as display and performance. In seeing through the evanescent quality of a persona, we are able to tune into the multi-layered flux of identities within the adolescent psyche. Thus, the question of persona is directly linked to the question of adolescent multiplicity.

I want to differentiate the notion of the multiplicity of identity in adolescence from a pathological reading of multiplicity, for example in multiple personality disorder or schizophrenia. The idea here is that adolescent identity is in a flux because it is not yet integrated and many sides of the self come to the fore. Testing out different personas on the world is a reflection of this eruption of identities.

In therapy, as an adolescent reveals different sides of herself, a dialogue occurs between the therapist and the multiplicity of voices spoken by the client. The contrast between these voices, their intricate interweavings, their opposing demands and expectations, become thematic as the dialogue develops. The transference happens in the context of this multiplicity. Many different transferences occur at the same time. Although this is true to some extent in adult analysis,[1] the amplitude of this multiplicity of voices and relationships is a distinguishing feature of adolescent psychotherapy. Over time, the adolescent internalizes the reflective voice of the therapist and starts to dialogue, question, and take an interest in the different sides of her personality. In doing so, there is less chance that one side will dominate as she develops her own capacity for self-reflection.

The adolescent therapist is asked to navigate among the differing relationships, being called upon one moment to respond as a deeply empathic, understanding friend and the next as an antagonistic, overbearing authority figure. A flexible stance is needed in order to adequately respond to this quality of shifting characterization. As a therapist, I may be speaking to a more adult part of the adolescent's self, one who can make connections between actions and feelings and suddenly, one interpretation later, find myself speaking to a much younger part of the self whose dialogical needs are vastly different. Staying attuned to this flip-flopping of identity is part of what makes the work with adolescents so demanding.

If, as a therapist, I insist upon a single unitary voice and implicitly in my body posture, tone, and style of rhetoric make demands for it, I can induce in the adolescent a false integration, premature, before its own time. This is another instance of not being able to tolerate what is unformed, as I noted in Chapter 2. The unformed presents itself in the multiplicity of identities, in the process of enacting various personas.

SHADOW

What has no shadow has no strength to live.

(Milosz 1988, p. 48)

Integration of the shadow, "the dark aspect, what we hate as incompatible with our ego personality, what we fear as a threat to our self-image and to our peace of mind" (Giegerich 1991, p. 87), is an integral part of the individuation process in Jungian psychology. It begins by recognizing the presence and reality of hidden aspects of the personality which have an autonomous emotional power and can potentially overwhelm and dominate the ego. The encounter with shadow brings us face-to-face with our potential to act destructively toward ourselves and others. Developing a relationship with the shadow brings forth an active recognition of life's malevolent powers, a sense of how evil plays itself out in the world. In this section, I will explore the emergence of the shadow in the life of a young person. I am making the claim that the foundation of one's capacity for shadow integration is set down in adolescence and is a central task of adolescent individuation.

Winnicott speaks of the discovery during adolescence of the destructive side of the self.

> If your children find themselves at all they will not be contented to find anything but the whole of themselves and that will include aggressive and destructive elements in themselves as well as the elements that can be labeled loving.
>
> (1968, p. 143)

Analogously, Guggenbühl-Craig (1971) points to a destructive urge which appears with notable openness in youth. He cites both their tendency to want to destroy not only the lives and property of others, but their own lives and property as well. I am interpreting these aggressive and destructive elements in adolescence as manifestations of the shadow. An individual expression of the shadow occurs when we personally repress those psychic contents that we cannot identify with because they go against what we believe or how we see ourselves; or it can occur collectively, when an entire culture or subculture effects this repression (Guggenbühl-Craig, 1980, p. 110).

Jamaica Kincaid's sensitive novel, *Annie John*, about a West Indian girl's youth on the island of Antigua, provides a compelling example of the encounter with the personal shadow in adolescence. As the main protagonist of the story, Annie, enters adolescence, she begins to feel a growing sense of distance between herself and her mother. This antagonism toward her mother peaks in the fourth chapter of the book entitled "The Red Girl." Here, contrary to mother's wish for her to become an upright, well-mannered young woman, Annie befriends a girl who embodies everything her mother disdains.

Annie describes her initial impression of the new friend whom she comes to call the Red Girl:

> Her face was big and round and red, like a moon, a red moon. She had big, broad, flat feet, and they were naked to the bare ground; her dress was dirty, the skirt and blouse tearing way from each other at one side; the red hair that I had first seen standing up on her head was matted and tangled; her hands were

big and fat, and her fingernails held at least ten anthills of dirt under them. And on top of that, she had such an unbelievable, wonderful smell, as if she had never taken a bath in her whole life.

(1983, p. 57)

The Red Girl essentially symbolized everything that Annie was not:

> I soon learned this about her: She took a bath only once a week, and that was only so that she could be admitted to her grandmother's presence. She didn't like to bathe, and her mother didn't force her. She changed her dress once a week for the same reason. She preferred to wear a dress until it just couldn't be worn anymore. Her mother didn't mind that, either. She didn't like to comb her hair, though on the first day of school she could put herself out for that. She didn't like to go to Sunday school, and her mother didn't force her. She didn't like to brush her teeth, but occasionally her mother said it was necessary. She loved to play marbles, and was so good that only Skerritt boys now played against her. Oh, what an angel she was, and what a heaven she lived in! I, on the other hand, took a full bath every morning and a sponge bath every night. I could hardly go out on my doorstep without putting my shoes on. I was not allowed to play in the sun without a hat on my head. My mother paid a woman who lived five houses away from us sevenpence a week— a penny for each school day and twopence for Sunday—to comb my hair. On Saturday, my mother washed my hair. Before I went to sleep at night, I had to make sure my uniform was clean and creaseless and all laid out for the next day. I had to make sure that my shoes were clean and polished to a nice shine. I went to Sunday school every Sunday unless I was sick. I was not allowed to play marbles, and, as for Skerritt boys, that was hardly mentionable.

(ibid., pp. 57–8)

Annie was keenly attracted to this girl who was her opposite. They would meet at sundown at the lighthouse on a hill overlooking the sea, a place Annie's mother had forbidden her to go. Under the influence of the Red Girl, Annie became a skilled marble player, also prohibited by mother, challenging the older boys on the island to games and beating them. Annie was so taken with the Red Girl that she began giving her the marbles that she won, as well as household items and money that she stole from her parents.

The Red Girl can be understood as an embodiment of Annie's shadow and therefore an essential source for a new kind of knowledge. This knowledge could not be acquired at school from her teachers, at home from her parents, or even from her best friend Gwen, all to whom she kept her relationship with the Red Girl a secret. The following passage illustrates how the encounter with shadow brings forth a secretive and illuminating knowledge of the world. Here, the Red Girl expresses her anger at Annie for missing their daily meeting at the lighthouse:

> Then, still without saying a word, the Red Girl began to pinch me. She pinched hard, picking up pieces of my almost nonexistent flesh and twisting it around. At first, I vowed not to cry, but it went on for so long that tears I could not control streamed down my face. I cried so much that my chest began to heave, and then, as if my heaving chest caused her to have some pity on me, she stopped pinching me and began to kiss me on the spots where shortly before I had felt the pain of her pinch. Oh, the sensation was delicious—the combination of pinches and kisses. And so wonderful we found it that, almost every time we met, pinching by her, followed by tears from me, followed by kisses from her were the order of the day. I stopped wondering why all the girls whom I had mistreated and abandoned followed me around with looks of love and adoration on their faces.
>
> (ibid., p. 63)

In this scene, Annie receives an education in the darker side of eros, its sadomasochistic capacity to intermingle pleasure and pain and in the process to create powerful bonds between people. Up on the hill, in an area forbidden by mother, Annie is initiated into mysteries that have no place in the brightly ordered world of her family home.

Annie's relationship with the Red Girl continues until her mother discovers her holding a prized blue porcelain marble she had won and was planning to bestow upon the Red Girl who was waiting for her at the lighthouse. Her mother, furious, figures out what has been going on and berates Annie, trying to force her to confess where she is hiding the other marbles.

> I couldn't remember my mother's being so angry with me ever

before; in the meantime all thoughts of the Red Girl vanished from my mind. Trying then to swallow a piece of bread that I had first softened in my gravy, I thought, Well, that's the end of that; if tomorrow I saw that girl on the street, I would just act as if we had never met before, as if her very presence at any time was only an annoyance. As my mother went on to my father in her angry vein, I rearranged my life: Thank God I hadn't abandoned Gwen completely, thank God I was so good at rounders that the girls would be glad to have me head a side again, thank God my breasts hadn't grown and I still needed some tips about them.

(ibid., p. 67)

It's interesting to note the psychological shift that occurs once Annie secret is discovered; her passion for the Red Girl suddenly abates. What is instructive here is the momentary nature of an encounter with the shadow, how it runs its own course and, in Annie's case, ends up allowing her to re-affirm and re-value the connections in her life which existed prior to this episode. Annie never tells her mother what happened with the Red Girl or the location of the other marbles, even after considerable pressure. Her memories of this period of her life stay secreted away and the chapter ends with Annie recalling a dream where she and the Red Girl live together in the wild on an island out at sea.

Annie's friendship with the Red Girl gave her a vantage point from which to see the rules and expectations that encompassed her life so that she could reflect upon them in a critical and challenging way. In this regard, Guggenbühl-Craig comments on the progressive developmental value of both the personal and collective shadow. He states:

The personal shadow works destructively against ego-ideals; the collective shadow tries to demolish collective ideals. Both these shadows also have a very valuable function. Both ego and collective ideals must be repeatedly subjected to attack since they are false and one-sided. Were they not continually being eaten into from the depths of the human soul, there would be neither individual nor collective development.

(1971, p. 113)

Adolescents are easy prey for consumption by the collective shadow. Hitler's mobilization of Germany's youth into a disciplined army enforcing the doctrines of the Third Reich is a good example. In this case, being a member of the youth party signified an identification with the collective ideals of Nazism. Today, the neo-Nazi/SkinHead movement also draws much of its strength from the support of young people. Adolescents can also find themselves the victim of a cultural shadow. The problem of homelessness in America has another face when it comes to the vast number of American youth currently on the run or living in homeless shelters. The AIDS virus is spreading more rapidly in the adolescent population, aged between fourteen and twenty five, than any other segment of society.

Conversely, adolescents possess an uncanny ability to see through and challenge collective ideals, recognizing the shadow side of what we hold to be most sacred. Some may refuse to participate in the American Thanksgiving tradition—why celebrate a holiday that signifies the unacknowledged genocide of Native American culture. Some may find the patriotism and fanfare of the Fourth of July hollow and empty given the social and economic inequalities in our culture. The political protests in the 1960s, including, of course, protest against the Vietnam war, all involved a heavy concentration of youth. Adolescents are not afraid to challenge long-standing traditions, matters we hold sacred, asking why something has to be that way, what is its sense and why can it not be done differently. This is also evidenced by their challenges to religious doctrine and religious authority.

In addition, adolescence brings forth experiences of the archetypal shadow. Guggenbühl-Craig amplifies Jung's understanding of the shadow at an archetypal level as an independently destructive force whose existence within the psyche is not exclusively a matter of individual or collective repression. Thus, for Jung, evil is inherent in the nature of human being.

The Grimm fairytale, "The Devil With the Three Golden Hairs," is used by Guggenbühl-Craig to illustrate the necessity of a confrontation with the archetypal shadow during adolescence. The hero of the story, a fourteen-year-old, is sent by the King to obtain three golden hairs from the devil's head as a test of his worthiness to be married to the princess. To move on with his life, and assume adult status, he must make intimate contact with the devil. Thus, contact with the archetypal shadow moves development forward. Guggenbühl-Craig states:

A young person is in a transitional state between childhood and adulthood. Of course the child has ample destructiveness in him; many children act like devils incarnate. But a child's overall situation is very largely determined by his parents. In wrestling with its problems he uses tools, images and attitudes given to him by his parents. An adult is naturally also formed by his parents; most of his attitudes have simply been taken over from them. But, in order to develop psychologically, the adult must pass through a phase of denial and destructiveness so that he can then, voluntarily so to speak, further cultivate his parents' values or find new ones for himself. A youth making the transition from childhood to adulthood must thus make contact with the Devil, with destructiveness; to fight his way through to freedom he must also experience the possibility of destroying.

(ibid., p. 117)

This element of destructiveness that arises in adolescence is ontologically an entirely different matter to what the child experiences. "How shall each one deal with something that is new: the power to destroy and even to kill, a power which did not complicate the feelings of hatred that were experienced at the toddler age" (Winnicott 1963a, p. 146). There is ample opportunity during adolescence for concretely living out this destructiveness.

Guggenbühl-Craig goes on to say:

Young people must have contact with the Devil, but they must on no account identify with him. A youth's ego must remain somewhat removed and aware of what it is doing. In most cases, when healthy youngsters destroy property, steal or let themselves in for other destructive activities, they generally know that they are involved in a temporary experiment. They are aware that all their actions, though interesting, are really bad.

(ibid., p. 118)

We witnessed this in *Annie John*. Annie's association with the Red Girl and her lying and stealing suddenly came to an end in the wake of being found out by her mother. Jung, especially in his alchemical writings, made many references to how the processes of the psyche play themselves out in the tension of the opposites. This model of understanding fits well with the necessity of encountering the shadow in adolescence. When one side is overemphasized, in Annie's case, the cleanliness and orderliness of life, the opposite pole becomes numinous and highly sought after. The draw toward the shadow allows one to move out of the safety and protection of the child's world and feel into the other side of what was valued by parents. We see this in Annie's excitement and enthusiasm for the Red Girl's freedom to make radically different choices about dress, comportment, and risk-taking. Thus, the encounter with the shadow has teleological significance—it is an attempt to redress an imbalance.

Allan Guggenbühl likens it to the lure frightening or violent stories have for children and adolescents.

> . . . if they get to hear stories that contain horror and terror, paradoxically, the children's good sides are constellated. The terrifying has found its place in the story so that the children can now be peaceful and relieved of the burden of having to produce their horrible sides.
>
> (1966, p. 134)

A psychological transformation occurs when images of terror and horror can be assimilated at the level of story, helping to contain the aggressive and destructive impulses of a young person. It is a way for the adolescent psyche to meaningfully encounter shadow material and work through it in the realm of imagination. This is exactly the role fairy tales play in the psyche of the child according to Bettelheim (1975) in his classic work, *The Uses of Enchantment*. It explains the adolescent's total fascination with watching horror films or violent movies, where the hero, on the side of justice, uses deadly force to annihilate his victim. Honoring the adolescent's desire for an imaginal encounter with the shadow is one possible remedy for reducing the need for it to be literally lived out. Much of the work in therapy utilizing expressive arts with adolescents is an attempt to use story, symbol and image as vehicles for containing shadow material.

Adults should not abdicate

What starts off as a temporary experiment, disobeying one's parents, skipping school, smashing windows, can suddenly jettison into a serious pattern of juvenile delinquency. I follow Winnicott here in stressing how extremely important it is for there to be an environmental response to such actions. Winnicott's writings on adolescence make it abundantly clear that he held adults responsible for being there and holding the line in the face of an adolescent's challenging behavior. The anti-social, destructive behaviors that occur as part of the youthful encounter with shadow call for such a response.

> In brief, it is exciting that adolescence has become vocal and active, but the adolescent striving that makes itself felt over the whole world today needs to be met, needs to be given reality by an act of confrontation. Confrontation must be personal. Adults are needed if adolescents are to have life and liveliness. Confrontation belongs to containment that is non-retaliatory, without vindictiveness, but having its own strength.
>
> (1968, p. 150)

[Parents of adolescent children face the task of confrontation daily as they respond to their son's or daughter's staying out past curfew, failing a class in school, getting into a fight, experimenting with drugs or alcohol, or any other behavior that challenges the rules and provokes authority. Adolescents, on the one hand, are hoping their parents will indulge them by caving in, pretending not to notice, forgetting about last evening's escapades, or abandoning promised consequences to their transgressions. Yet, given all of that, I am convinced that they are also looking for containment and a sense of limits, a safe boundary in which they can experience the intensity of these newly developing urges.]

Many parents seek professional help for their adolescent children when they are no longer able to effectively contain these behaviors. They may have surrendered the fight, no longer setting any limits at all, which results in real fear for their children's safety. Therapy seeks to redress the shattered boundaries between parents and adolescents. These kinds of problems are seen everyday as therapists work with families to re-establish balance in the home. A similar breakdown exists in our society where responses to teen-age delinquent behavior are either vindictive and retaliatory or completely absent.

One disturbing example of this trend can be found in Edward Humes' (1996) book, *No Matter How Loud I Shout*, which chronicles the year he spent as a writing teacher at Los Angeles' Central Juvenile Hall, investigating the everyday workings of the juvenile justice system. His work, as a whole, provides a living portrait of our culture's failure to acknowledge adolescents, who through anti-social, delinquent and increasingly violent behavior, are trying to compel a response. Overwhelmed by the growing number of juvenile offenders each year, juvenile courts pay scant attention to the behaviors I have been characterizing as temporary experiments; the system waits for someone to be seriously hurt before they are willing to act.

A former Los Angeles probation officer describes the progression of those kids who end up in jail as violent offenders:

> Typically, they start out demanding a lot of attention in school, behavior problems, academic problems, they disrupt. Gradually, they get shunted aside. That's the first time. Then when they reach age nine to eleven, maybe twelve, they commit a crime, usually a low-grade misdemeanor. At that point, there is a tendency to overlook the offense. The police counsel and release him without making an arrest, or the Probation Department looks at the case and decides to give the minor a break. That's the second time they are pushed aside. This is not such a break, though. In fact, that young person might have been better off being provided services then and there, intensive probation, supervision, special classes, counseling—something to keep them from becoming habitual offenders. But the opposite is done.
>
> (Humes 1996, pp. 176–7)

What typically happens is that by the time this young person reaches age fourteen and has committed three or more crimes, the system takes action and metes out a harsh punishment and forgoes the possibility of rehabilitation.

I personally witnessed the arbitrariness and lack of responsiveness of the juvenile court system while working with a client who was initially picked up by the police for spray painting graffiti. Since it was a first time offense, his case was dismissed and months later he was hauled back into juvenile court after being arrested for shoplifting. This case was also dismissed because the arresting officer failed to appear in court. Two weeks later, he was again arrested for shooting a BB gun off the top of a roof situated across the street from a crowded subway stop. This case was pending when he was arrested for the fourth time for trying to steal a car. These latter two charges forced him to make intermittent appearances in court over a three-month period. On one such occasion, sitting with his friends on an old dilapidated couch, waiting to see the judge, he began pulling at the foam stuffing and throwing it at his friends. It was this final charge, malicious destruction of government property, for which he was finally sentenced and sent away to juvenile lock-up.

We unwittingly push adolescents further into the shadow when we grant their destructive actions complete immunity through a failure to respond.

Every year in America about 2.3 million kids under eighteen are arrested for crimes ranging from shoplifting to murder. Less than one quarter of them actually, in the end, face a meaningful consequence. Thus, when a minor is arrested, there is less than a one in four chance someone will respond. Three out of four times they walk away (Humes 1996).

Geoffrey Canada highlights the importance of adult authority in confronting street violence. Many of the youth that Canada worked with grew up in inner-city neighborhoods in Boston and New York and had "never run into an adult who could control them, who was not afraid of the obvious layer of violence that was always so close to the surface of their actions" (1995, p. 25). The unpredictability of kids carrying weapons ups the ante in the confrontation between adolescents and adults. Under these circumstances, adults feel powerless and immobilized in the face of the mayhem on the streets. Adult fears directly intensify the fears and insecurities of children and adolescents; they do not feel safe, and carry knives or guns to school not for provocation but for protection.

The shadow in group life

In a peer group with anti-social tendencies, it may be the case that only two or three of the individuals are actively engaged in destructive or criminal activities while the other members of the group vicariously participate simply by hanging around and hearing about what happened. Or a small group of friends becomes intimately involved with a close friend's suicidal feelings and thus vicariously touch upon those feelings in themselves. In both cases, group life has the effect of diffusing contact with the shadow. In the psychology of adolescent groups, one individual may implicitly agree to live out the shadow for the benefit of the group.

Asking an adolescent where she hangs out, what her friends are like, and how they spend their time together is an important part of therapy. If we assume that different members of the group carry different parts of the self, it is essential to get a real sense of the peer group in order to perceive how it magnifies and reflects the self. A good portion of adolescent psychotherapy revolves around the client's complex interweaving of narratives about others in the context of the self. Undisclosed aspects of the adolescent's psyche are revealed by what she says about her closest friends.

It is striking to watch how the shadow is projected in the context of these friendships. One member of the group can suddenly become the recipient of the group's shadow projections; he is identified with all the negative and destructive energies to which his friends are blind within themselves. Or, you might hear, "This one friend I know, he's the one with the real substance abuse problem, not me. He is out of control with his drinking." The way to go here is not to abruptly confront the projection, but rather to help him explicate just what it is about the other that strikes him this way and to discuss how he feels about it. As the character of the other becomes more fully realized, an adolescent can, at times, be more forgiving and understanding of a friend's behavior, seeing the reasons behind it, than he can for the same behavior in himself. The focus on the other is a safe place to begin the process, especially with a resistant client. The projection is there and it is ripe, which also means there is opportunity to see through it, or take some of it back as the therapy progresses.

As an example, I worked with two young women, both seniors in high school, who had been best friends since early childhood. Two months before graduation, they had a fight, filled with screaming, yelling, pushing and accusations, and after being separated by teachers, refused to talk to each other ever again. As they spoke separately to me, it was uncanny how they accused each other of bearing the same behavior traits: being untrustworthy, two-faced, and dishonest. Each was the perfect foil for the other and it was clear that in order for the friendship to mend and development to proceed, this mutual shadow projection needed to be worked through. Each saw in the other qualities that were difficult to accept within themselves and the therapy became a place to struggle with owning those split-off sides of the self. Adolescents project the shadow onto peers, parents, and authority figures, and thus a therapy that works on helping them take back those projections is aimed at integrating the shadow.

In this regard, it is important to note the adolescent impulse to partake in extremely cruel and brutal scapegoating. The psychology of the scapegoat is congruous with the dynamic of projecting the shadow. A scapegoat temporarily relieves an adolescent of the emotional burden of bearing those traits that he finds reprehensible in himself, be it physical weakness, emotional vulnerability, or feeling the fool. He searches for a victim who will hold these projections and with relish attacks that person for expressing the very emotions and behaviors that he cannot face in himself. Adolescent homophobia and racism are firmly rooted in this dynamic.

Scapegoating comes up in the transference with adolescents as well. I remember one fifteen-year-old female with whom I played chess every week in therapy. Whenever I made a bad move, she would attack me with jaunts of "stupid," "idiot," "asshole." Rather than duck the assault, I tried to intensify the emotion by having her describe in exacting detail how stupid and idiotic I was being. This process of intensification and exaggeration put the emotion out there as something between us that either of us could own. By then finding a way to claim it in myself and acknowledge it, "Yes, that was a really dumb move I just made. I feel very foolish," I was modeling a position of being able to have a relationship with the less than perfect parts of oneself and still go on. This way of psychologizing the attack, rather than denying it or retaliating, offered the adolescent a chance to reclaim the projection so that she could eventually talk about how stupid she feels whenever she makes a mistake or fails at something. By engaging the scapegoat role, the projective process is slowed down and there is an opportunity to work with the emotions that the adolescent is seeking to dissipate.

Another way of fostering shadow integration so that an adolescent can learn to tolerate and own the hateful and destructive sides of himself is to point out the times when he has behaved in a constructive manner in an attempt at reparation. The move toward reparation is common in therapy. For example, after a session in which an adolescent client has treated the therapist in a particularly brutal manner, one notices at the following week's session his attempt at making some kind of constructive reparation for how he acted. He might be more soft-spoken or inquire into the well-being of the therapist or give a gift, even if it is as simple as sharing some of the food he has brought with him. It is important to be open to receiving this gesture so that the adolescent feels the constructive counterpart to his destructiveness. Winnicott, who was influenced by the work of Melanie Klein, detailed his observations concerning the reparative gestures of the infant and small child. He writes of this phenomena as "the complex way in which, under favorable environmental conditions, a constructive urge relates to the growing child's personal acceptance of responsibility for the destructive side of his or her nature" (1939, p. 96).

Throughout the book, I have been pointing out the adolescent's uncanny ability to focus on aspects of ourselves as adults where we are less developed or in continued conflict. We saw this in our discussion of how an adolescent's uncompromising gaze penetrates and exposes a fragile or rigid persona. The same holds true with the shadow. Adolescents test the strength and integrity of an adult's character by knocking up against her shadow. They can sense those adults who possess a well-integrated shadow, for example, a teacher who does not need to yell or threaten punishment as a way of maintaining classroom order. Students instinctively respect her authority. In contrast, teachers with split-off shadows get into a lot of trouble when it comes to matters of asserting power and control. Adolescents pick up on their vulnerability and push them into situations where their authority is challenged. In these cases, it is easy for the teacher to project her shadow onto a particular student, seeing him as the whole reason her job is so bad and her classroom so out of control. Adolescents, as well as children, willingly step into this role and the stage is set for an on-going confrontation that usually does not cease until the student is kicked out of school or the teacher switches classes.

CONCLUSION: HERMES AND ADOLESCENCE

The Hermes/Trickster archetype constellates in adolescence and is distinctly related to the manifestations of the persona and shadow which we have been discussing. In Greek mythology, Hermes is known to show up wherever change is imminent. He is the mobile, volatile element in any transformation (Paris 1990). Hermes' own nature is one of paradox: he is god of communication as well as patron saint of liars and god of merchants and thieves. Hermes is a trickster god whose cap of invisibility and winged sandals allow him to mercurially maneuver through the world, carrying the messages of the gods and goddesses to human beings. Given his changing and unstable nature, Hermes as quicksilver is in accord with our characterization of adolescence as a time of fluctuation in identity and character.

One of the best portrayals on film of the hermetic quality in adolescence is in the 1995 movie *Kids*. In it, we witness how the normal, everyday boundaries of adult living do not hold sway for the group of adolescents depicted in the film. Their movements through the streets of New York City display a hermetic grace that discovers new paths at every twist and turn in the road and allows easy passage through the doors, gates, locks, and barricades of adult life. For example, one hot summer evening they wish to swim after the local pool is officially closed. With great ease, they climb over a tall metal fence, as if, with no doubt, this is the way to enter the pool for an after-hour swim. The two main protagonists, Telly and Casper steal a ride on the subway by quickly and elegantly jumping over the turnstyle in the subway station when the man at the ticket counter is distracted. Later, the two boys are thirsty for beer so they set up a diversion in a mini-market: while Telly distracts the owner of the store with senseless mumbo jumbo, Casper effortlessly places a quart of beer down the leg of his baggy pants and walks out of the store. On their way out, they overturn the fruit vendor's perfect display of summer fruit and in the ensuing mayhem snatch a peach.

This kind of thieving, under the tutelage of Hermes, is prominent in adolescence. The fascination with tricking expresses itself in the allure of scamming younger kids or shoplifting. At the same time, adolescents are often on the receiving end of being tricked. They are cheated or taken advantage of due to the naivety of youth. In the following passage, Scott provides an image for the adolescent vulnerability to an unforeseen hermetic theft:

> Hermes is thief. One struggles to gain independence from a parent, say, and does, and in the possession of new independence finds that he/she has lost something too, other than dependence. Perhaps he/she has lost an old security or a certain youthful charm or a kind of optimism. Hermes. And if one laughs, as well as grieves, and feels a little tricked and stays with the sense of loss or the unexpected emptiness, one is with Hermes.
>
> (1982, p. 19)

This description provides another angle from which to approach the point I made in Chapter Six regarding adolescent grief over the loss of innocence and the shattering of one's ideal image of parents. The adolescent's demand for independence and a severing of family ties is susceptible to Hermes' trickery: the unexpected and painful realization of something lost in the quest for adult freedom.

As we have seen, adolescents possess fluidity with their personas and understand the power of masks. They use their hermetic ability to deftly maneuver between different styles of self-presentation, to trick and throw outsiders off track. Adolescents can lead a dual life: appearing one way to family, teachers, and neighbors while presenting a radically different face to their close circle of friends. They are masters of disguise. It is generally quite easy for them to con an adult, convincing them, for example, of contrition, whereas in actuality, they feel no remorse for their actions.

Adolescents delight in playing with the truth; they are hard to pin down and nothing seems to stick to them when they are accused of wrongdoing. They can twist words, taking advantage of the multiple shades of meaning, finding the gray zone in what appears black and white. One senses a mercurial quality in how adolescents argue and defend themselves, similar to Hermes' seductive and playful account before Zeus of his first day's activities, which included stealing his brother Apollo's cattle. Zeus is so taken by his story that he bursts out laughing and forgets the punishment. How many times have parents been thwarted in their attempt to lay down the law and impose a punishment after hearing the adolescent's "side" of the story.

Hermes had his own special way of dealing with harsh authority, never meeting it head on, but rather using humor and ridicule to defuse a situation. Adolescents delight in this kind of play in response to strong-willed authority figures. The more forceful the encounter, the more motivated they are to plunge into their bag of hermetic tricks and taunt the authoritarian with insults or ridicule. Or, they use their charm and cunning to broker a deal which leaves the person in charge feeling tricked, as if they have lost some of their power.

Hermes is God of the borders; his domain is considered a no-man's land, an indeterminate realm outside of established limits. Adolescents move about in a town or city in just this way, finding the most unlikely places to congregate. The film *Kids* depicts a group of adolescents walking in the median between two lanes of traffic. As the cars speed by, determined and on course, the group charts its own path through what is ostensibly a "no-man's" land. This scene powerfully depicts that sense of indeterminacy and moving against the collective tide. Adolescents gain access to places that seem nearly impossible to traverse; think of the seemingly unreachable places where we discover graffiti—the mark of the mercurial adolescent!

Contact with Hermes brings an adolescent into the realm of shadow. Although he conceptualized it in different terms, Winnicott was well aware of the hermetic aspect in the work with adolescents. He spoke of the developmental necessity of adolescents doing "a bit of thieving and lying" (1963a, p. 149) as a way for them to challenge their instincts and develop their own moral sense.

Winnicott advises the practitioner working with adolescents: "Whoever asks questions must expect to be told lies" (ibid., p. 148). Thus, the therapist must find a way of tolerating the hermetic lying, half-truths, and changing stories that pervade therapy. If a therapist depends upon the straightforward, clear communication of Apollo, she will be greatly frustrated in her work with adolescents. Recognition of the hermetic also speaks to the art of differentiating between those stories which need to be taken literally and those that do not. Hearing the metaphor embedded in a story, whether or not it is literally true, is one way of engaging the hermetic.

Winnicott's theory of the anti-social tendency has its own hermetic twist. The impulse to steal is not what it appears to be. The child does not really want what he is stealing, rather he is attempting to possess what he a priori has a right to, namely adequate care by his mother. When he is in a situation in which hope arises, there is an unconscious compulsion to steal. That is why kids steal from those that treat them the best. They are reaching over a developmental gap, making a claim on what they once had because the new situation holds out the promise of getting it again. From the perspective of this dynamic, Winnicott describes the difficulty of working with juvenile delinquents:

> In the period of hope the child manifests an anti-social tendency. This may be awkward for society, and for you if it is your bicycle that is stolen, but those who are not personally involved can see the hope that underlies the compulsion to steal. Perhaps one of the reasons why we tend to leave the therapy of the delinquents to others is that we dislike being stolen from?
>
> (1956, p. 123)

Thus, our resistance to working with juvenile delinquents is, in part, a resistance to the hermetic nature of the work. Depth therapy with adolescents requires that we tolerate being stolen from without retaliating.

Chapter 8

The development of conscience

All passions have a phase when they are merely disastrous, when they drag down their victim with the weight of stupidity—and a later, very much later phase when they wed the spirit, when they "spiritualize" themselves. Formerly, in view of the element of stupidity in passion, war was declared on passion itself, its destruction was plotted: all the old moral monsters agreed on this: il faut tuer les passions (One must kill the passions).

Frederick Nietzsche

PROHIBITION OR INHIBITION?

I now turn to a little known essay of James Hillman's appearing in his book *Loose Ends* entitled, "Towards an Archetypal Model for the Masturbation Inhibition." In reviewing both historical and contemporary views of masturbation, Hillman notes that implicit in these accounts is a condemnation of masturbation resulting from the fundamental sense of guilt it evokes. Pondering the origin of masturbation guilt, Hillman writes:

What is the origin of this discomfort and disapproval, this widespread guilt in conscience? Can we lay it entirely to the prohibition imposed by the parental representatives of culture? Has masturbation become associated with an introjected restrictive authority, so that the two—impulse and prohibition—appear ever after together? Or has masturbation a sui generis inhibitor, as part of the drive itself? Prohibition or inhibition?

(1975a, p. 112)

Hillman is seeking to discover the particular set of dynamics that are in play when one has a guilty conscience in relation to masturbation. If we enlarge the frame of reference we can see that this inquiry into the masturbation inhibition has relevance for the whole question of how one comes to terms with instinctual life itself. Such an investigation has an important bearing upon our study of the adolescent psyche. Since the pubertal changes accompanying adolescence bring forth a dramatic surge of instinctual energy, this fundamental question—prohibition or inhibition—has important ramifications for how we understand adolescent development, especially in relation to sexuality, aggression, substance abuse, and identity formation.

If we view the adolescent psyche as being at war with itself (as in Anna Freud's vision of the adolescent ego caught in a defensive battle against incompatible and incestuous id impulses), then our cultural aim, as parents, educators, probation officers, and judges, is to help fight that war by erecting ever greater external prohibitions to defend against adolescent impulses. This is the situation we find ourselves in today, where the main avenues for dealing with "troubled" adolescents are incarceration, psychiatric hospitalization, and residential treatment.

In the Freudian imagination, instincts are blind cataclysms of id energy seeking discharge through the libidinal zones of the body. They have neither consciousness nor intelligence and it is the developmental task of adolescence to take advantage of the newly acquired ego and superego capabilities in order to once again get the upper hand in coming to terms with their power and demands for satisfaction. Thus, the theory of recapitulation, that this is the second time in our development when we have had to wrest control away from the forceful impulses of the id, implicitly concurs with a prohibitory approach.

Hence, our model of the psyche, in large part, determines whether we emphasize prohibition or inhibition. Hillman, vis-à-vis Jung, envisions the psyche as a self-regulating system:

> If we assume the psyche to be a goal-directed, relatively closed, individuating system, a basic model of which is the self as a circulating flow of psychic life within the person, then this system is also self-steering, self-guided.
>
> (ibid., p. 112)

This idea of a homeostatic psyche can be traced back to the conflict between Jung and Freud regarding the psychology of the instincts. According to Jung, the natural condition of instinctual life is always opposed by a spiritual principle which asserts itself with tremendous force. Jung faults Freud for denying that the spiritual principle is an equivalent counterpart to the instinct. He states:

> Freudian theory consists in a causal explanation of the psychology of instinct. From this standpoint the spiritual principle is bound to appear only as an appendage, a by-product of the instincts. Since its inhibiting and restrictive power cannot be denied, it is traced back to the influence of education, moral authorities, convention and tradition. These authorities in their turn derive their power, according to the theory, from repression in the manner of a vicious circle. The spiritual principle is not recognized as an equivalent counterpart to the instincts.
>
> (*CW* 8, para. 104)

Each of the psychoanalytical theorists I have reviewed, in his or her own highly distinctive manner, elucidates the instinctual processes that become activated during adolescence. The concept of a spiritual principle serving as a counterbalance to the instincts is not present in these theories. Because they have no conception of such a force, greater emphasis is given to the myriad defenses that are employed by an adolescent for the very same purpose, that is to counterbalance the powerful instincts that become activated in adolescence. Consequently, a psychology of adolescence that fails to understand the spiritual principle as being equiprimordial to the instincts results in viewing adolescence as a primarily defensive time of life.

Jung (*CW* 10), in his essay "A Psychological View of Conscience," challenges Freud's assertion that the superego is not a natural and inherent part of the psyche's structure, but rather is consciously acquired from the moral codes of the time. Jung says of conscience, " . . . the phenomenon of conscience does not coincide with the moral code, but is anterior to it, transcends its contents . . . " (ibid., para. 840). Following Jung, Hillman makes explicit the connection between conscience and inhibition.

> Conscience is the experience of the spiritus rector function of the self-guidance system. Guilt in conscience is inhibition in function: inhibition of function is felt as guilt in conscience. Inhibition is self-imposed by the self-regulatory activity of the psyche.
>
> (1975a, p. 112)

Thus, for Freud, we have developed a superego because we were able to internalize parental prohibitions. Whereas for Jung, this internalization is possible only because it echoes a prior self-regulatory function of inhibition which is a structural component of the psyche.

Along these lines, Jung conceives of impulses, desires, and passions as containing within them a telos, a directing intelligence, a self-regulating mechanism that seeks not only physical discharge, but has spiritual, moral, and aesthetic aims also. Attending to the psyche's ability to self-regulate as a directing intelligence, a ruling spirit, is a central aspect of the individuation process. Jung, drawing upon the opposition between the instincts and spirit, articulates this connection between individuation and the self-regulating nature of the psyche. He states:

> Over against the polymorphism of the primitive's instinctual nature there stands the regulating principle of individuation. Multiplicity and inner division are opposed by an integrative unity whose power is as great as that of the instincts. Together they form a pair of opposites necessary for self-regulation, often spoken of as nature and spirit.
>
> (*CW* 8, para. 95)

In the model of the adolescent psyche proposed by the psycho-analytical theorists the impulses are held in check by prohibitions, that is, forbidding, external authorities (although they have the potential to become internalized vis-à-vis the superego). In contrast, Hillman offers a vision of impulses counterbalanced by an inhibitory, self-regulating mechanism which is part of the impulses themselves, much in the same way that Jung envisions instinct and spirit as equiprimordial. In this view, the self-regulating nature of the psyche is emphasized rather than ego defenses which protect against id impulses. Hillman states:

> I hope by now the difference between "prohibition" and "inhibition" has become quite clear. A prohibition is a negative command, a forbidding by authority. An inhibition is the action of hindering, restraining, checking, preventing. A prohibition requires authority. . . . [A]n inhibition on the other hand, can be conceived as native to, as part of, a function itself, as a built-in check and balance necessary for self-regulation.
>
> (1975a pp. 113–14)

Experiencing the inhibition as originating from inside (as opposed to an external prohibition) is a psychological experience that has tremendous therapeutic import. In Chapter 10, I will draw out the implications of such an approach at the level of praxis with adolescent substance abusers. For now, I want to explore the connection between the psychological process of experiencing the inhibition in the impulse and the development of autonomy as constitutive of an innate guiding conscience. Hillman's remarks about the masturbation inhibition sheds light on this connection. He states:

> Masturbation and its inhibition are aspects of the same activity. The lower end is the impulse to action, the upper end consists of fantasies and the spiritus rector of conscience . . . . The therapeutic return of masturbation means the reunion of the two ends of the instinctual spectrum. It means the return of the inhibition as well, in the form of reawakened fantasy life, and a sense of one's own autonomy, one's own innate guiding conscience, rather than an imposed superego morality.
>
> (ibid., p. 114)

Hillman's notion of inhibition is rooted in the phenomenon of masturbation. Perhaps in no other activity is there such a strong connection between fantasy and physicality. As I continue to explore the ramifications of the inhibitory impulse in adolescence, the intimate pairing of imagination and instinctual life will become apparent.

THE AWAKENING OF CONSCIENCE IN ADOLESCENCE

Conscience is awakened by those episodes in life where there is a conflict between the dictates of the traditional moral code of the culture and one's inner sense of right and wrong.[1] Events that activate one's conscience and put it to the test occur with marked frequency during adolescence. There are a myriad of situations that arise when an adolescent's own individual responses are at odds with the moral code upheld by parents, teachers, and school officials and enforced by the government and police. A clash of values ensues. In moving against the collective tide, an adolescent may act in ways that are judged as immoral or unlawful. Awakening to one's own inward sense of conscience challenges unthinking submission to the morality and ethics of the parent's world. A transition from collective authority to individual authority and autonomy is effected; Bosnak (1977) characterizes this as a move from passive morality to dynamic conscience.

It is clear that obtaining a personal sense of morality and values is a life-long task. Winnicott understands the move from passive morality to dynamic conscience as an essential part of the developmental process. For him, dynamic conscience involves the feelings of right and wrong a child has apart from compliance. He states:

> I like to think that there is a way of life that starts from the assumption that morality that is linked with compliance has little ultimate value, and that it is the individual child's own sense of right and wrong that we hope to find developing along with everything else that develops because of the inherited processes leading toward all kinds of growth . . .
>
> (1966, p. 107)

With children, there is a vast difference between one who precariously moves through the world, reaching for this and that, and can only feel a sense of limitation when complying with a parent who barks out prohibitory commands, "No, you can't have that," "No, you can't do that," versus a child whose internal sense of limits is evident in how they are able to stay relatively contained in the absence of monitoring forces. In this case, a gentle admonishment from a parent resonates with a pattern of response already existing within the child.

In terms of adolescents, the question arises as to what is needed from the environment to help awaken those psychic functions which contribute to the development of personal conscience and autonomy. In other words, how do we aid an adolescent in the process of extracting her personal conscience from its absorption in and by the moral code of the times (Bosnak, 1977)? This process of extraction is what enables passive morality, unthinking compliance to moral precepts to be transformed into dynamic conscience, that is, the sense of working through and claiming one's own moral stance.

A purely prohibitive approach is bound to fail because an outside authority cannot always be there to monitor an adolescent's behavior. Winnicott states:

> The gradual withdrawal of authority is an important part of the management of adolescents, and adolescent boys and girls can

be grouped according to their capacity to stand withdrawal of imposed authority.

(1939, p. 91)

The process of vitalizing one's personal sense of conscience is central to adolescent individuation. Adolescents are deluged with serious moral choices. The values which have been inculcated in them by their parents and society are put to the test. It is startling to consider the plethora of decisions that adolescents must contend with in today's world. They must make choices involving their education and a vocational future, including whether or not cheating in school is permissible; they must decide about graduating from high school and possibly going to college or dropping out of school and getting a job; they must decide whether to participate in under-age drinking and the use of illicit substances, whether to steal, vandalize, or engage in street crime, whether to join a gang, carry a knife or a gun, or engage in fighting and violence; they must decide how they will express their sexuality and if they will protect themselves from pregnancy and disease; and finally, they must figure out where to draw the line between what they want for themselves and what they are being urged to do by their friends, parents, and the prohibitive voices of the culture.

Can we guide adolescents in sifting through what is important for psychological development amongst these choices, helping them to differentiate where their own values differ from their parents, peer group, and society? One therapeutic technique which I have found useful in this regard is to create a "Self Chart" with an adolescent.[2] On the top horizontal axis, all of the current dilemmas with which he is struggling are listed, for example, drugs/alcohol, school, sexuality, curfew, stealing, etc. On the left vertical axis, a list is made of all the important influences in his life, for example, parents, teachers, school administrators, boss, peer group, best friend, and finally, at the bottom, the category of "self" is written in. The adolescent then fills in what each one of these figures believes about the topics on the top of the list and notes the similiarities and differences in opinion. The most interesting part of the exercise comes when it is time to fill in the self column at the bottom of the chart. Many adolescents pause here, uncertain what they feel about a topic as opposed to what everybody else is telling them to feel. The visual lay-out of the chart affords them an opportunity for reflecting upon where their own voice gets drowned out by the other voices around them.

As therapists, we promote individuation by nurturing an adolescent's awareness of his authentic responses to the world in the face of collective pressures to conform to normative standards. This approach centers upon the evolving consciousness of one's own inhibitory responses in the face of an imposed superego morality. Is there a part of the self that recoils in the contemplation of an intended action or in the aftermath of a major life-event? Much of the therapeutic reflection that naturally turns up with adolescents implicitly follows along these lines. For example, the opening of a pathway for an adolescent to feel into the remorse, bitterness, or sadness after engaging in an activity that just did not sit right: "I don't want to do that again not because I am told it is wrong or I will be breaking the law, but because it goes against my own grain, it doesn't feel right to who I am." In other words, the remorse speaks to the sense of having transgressed an inner law. This inhibitory response—feeling a sense of limit or restraint in regard to a behavior from an inward place—is crucial for self-regulation.

THE PROJECTION ONTO PARENTS

According to Jung, an inhibition is given as an innate counterforce to a drive. A child's first experience of this inhibiting force is external, namely, the obstructing behavior of mother and father. Parents are the hook for the projection of the inhibition. Jung comments:

> At first he (the child) is conscious only of the instincts and of what opposes these instincts—namely his parents. For this reason the child has no notion that what stands in his way may be within himself. Rightly or wrongly it is projected on to the parents. This infantile prejudice is so tenacious that we doctors often have the greatest difficulty in persuading our patients that the wicked father who forbade everything is far more inside than outside themselves. Everything that works from the unconscious appears projected on others.
>
> (*CW* 8, para. 99)

Bosnak, commenting on this passage of Jung's, makes clear the juncture between the inhibition in the drive and the parental archetype.

Jung says how difficult it is to show a patient that the evil father who forbids everything is less the historical father than the inner father. This inner father is functionally the drive inhibition. It is the inner authority of the person imagined as Father, who is the ordering principle of the psyche. Ordering seen as both forming the laws as well as giving orders.

(1977, p. 84)

For some adolescents, the drive inhibition cannot be felt in an inward sense so that a literal encounter with a prohibitory force is a psychological necessity. One must cross external limits in order to discover them inside. A confrontation with the police serves the function of letting an adolescent feel first-hand society's prohibitory restrictions on their actions and behavior. The same holds true for a parent grounding an adolescent for two weeks because she skipped school and came home past curfew. The prohibitive confrontation is a barometer for where one is in the world, a warning for when one has crossed over an impermissible line.

In adolescent psychotherapy, one method for accessing an adolescent's own inward sense of inhibition is through an exploration of the prohibitory voice. The voice of prohibition enters the therapy session in a bossy and demanding way, forcing itself into the room as an unmistakable presence. If the adolescent is incapable or unwilling to engage it, the therapist has to be relied upon to honor it in order to insure the adolescent's behavioral accountability. In other words, the therapist has to find a way of calling attention to the fact that the adolescent's actions have real consequences both for the adolescent and those in his environment. Some adolescents force the therapist to always carry the prohibitive voice. The adolescent stays in the role of innocent victim, blaming everyone else for what is going wrong in his life.

One common motif that repeatedly surfaces is the adolescent's perception of herself as a victim of the parent's failure to consistently and fairly enforce the rules at home. For example, the adolescent may feel she is being unjustly punished for breaking an arbitrary rule enacted in a blatantly unfair manner by two-faced parents with double standards. She feels betrayed and refuses to accept her parent's authority. Disavowing parental authority can be actualized in adolescence, where the possibility of moving out, running away, living with other relatives or friends is a living reality. By focusing on the parent's inconsistencies as rule enforcers, the adolescent fails to examine her own accountability.

This brings us to the crucial question of how to work with an adolescent who has abdicated all responsibility for his actions and behaviors. Typically a parent or teacher confronts this problem exclusively from the side of prohibition: "Don't you ever let me catch you doing that again, or else." I am suggesting here that as therapists it is a mistake to try and repeat these failed attempts by wholly identifying with the prohibitory force. Rather, I believe, the voice of prohibition has entered the therapy room because the adolescent is seeking to encounter it at a deeper level through the process of therapeutic reflection. The whole scenario of anger, blame and victimization which is repeatedly enacted in therapy sessions is often an expression of the adolescent's unconscious longing to hear the voice of prohibition in a different way.

The compulsion to repeat the diatribe against mother and father, their failures and inconsistencies, is, in essence, an attempt to move past the resentments, entrapments, and disagreements with the personal parents in order to make contact with a sense of one's own inner authority. This is what I have been referring to as the inward sense of the drive inhibition which Jung, Hillman, and Bosnak contend is archetypal. In railing against the personal parents, one seeks to discover the ordering principle that is unique to one's own psyche. The therapist's willingness to engage a parental transference, where the adolescent turns the therapist into a prohibitive parent, or to tolerate hearing the incessant vilification's against the personal parents, underlies a belief that an adolescent is searching to locate these forces within herself. Thus, how a therapist responds to and embodies the prohibitive voice is a crucial part of the process.

An overly empathic therapist can prevent an adolescent from discovering this voice as an archetypal force within himself. This is the result of too strongly identifying with the victimized adolescent over and against the corrupt parents, teachers, probation officers, etc. who are out to get him and do him wrong. Adolescents can coerce a therapist into taking this stance by painting themselves as innocent victims or the therapist may have a need to find salvation for his own wounded adolescence and play this out in the therapy. In either case, too much empathy leaves the adolescent with no ability to come to terms with the prohibitive voice as an intrapsychic reality. It collapses the tension and affirms the adolescent in denying that he will ever need to take responsibility for his actions and thus keeps him in the role of a child.

Other therapists react to this dynamic by battling for superego supremacy. A moralistic approach toward getting an adolescent to take responsibility for herself blocks her from doing any kind of psychological work other than paying lip service to the therapist's need to enforce his moral system. In Winnicott's sense, this would be a case of forced compliance. Also, if one enters the relationship with a moral horn to blow, an ideology to be adopted, one may unduly influence the adolescent's developing sense of values.

CLINICAL VIGNETTES: GETTING TO KNOW THE "FUCK-IT" VOICE

The lack of "impulse control" in adolescence takes on a new meaning once we understand that the impulse itself contains within it an inhibitory force. Our therapeutic approach shifts from strengthening defenses against the onslaught of impulses to an engagement with adolescent impulses; they are personified and worked through at the level of image. Once inside the image of the impulse, we can ask what it wants, what kind of expression it is seeking as well as uncovering its inhibitory counterpart which is most likely, in adolescence, to be split off from consciousness. To illustrate this method, I will present two clinical encounters where I used an imaginal approach.

Kirk, soon to be eighteen, experienced tremendous difficulty controlling his angry outbursts which frequently resulted in violent action toward others. Since the age of sixteen, he had been arrested for disorderly conduct, drinking in public and threatening a police officer. As a result of these arrests, he was placed on probation. When I began seeing him, he let me know that if he was picked up one more time for such behavior, in the four months before he turned eighteen, he would be locked up in a youth facility by his probation officer.

Kirk described how his mind went blank whenever he became enraged, leaving him with no capacity to work through his anger in any way other than getting into a fight or smashing something. An unyielding force emerged inside of him which Kirk was able to describe in words: "I don't care. Fuck it." This attitude overpowered all other feelings or responses.

A central piece of the therapy took place in reflecting upon the image of this force inundating Kirk's consciousness which we came to call the "Fuck It" voice. The "Fuck It" voice personified what Kirk felt as a real presence in his psyche. I approached it at the level of image by asking: if the "Fuck It" voice were a person, what would he be feeling? Does he find the anger and rage comforting? What else can be done to soothe him?

The act of personifying, finding just the right name for this complex, was the first step in decreasing its psychological grip. It is analogous to what happens in the fairytale Rumpelstiltskin when the miller's daughter discovers the little man's name. Her speaking the name Rumpelstiltskin aloud causes him, in a fury, to tear himself in two and thus lose his hold on the miller's daughter's newborn child. For Kirk, our discovery of the correct name provided us with a way into the image. With adolescents, this method of finding the right name for a complex is a powerful tool in lessening its psychological intensity. Asking the question: "What would you call that part of yourself?" offers the adolescent a tangible image to hold onto that can be perceived as an aspect of his experience and reflected upon as the therapy proceeds.

I made the interpretation to Kirk that part of becoming an adult was establishing a relationship with the "Fuck It" voice, the part of the self that does not care and easily dismisses whatever one has worked hard to achieve. Kirk reacted to this idea by explaining how the "Fuck It" voice for him was also a strategy for survival. In the past, for example, when he was physically threatened by someone, this part of himself would "click" in and take over, readying him to fight full force without being afraid. It was important for me to understand its positive function and acknowledge its adaptive aspect before we could go further in exploring its dangers. This led us into an examination of specific situations that elicited this response, asking whether or not, in the long run, it was useful.

For Kirk, the "Fuck It" voice interfered with the expression of other parts of his personality that may have functioned to inhibit his impulsive aggressivity. The power and force of this unitary voice was completely overwhelming. One valuable outcome of dialoguing with the image of the "Fuck It" voice was that other attitudes and feelings surfaced and found expression. For example, Kirk learned to draw upon a calmer, more centered part of himself when he began to feel out of control with his anger. In response to a provocative situation when he sensed his impulse to fight, he could reason with the "Fuck It" voice by saying: "If you fight, you'll end up in jail, and destroy your chances of graduating high school. That's not what I want. It's not worth it." The therapy allowed for the emergence of new attitudes in relation to the aggression so that Kirk had some choice in deciding whether or not to take action. It was as if the impulsivity itself became denser and more filled out and not so easily subdued through rageful action.

Andy, sixteen, a heavy pot smoker, told me the story of how, being weeks away from taking the test to get his driver's license, he decided to sneak out of his house in the middle of the night and take his parent's car for a joy ride with his friends. I asked him if there was any part of himself that was hesitant or uncertain about his decision.

"Nope," Andy said, "but my younger sister was there and she said, 'Don't do it. You'll get in trouble.' "

At first, Andy denied that this voice was in any way a part of himself. As I pushed him on this point, he repeated his sister's phrase, "Don't do it, you'll get in trouble," in a snotty, falsetto tone.

"And what do you call that kind of voice?" I asked.

"A pussy."

"But is it part of you?"

"A tiny, tiny part," he replied. "Way in the back, like a burnt-up piece of weed that didn't get smoked."

Reflecting upon this interchange, Andy's reasons for smoking so much marijuana took on a new significance. I viewed the "burnt-up piece of weed that didn't get smoked" as an image of an aspect of himself that survives his attempt to quell his affective life through his daily ritual of getting high. A very small, tightly compacted piece survives the anesthetizing process. It will not yield and give itself up to the flame by turning into smoke. In working with the image of this tiny piece of himself, I pointed out how much wisdom I thought it contained. After all, it was the part of himself that was able to assert, "You really like driving. If you only wait a few more weeks you can take your parent's car out whenever you want. One night of fun is not worth blowing the whole thing now." Andy replied to my attempt to speak out of this image with the words: "Fuck it."

This led us to focus on the same dynamic that Kirk faced, that is how the "Fuck It" voice had become the single, solitary spokesman for Andy's entire self. With Andy, I sensed his strong compulsion to find a way inside of this image. Any time I pointed out to him the unpleasant consequences of his impulsive actions, he would mockingly assert, "Fuck it, who cares." This particular interaction played itself out as a little performance where Andy forced me to submit to the dynamic power of an aspect of himself that had an answer for everything. "Fuck It, Who Cares" covered every conceivable situation where Andy felt at a loss. The way it worked to keep me silent, keep me shut up and shut out was parallel to how it silenced all of the other parts of Andy's self that could possibly respond to this voice. I was left feeling the split-off sadness, frustration and rage that Andy kept at bay in his overidentification with the power of this stance. By repeatedly enacting this scene, Andy was unconsciously using me and our relationship to gain a new vantage point from which to witness how this force dominated his life. This was critical for Andy since it was this very aspect of his personality that greatly exacerbated the pain and difficulties he was already facing.

ACTING-OUT VERSUS ACTING-IN

We are now in a position to investigate the denunciatory characterization of adolescent impulsivity as "acting-out" behavior. This term, which predominates the typical adolescent case report, is conceptually problematic for two main reasons. First, it is rooted in the psychoanalytical vision of the adolescent psyche as being primarily defensive in nature. Acting-out is commonly understood as a mode of behavior that defends against an inner conflict or is an attempt to externalize a painful affect. In this model, behavior is enacted defensively in order to depotentiate intolerable feelings. The second difficulty with this concept is that it indiscriminately devalues all outward behavior in favor of inward states of mind. Taking action comes to be seen as an inferior mode of expression.

In its typical usage, acting-out specifies only two elements: affect and behavior. Adolescents act in order to avoid feelings; outward behavior masks inner feeling states. What is left out of this equation is a third element, that is the play of tension between feeling something and putting it into action, which I have been calling "inhibition." What if we imagined acting-out as a mode of behavior where impulse and inhibition are split off from each other. In that case, it is not the fact that an adolescent is taking action in the world that is problematic, but rather the premature collapsing of the tension between a feeling state and an action. In other words, the unconscious enactment of a behavior without meaningful self-reflection (Bernstein 1987, p. 138). The term used by some Jungians, acting-in, describes in a positive sense behavior that originates along the ego–self axis. I want to expand on that idea by stating, in addition, that acting-in signifies behavior that does not prematurely collapse the inhibitory tension.

The middle region between impulse and action is demarcated by Hillman (1975a) with his idea that experiencing the inhibition in the impulse is akin to making a natural instinctual process psychological. This idea is intrinsic to Jung's notion of the inseparable nature of images and instincts. Hillman states:

> Jung places images and instincts on a psychological continuum, like a spectrum (*CW* 8: pp. 397–420). This spectrum, or color-band, ranges from an infra-red end, the bodily action of instinctual desire, to the ultra-violet blue end of fantasy images. These fantasy images, according to Jung's model, are the pattern and form of desire. Desire isn't just a blind urge; it is formed by a pattern of behavior, a gesture, a writhing, a dancing, a poetics, a coming-on of style, and these patterns are also fantasies which present images as instinctual behaviors.
>
> (1995, p. 50)

Nietzsche (1888), in the opening quotation of this chapter, alludes to the same phenomenon with his image of the wedding between the passions and the spirit. The implication for adolescent psychotherapy is that by working with the inhibition that arises within the impulse toward action, we allow adolescents to connect to the other side of the instinct–image spectrum. In doing so, the natural fantasying activity of the psyche is activated as an adolescent dips into the stream of her inner life.

The inhibition of action produces imagination. Experiencing an inhibition is feeling into the imaginative pattern that contains the impulse toward action. Engaging an instinctual impulse imaginally, feeling where it is rooted in the body, may reduce the need literally to take action. Thus imagination is one of the most effective tools we have in working with adolescents who are prone to impulsive behavior. Helping them express the imaginative form of their impulses re-connects the two ends of the instinctual spectrum.[3]

As an example, take anger. An adolescent can "act-out" anger by hitting, shoving, or screaming obscenities at the object of her anger. Or she can repress the angry feelings, and project them onto another. This latter alternative characterizes the passive–aggressive move which adolescents are notorious for making. The extreme passivity is the vehicle for splitting-off anger and unconsciously imposing it onto someone else so that an adolescent can sit back and watch as those around him become more and more enraged. The third alternative is to help an adolescent give form to the anger, finding out how it is shaped, discovering its rhythm and sense of timing, and most importantly, what it is seeking. This approach fosters the adolescent's ability to bear the tension between repressing anger and discharging it. Thus, it is therapeutically effective to help adolescents find a form of expression that can contain the angry impulses whether it be artistic expression such as painting, poetry writing or modeling clay, or a more visceral form, such as beating a drum, shaking a tambourine or imagining the object of anger and expressing in words exactly what one is enraged about. This is putting into practice the idea of discovering the pattern or form of the emotion so that it does not require immediate discharge which collapses the tension and precludes the possibility of therapeutic engagement.

However we characterize the passions that arise in adolescence, whether we call them drives, impulses, instincts, libido, etc., it is clear that they are a central life-force intimately connected to desire. And as we have seen, desire itself manifests in a new way, with a new kind of reality. Hence, the work with the impulses as imaginal realities allows an adolescent to come into contact with his desire.

Mary Watkins (1990b), in her essay, "Mother and Child: Some Teachings of Desire" explores the claim that one crucial aspect of parenting is finding time where the child can be given a space and allowed to be present to her own desires, letting her experience in a bodily and emotional way the texture of these desires. It is crucial for a child to learn that she can survive the eruption of intense emotion because contained within it is a guiding pattern that allows for its own organic sense of resolution.

Treating impulsive behavior by strengthening an adolescent's trust in his own sense of inhibition is a parallel method for allowing him to come to know his desirous responses to the world. Inhibitions pull one in a certain direction. They serve as guides, steering one away from what does not accord with the rhythms and impulses of the self. Jung's negative evaluation of a persona that feigns individuality along with Winnicott's notion of the false self both speak of an individual who has lost touch with desire. Compliance to a role or mirroring the desires of another takes the place of being steered by the subtle adjustments of an inhibitory response. Given all that happens in adolescence concerning the development of conscience and the struggle with shadow, as well as the pressure to conform and overidentify with a persona, speaks to the importance for therapists of having a vision of the psyche as self-regulating. The more we can help the adolescent discover from inside a capacity for self-navigation, the less need we have to anxiously perpetuate prohibitive interventions that attempt to fix the adolescent's course.

Part IV

Adolescent psychotherapy: shifting the paradigm

INTRODUCTION TO PART IV: ADOLESCENCE AND PSYCHOPATHOLOGY

Adolescence is a time of extreme turmoil and profound emotional suffering. Unlike a therapeutic encounter with an adult client where there is a tangible sense of distance, adolescents are inclined to present themselves in the context of their own turmoil in an overwhelming way that impinges upon the prescribed boundary between therapist and client. What breaks through is an outpouring of highly charged, unprocessed, affective material that leaves a therapist feeling disoriented and ungrounded. In the pressing need to organize and structure the chaos, attempting to find some secure ground on which to stand and continue with the work, our therapeutic focus narrows to the particularities of the case before us. We are then inclined to rely on (to a far greater extent than in work with other clients) diagnoses and categories of psychopathology as a way of containing the material and re-establishing an appropriate sense of distance. The inevitable consequence of such a move is that we fail to grasp the particular suffering of the adolescent before us in the context of the more universal, existential suffering which I have been exploring throughout the book.

Another consequence of too quickly fitting an adolescent's symptom picture into a particular diagnostic framework is that no consideration is given to the teleological meaning of his symptoms. In many cases, what appears initially as "pathological" in adolescence—a particular behavior or symptom—has a prospective function, that is, contained within it are intimations about future growth and development. When pathology dominates our vision we miss the chance to see that a certain behavior or symptom hints at a deeper process of change. In this regard, we can envision the function of psychotherapy as helping the troubled adolescent to meaningfully engage a crisis so that its inherent potential for transformation can unfold.

Adolescents frequently come to therapy as a result of banging heads with the system. They have behaved in ways that are not acceptable to society, whether through theft, truancy, fighting, or drug use. Because of the current confluence of mental health treatment and the legal system, psychotherapeutic treatment is presented as the least noxious option among few possibilities. For example, an adolescent may be a first-time law breaker and rather than face criminal punishment, she may opt for ten sessions of psychotherapy. Another may come at the behest of an anxious parent or demanding school official with the threat of being grounded or kicked out of school. It is rare that an adolescent initially starts therapy without some form of external pressure.

Consequently, therapists find themselves caught between the conflicting needs of their adolescent clients and the outside forces who have high stakes in the outcome of the treatment. This situation places pressure on the therapist to "straighten out" the adolescent and eradicate "negative" behaviors. In my own practice, I have received dozens of phone calls from teachers, school administrators, and parents demanding that I get an adolescent to stop his intolerable behaviors. Because of this external pressure, one is vulnerable to unconsciously setting off on a course of socialization with an adolescent client, using the therapy as a rehearsal for social conformity.

Once we can unequivocally say what is causing the aberrant behavior, we have something definite to give back to those on the outside pressuring us to produce tangible results. In this case, the tendency to overpathologize is a result of the quick-fix mind-set. For example, the diagnosis of major depression not only explains away a whole host of behaviors and symptoms (not to mention the lack of attention given to family and school dynamics), but sets into place a medicalized treatment regime that allows everyone in the adolescent's environment to narrow their range of focus to the single issue of whether or not the anti-depressant medication is being taken on a regular basis. This seems to all concerned a clear, clean, and containing solution in response to the turmoil that is so difficult to bear.

When we, as therapists, become a socializing force in service to societal pressures, our ability to engage therapeutically is compromised. One cannot entirely escape this conundrum in any work with adolescents; however, gaining a visceral awareness of the pressure this bind creates has significant effects on how we envision our work. In this section, I will focus on those places where the conflict between eliminating aberrant behaviors versus exploring their underlying meaning is most pronounced. My practice of dwelling openly and patiently with the kinds of problems, fraught with paradoxes and dilemmas, that adolescents bring to a therapist, emerges from the ideas developed thus far in the book. Overall, I want to explore ways of listening and responding to the material brought in by an adolescent in crisis so that its implications for individuation are given value and voice.

Chapter 9

Countertransference in the treatment of adolescence

Don't we reveal our essential selves most explicitly in the unguarded enthusiasms of our teenage years? Isn't that why the memories later fill us with such a prickly sense of shame?

Sven Birkerts

INTRODUCTION

In working with adolescents, perhaps more than any other client population, the path into the heart of the work, where new possibilities for listening and understanding can arise, is through an analysis of one's own countertransferential responses. Staying with what personally feels most uncomfortable and distressing and in like manner most provocative and engaging leads into the central dilemmas facing each of us in our attempts to make a therapeutic connection. How we balance the demands of external adaptation with the urge toward individuation in our adolescent clients plays itself out in the particular countertransferential responses that arise during the course of therapy. What follows is an examination of how these responses serve to open up the dialogue between adolescent and therapist so that it is mutually transformative.

ADOLESCENCE AS A MODE OF EXPERIENCE

[In a peculiar way, adolescence is not over even though we have finished passing through its developmental entanglements. Like childhood, adolescence is not overcome by time. Both are modes of experience that linger on in adult living.] Thus, it is possible to envision adolescence as an interior realm within an adult. Consider for a moment how we might mockingly say to a friend, "Oh, you're acting so adolescent," or in reaction to certain youthful behaviors like driving a car very fast and somewhat recklessly, we might critically exclaim, "What are you doing, re-living your adolescence?" Such statements are usually in response to a display of exuberance, a mode of moving through the world where total absorption in an activity is still a possibility. The appearance of adolescent modes of experience in adulthood are met with disparaging words and leave their victim feeling embarrassed and ashamed. Adolescent intensity is an awkward and uncomfortable energy to bear at any age.

As therapists working with adolescents, listening closely to their stories, we recover images of our own adolescence. The initial countertransferential response lies in the sudden, sometimes shocking realization that to sit therapeutically with an adolescent entails coming face to face with uninvited stories and emotions from that difficult period in our own history. Often these memories carry a highly affective charge. A seasoned therapist expressed what it was like when she first began taking adolescents into her practice: "Every problem I ever had as a teen-ager came back and slapped me in the face." If we are resistant to this outpouring, struggling against the ascent of our own memories into consciousness, we are all too likely to unconsciously project the most disturbing and raw aspects of this material onto our clients. Furthermore, we foreclose the possibility of in-depth listening when we bar the door to the living memories of our own adolescence.

In a course I teach on adolescent psychotherapy with graduate students training to become therapists, my first assignment is for them to write a one-page memoir of their adolescence. The assignment is typically met with resistance. In the end, however, by reminiscing about their own adolescence, my students are catapulted in a stirring way into the affective space of that period of life. Within the interiority of their recollections, I have them imagine a therapist approaching their adolescent self. I then proceed with an active imagination based upon what could potentially occur between them. I ask: What kind of bearing on the part of the therapist would allow for a connection to be established? Which questions would feel appropriate and which would feel violating and intrusive? What style of pacing would be necessary, and how could this imaginal therapist express that he or she is truly listening and taking in what is being said in a non-judgmental way? In doing this exercise, there is an assumption that sensitivity to our own

adolescent process is the key that allows entrance into the heavily
barricaded inner world of an adolescent client. Staying in relation
to the vulnerabilities we felt as adolescents engenders in us the
necessary therapeutic sensitivity from which to ground the work.

A former colleague of mine working with adolescent substance
abusers had the following dream:

> I am sitting in my office talking to one of my clients about his
> marijuana use. I reach into my desk to get a pen to write some-
> thing down and to my shock and horror I discover a bag of grass
> sitting in the back of the drawer. I realize it is my own stash and I
> feel great shame.

Now this particular clinician, although very caring, took a cool
and distant approach toward her clients' use of drugs and alcohol,
focusing in a somewhat perfunctory way on the risks they were
incurring. She had a difficult time establishing a strong enough
connection to weather the intricacies of counseling substance
abusers; her clients would stop coming after a few sessions. The fact
that she too, in her dream, had a secret stash that brought forth feelings of shame and embarrassment seemed to me to be her psyche's
attempt to compensate for the emotional aloofness that surrounded
her work. The dream was pointing to the idea that somewhere
secretly stashed away inside, as close at hand as her desk drawer,
were her own experiences and emotions that paralleled what was
being brought in by her clients. Thus, some of the shame, a key
ingredient that surrounds adolescent substance abuse, was transferred back to the therapist as the dream beckoned an awareness to
take seriously her own illicit carrying on.

Thus, therapeutic work with adolescents asks that we be attentive
to the emotional complexes that are being touched off in us as we
make contact with the turbulent energy that adolescents embody.
(Parents of teen-agers face a similar task). We must be attentive to
the imagery, thoughts and feelings that spontaneously arise as we
listen to the stories being told in therapy. A reinvestigation of our
own adolescence is important, feeling how that realm continues to
move inside of us. The work with adolescents also becomes work on
ourselves. We must remember the foolish and painful things that
happened to us as youth. Rather than repressing the raw emotions
of these memories, we must actively work at refining them,
empathizing with our own adolescent suffering so that we can be
open to that suffering in our clients.

For example, if at fifteen we were shy, withdrawn, and isolated, and had difficulty in social situations, what would happen if an adolescent with a similar profile came into our office? The way we would respond is to a large part dependent on how we currently respond to that part of ourselves. Do we try to rouse our own dull adolescent into action through a self-motivating internal voice, or are we overcome by her depression? Have we found it best to give lots of advice? The trap to avoid is treating the adolescent client in the same manner in which we treat our own disenfranchised adolescent. Moreover, if that place inside ourselves is split off from consciousness then we experience our clients as irritants and unconsciously direct the therapeutic process away from whatever threatens to touch our adolescent wounds.

This kind of awareness is painful to develop because it forces us to face the myriad ways in which our own adolescent processes were impinged upon by those closest to us. Winnicott describes how involvement with adolescents can bring forth feelings of jealousy, envy, and resentment over the obstructions that prevented us from ever truly living out our own adolescence. He states:

> The big threat from the adolescent is the threat to the bit of ourselves that has not really had its adolescence. This bit of ourselves makes us resent those people being able to have their phases of the doldrums and makes us want to find a solution for them.
>
> (1963a, p. 155)

In addition, there is much to be gained from helping parents recall the stories of their own adolescence. It is striking how some parents who had a difficult adolescence attempt to keep the past hidden from their family. In their role of parenting an adolescent, the suffering and shame resurfaces and unconsciously influences their interactions and responses. Parents, who as youths experienced acute suffering, carry with them the sentiment, "I never want my child to go through what I went through." Those who engaged in anti-social or delinquent behavior worry that if it ever gets out, their children will use this knowledge as justification for participating in similiar activities.

In one family with which I worked, consisting of a mother, father and two daughters (one twelve, one fifteen), the eldest daughter was caught in a severe conflict with her father. Her staying out late at night, having admitted to getting drunk on two different occasions, flunking one of her classes, caused her father to become almost militaristic in his approach to her. When she stayed out past curfew, he would get in his car and drive around the neighborhood looking for her. Once caught, she would be grounded and her privileges would be taken away for months at a time. This caused increasing animosity on his daughter's behalf and they became locked in an vicious cycle of resentment and ill will toward each other.

As we pursued this conflict in a family session, I asked if anyone in the family could tell me what it was like for Dad when he was an adolescent. The two daughters looked stunned and perplexed, but I noticed a slight, sheepish grin on Mom's face. She grew up in the same neighborhood and started to tell stories of what a hellion Dad was as a teen-ager, stealing cars, running away from home, dropping out of school. As she spoke, Dad appeared sullen and withdrawn and I asked him what he was feeling. He spoke of his wish to keep this information concealed from his daughters so as not to be a bad role model. In turn, I asked his eldest daughter what is was like to hear these stories about her father. She said she felt relieved that her dad wasn't so perfect and that it alleviated the pressure she felt to always do everything right. Lifting the repression on these stories was the true agent of change in this family, allowing father and daughter to discover a common ground upon which they could meet.

[When parents are able to reclaim some of the memories and emotions that occurred for them as adolescents, it can cause a shift in how they perceive and interact with their adolescent children. Often, it increases their capacity for empathy. At that moment, the lectures and threats give way to the possibility of genuine engagement. When parents have less of a need to defend against these affects within themselves, they can express their legitimate concern in a way that is more likely to be heard and received.]

THE PUER–SENEX ARCHETYPE

Another countertransferential response stems from the inevitable clash that occurs between youth and adults, what Bettelheim (1961) refers to as "the problem of generations." Obviously, this confrontation between the youths of a society and its elders does not only occur in psychotherapy. We see it repeatedly in the conflicts, fights, and disharmony that ensue when children become adolescents and their parents struggle to properly rear them. [Parents fail to comprehend the music, clothes, and language of their teen-age children. They demand stability, regularity, and acknowledgment of boundaries, while their adolescent sons and daughters seek change, discovery, and disruption of conformist standards. Raging battles erupt as every conceivable boundary is challenged: choice of friends, choice of career, curfew, style of clothing, sexuality, drugs and alcohol, etc. Battle lines extend far beyond the perimeters of the home as the local police force and school administration, the television and music industry, all come down on one side or the other in the war waged between two conflicting perspectives of the world.

This universal conflict between youth and old age is expressed in Jungian psychology by reference to the puer–senex archetype. In Chapter 2, I used the psychology of the puer to illuminate the spiritual inclinations of adolescents, and out of that perspective, offered a teleological approach to their symptomatology and erratic behavior. In this section, I will move further down that road by examining the constellation of the puer–senex archetype in adolescent psychotherapy through myth, image, and story to help us better understand our countertransferential responses.

The puer aeternus is defined by Jung (*CW* 5) as the eternal youth, and is personified in a myriad of mythological figures including Phaethon, Bellerophon, Narcissus, and Icarus. It bespeaks an image of the "defenselessness and vulnerability of incipient developments in the psyche" (Moore 1979, p. 190). Care and sensitivity is required in traversing the region of a non-defended psyche. Moore echoes this sentiment in his description of the puer. He states:

> Whenever new movements of the soul come to life, stir, and press upon consciousness, puer may constellate. One is then close to virgin soil, filled perhaps with the spirit of adventure, excited, nervous, and unsteady—like a colt on shaky legs, eager to run but awkward and unpredictable.
>
> (ibid.)

The lofty idealism and spiritual longings that we have been examining as an integral part of the adolescent psyche are qualities attributed to the puer. Hillman contends that "puer figures can be regarded as avatars of the Self's spiritual aspect, and puer impulses as messages from the spirit or as calls to the spirit" (1967, p. 23). The call of the spirit awakens one to the present moment. The "now" is given supreme value; past and future have little signifi-cance. In this regard, the puer experiences time in a non-ordinary way.

The experience of the "now" as eternal is closely aligned to the movement of the puer along the vertical axis. Phaethon, Apollo's son, tries to drive his father's Sun-chariot straight up in the sky. Icarus, in his desperation to escape the starry-eyed bull at the center of Minos' labyrinth flies upward toward the sun on waxen wings constructed by his father. Both figures fall to their death on a reverse traversal toward the earth. Vertical flight and free falling characterize this aspect of the puer spirit.

The senex archetype, which originates in the Greek god Saturn–Kronos, (Kronos is the Greek word for time) stands in diametrical opposition to the puer. Situated in time and history, giving credence to the past and future, the senex is connected to the horizontal axis.

A common image of the senex is an old man; he serves as a father figure, in that he provides a sense of order and authority. Often, the senex insistence upon order, history, and authority finds itself in conflict with the puer's impulse for wanting it done now, immediately. As Moore describes:

> The puer strives for vertical flight. His feet are not on the ground. He has little patience for development, for working things out. Puer wants things done immediately, and his impa-tient idealism finds the sage counsel of the senex establishment an anchor and a weight. As the street pueri like to say: "It's a drag!"
>
> (1979, p. 191)

There is a strong propensity in our therapeutic work with adoles-cents for polarization into puer and senex sensibilities. Adolescents, male and female alike, often identify with the puer, and unwittingly constellate the senex in us. Likewise, our dour senex responses to adolescent flightiness creates within the adolescent an intensified fixation and fascination with a puer-like style of consciousness. What I am explicating here is a tandem archetype, in other words, puer and senex are always together, yet it is very common for one to be split off from the other. To grasp this potential for splitting, let us take a closer look at the phenomenology of the senex.

Kronos, son of Uranus (the Sky) and Gaia (the Earth), in response to the tyranny of his father, castrated him and took over his rule. But Kronos quickly became as brutal as his father and worried that one of his children would depose him in the way he himself had deposed his father. To prevent this from happening again, he swallowed his children one by one as they were born. Only Zeus escaped and eventually, through a war with his father, took his place.

Hillman, in commenting on this classical story, provides an entry into the implications a senex style of consciousness has for psychotherapy. He states:

> Saturn is at once archetypal image for wise old-man, solitary sage, the lapis as rock of ages with all its positive moral and intellectual virtues, and for the Old King, that castrating castrated ogre. He is the world as builder of cities and the not-world of exile. At the same time that he is father of all he consumes all; by living on and from his fatherhood he feeds himself insatiably from the bounty of his own paternalism. Saturn is the image for both positive and negative senex.
>
> (1967, p. 16)

We unconsciously form an identification with the senex in the context of doing therapeutic work with adolescents. This is a primary, inevitable countertransferential response given the tandem nature of the archetype that has both positive and negative ramifications.

One of the most important positive traits of the senex archetype is that it provides a genuine sense of order and authority. Adolescents are constantly creating situations where they put themselves in a position of challenging the existing order, whether it be the authority of an individual in power, the rules and regulations of an institution or the laws of society. Disrupting and clashing against fixed orders is certainly part of the landscape of adolescence and is commonly interpreted to mean that adolescents have no respect for authority. In many instances, though, such recalcitrance is in reaction to what adolescents perceive as detached authority. Ungrounded authority that is based on the need for power and control is a trait of the negative senex.

Take, for example, an adolescent who is forced to attend therapy and arrives at the first session bearing the most unequivocal form of resistance there is: "I don't want to fucking be here and I'm not going to say anything!" This particular piece of communication can manifest itself in words, body language, or a dead cold stare that sends a shiver through whoever is in its path. As therapists, with sincere intentions to listen and help, we are caught off guard and knocked back, and larger archetypal forces come into play. I cannot imagine a clearer invitation to the negative senex. The teen-ager before us, having communicated his piece, now leans back passively and waits, watching to see what kind of response this unprovoked challenge to our authority will bring about. It shakes us up to consider the bind we are put in and the innumerable ways we can go wrong.

What is the adolescent actually hoping for at this point? Is there a part of him that secretly craves a harsh, authoritarian response: "You goddamn better talk or we'll sit here in silence till the end of the session." It is just this response that allows the adolescent to feel justified in further enacting the polarization by staying self-righteously stuck in an angry, closed-down position.

But isn't there at the same time a yearning for something else? Boss provides a contrasting portrait of what is at stake, at the level of psyche, when adolescents challenge and provoke authority. He states:

> One is always hearing these days that the young are hostile toward authority. But with every single one of these rebellious young people (who is not constitutionally impaired) the exact opposite happens as soon as there is someone they can come to trust, with whom they can be open. They would like nothing better than finding authority worthy of the name. The word itself comes from the Latin augere, which means "to increase or multiply." For the young, then, a genuine authority is only someone who can existentially enrich their Da-sein (human being), who knows how to help them become the human beings they could, according to their own inborn potential, be. The best among the rebellious young despair, grow outraged and destructive, only because their search for such authority is fruitless and they must experience again and again the fact that those adults who would be their authorities are hindering instead of furthering their efforts to lead meaningful lives.
>
> (1983, p. 287)

Detached, ungrounded senex authority arises from the fear of encountering a challenge to one's power and superiority. Adolescents are keenly sensitive to this fear and almost instinctively provoke it. I once ran a weekly psychotherapy group with five male adolescent members. I was anxious about the group being successful, which at the time I narrowly defined as maintaining a certain amount of control over the group process by being seen as an authority figure. Hence, I approached the group with the attitude that I was somehow above the childish antics and twisted vulnerabilities of the group members. Fighting the influx of these emotions within myself, it was as if I was looking down at the group from a raised perch, high above all the participants. In order to differentiate myself from them and thereby insure my exalted position, I sat on the only chair in the room which had a padded seat. Minutes into the session, the following dialogue occurred:

GROUP MEMBER NO. 1:   How come you get that chair? What makes you so special?

THERAPIST: (*hesitantly*) I am the leader.

GROUP MEMBER NO. 1:   What qualifies you to be the leader? You mean if I get in that chair, I could lead the group? What do you have that we don't have?

THERAPIST: Let's get going. We have a lot of work to do.

This next interchange followed five minutes later:

GROUP MEMBER NO. 2:   (*intently looking down at my feet*) Hey, where did you get those shoes? (*Everyone in the room laughs.*)

THERAPIST: What are you talking about?

GROUP MEMBER NO. 2:   Those are the funniest looking shoes I have ever seen.

THERAPIST: I don't know what my shoes have to do with what we are supposed to be here for. Can we please get back to having our group.

GROUP MEMBER NO. 2:   Yeah, sure. But I wouldn't be caught dead in those shoes. (*The entire group joins in, insulting my shoes and laughing uncontrollably.*)

Being attacked in this way by the group members forced me to choose: either let go of my quasi-dignified superior attitude and respond in a more human manner or walk out of the room and abandon the group. These were no random attacks—the dynamic meaning was an imploration for me to be present in a less haughty and distant manner. Making fun of my shoes and questioning my right to the special cushioned chair challenged the barrier I had set up between myself and the group members. Letting go of my superior attitude did not mean giving up my authority as group leader;

instead, it was about allowing a sense of confidence and leadership to exist alongside a consciousness of my own vulnerability, that is my feelings of inferiority, anxiety, and fear. Such a move decreased the group's need to attack me as leader, and a more genuine connection developed between us.

Adolescents crave authority that is related and grounded. I am reminded of one teacher in an alternative high school who spent most of the day in close contact with a group of eight students who were labeled by the school system as having "severe behavior problems." What was most striking in entering this classroom was the vast distance between the teacher's large iron desk and the smaller wooden tables where the students sat. A similar feeling of distance was expressed in the paternalistic tone of voice this teacher used when addressing the students and the rigid authoritarian position he manifested whenever conflict arose in the class. One day, one of the students put a tab of LSD into the teacher's can of coke, and under the influence of a mild dose of this hallucinogenic drug, he arose from his desk, and settled himself directly in the middle of the students. He then proceeded to spend the next two hours, before realizing what had happened, talking and working with them on their lessons in a loose, casual manner that was completely uncharacteristic for him. Amidst the chaos that followed the discovery of this dangerous prank and the eventual punishment, the one thing the students could not stop commenting on was that move by the teacher into their space and the authenticity of his connection to them.

Two other senex qualities are coldness and distance. Classically, Saturn was believed to be the furthermost planet from the sun and thus the most distant and cold. How can these qualities, seemingly so antithetical for therapy, positively influence our work with adolescents?

As we have noted, more often than not, adolescents are forced to enter treatment and come with the expectation that they will be misunderstood and harshly judged by the therapist. In this respect, a sense of distance between therapist and client plays an important role. Hillman describes it in the following manner:

> But above all we do not want to rouse fear, and there is always tremendous fear—flight-or-fight—when the soul is concerned. The danger of its loss, of damage to it, of its being misled, falsely advised, judged, damned—all are present during the therapeutic encounter.
>
> (1967, p. 33)

Hillman goes on to discuss how a therapist keeping her distance, staying contained within herself, "constellates the other person as 'other,' as different, separate, with its painfulness of being himself, alone" (ibid.). Such a stance on the part of a therapist can nourish an adolescent who lives in a world of peers where conformity and allegiance to group norms is demanded, and simultaneously, in a world of teachers and parents where there are constant attempts to rush in, straighten out, and educate. There is something about the adolescent psyche, its sense of flux and disorder, that calls forth these regulating "step-in-and-take-over" responses. This accounts in large measure for the resistance adolescents have in therapy toward revealing themselves. It is self-protective! Imagine how vulnerable their experience and understanding of the world is next to the over-powering force of adult logic and clarity. It is no wonder that the number one complaint of parents in relation to their adolescent children is: "She never talks about herself with me; she never shares what is going on in her life."

Furthermore, Hillman notes:

> . . . my distance gives the other person a chance to come out, to make a bridge, to bring into play his own extroverted feeling and emotion . . . it constellates dignity and respect for the problems. Nothing gives soul more chance than quiet; it cannot be heard above noise.
>
> (ibid.)

To provide the adolescent with enough space and stillness to come out of herself and create a bridge marks the beginning of a genuine connection. That bridge is sometimes anxiously and prema-turely sought by the therapist who is convinced that the task of making a connection falls primarily upon his shoulders. The coolness in the room is too hard to bear and he cannot keep quiet. His anxiety manifests as a racing mind, eager to fill up the spaces of silence or a probing detective, firing questions aimed at quickly getting to what is wrong. Quieting this anxiety, and allowing the other a space in which to reveal herself at her own pace is one of the most demanding aspects of the work. Adolescents stir up a deep level of apprehension that can unwittingly cause us to demand a connection even if our bearing in doing so is felt by the client as intrusive and violating.

Since we are dealing with archetypal energies, we should be aware that a positive senex expression of distance and coolness can

idation of our later relationship. The adolescent does the
ing when he comes into contact with me. He wants to
ght away what kind of person he is dealing with.
usually try to orient themselves quickly, but for the
t they are not clever about it. The adolescent, however,
elops an amazing ability at this. *We observe a momen-*
n in the eye, a hardly perceptible movement of the lips, an
y gesture, a "watchful waiting" attitude, although he
a state of conflict.

(1925, p. 128) (Italics mine)

in our anxiety about an adolescent's resistance and
bear the burden of establishing a connection, we miss
gns that reveal his interest in making contact.

associated as well with providing order through the
aws and the establishment of rules. It is clear that
ense of structure, rules that set forth the boundaries
hip, it is impossible to bring a sense of containment
. Thus, we can ask the question: What kind of order
work with adolescents? Can the senex archetype, as
ciple, ground the work? Paradoxically, it is exactly
cern for rules and limits that many treatments miss
unsuspectingly slip into a negative senex position,
nd break the connection. Let us explore this in
at which a treatment relationship unfolds.

that the less effective I feel as a therapist in a
e more rigid I become about my client showing up
ment and being on time. My sense of ineffective-
oncern that therapeutic change is not occurring
ves rise to feelings of therapeutic inferiority and
gative senex. I am not advocating that we no
ents responsible for showing up for their weekly
am simply pointing out that when a treatment
own, for whatever reasons, this can readily
a battle about time. I observed one adolescent
l wait by the door of her office, wristwatch in
t was even a minute late for their appointment,
uld be devoted to her angrily confronting what
breach of contract. Here, I am pointing to the
egative senex as providing us a focal point for

reverse itself into something destr
remoteness as self-protective arma
extend only so far; we can become
and out of reach. The relationshi

Finding the right balance be
the adolescent as other and m
complex matter. The complexit
nation of defiance and depend
we meet an adolescent's defiar
the possibility of making cc
side. The blank screen approa
to mask our anger in the rati
tension in the name of spur
commences and the therap
crack first? Let us not forg
the ability to create an af
can emerge as other and
taining power and contro

Winnicott's notion o
context. With some ad
take an active role in a
tions and making con
engagement, and inte
environment. The str
around the client m
respond at her own
mistake to always t
for what goes on ir
treatment, she mig
the communicatio
the room is create

As we have no
be a cover for th
take place. Aug
of a treatment
first reveals its

I consider t
importanc
must have
put throu

the four
same th
know r
Children
most par
often dev
tary glear
involuntar
may be in

Too often,
our having to
those subtle si
The senex i
setting up of
without some
of the relations
to the treatmen
is necessary in
an ordering prin
around this conc
the mark. We ca
force the issue,
terms of the pace
I have noticed
particular case, th
for every appoint
ness, that is, my o
quickly enough, g
constellates the ne
longer hold adoles
therapy sessions. I
begins to break c
displace itself into
therapist who would
hand, and if her clie
the entire session wo
she perceived of as a
constellation of the r

reflection when we suddenly shift into a rigid stance with a particular client.

The negative senex finds expression in relation to other aspects of time. If, for example, we find our therapeutic efforts continually thwarted by a client who continues to engage in dangerous, risk-taking behavior, we may feel boxed into a corner in such a way that we begin making provocative statements about time. For example, a common response to an acting-out adolescent is the angry, "Your clock is ticking away . . . . You don't have much time! It's your choice to get it together or not." We need to be careful with such statements for we must remember that the part of the adolescent identified with the puer lives in a vertical relationship to time, where a sense of past and future may be absent. When the senex concern for the future is communicated so caustically, adolescents react by closing themselves off and thus have no ability to hear the real concern underlying what is being expressed.

This is evidenced in the common observation that adolescents engage in all forms of risk-taking behavior without any concern for their future well-being: "It is no wonder that AIDS is rapidly spreading in the adolescent population! Adolescents live for the moment." As therapists, we perceive how dangerous and out of hand things are getting because of this lack of consciousness about the future and feelings of invincibility. We express our fears and worries in a bristling, overpowering manner and find that the louder we speak, the more shut down our adolescent client becomes. To help an adolescent become conscious of the riskiness of her behavior, it is essential to approach her from a different place than where the angry senex and the risk-taking puer stand opposed to one another. This is an archetypal moment, and therapists who have spent any time at all around adolescents have found themselves stuck in this very stand-off. As with many aspects of treating adolescents, timing is crucial. In this case, there is good reason to wait for a less polarized moment to make an interpretation or share one's worry and concern, thus allowing time for this archetypal stand-off to recede. The senex's advice to the risk-taking puer falls on deaf ears. Icarus could not heed his father's warnings about flying too close to the sun.

THE NEGATIVE TURN

I have been describing positive and negative aspects of the senex which are constellated in work with adolescents. As we have seen, positive senex qualities, those that help to establish a connection and allow for containment and increased therapeutic engagement, have the potential to unsuspectingly slip over into their opposite and create a profoundly deleterious effect on the treatment. We are now in a position to ask what contributes to this slip into the rigidness of a negative senex position: rigid rules, a rigid moral stance, and a sense of authority based on a need for power and control. For Hillman, "the difference between the negative and positive senex qualities reflects the split or connection within the senex–puer archetype" (1967, p. 23).

In other words, the puer–senex archetype is the union of youth and old age, a composite where one is always influencing the other. As therapists, in order to avoid the fall into the negative senex, we must be conversant with youth and listen and respond with an openness to the puer spirit. When we are completely identified with senex authority, we end up constellating the opposite in our adolescent clients. They rebel, and their identification with the puer grows stronger. How do we allow for a position within ourselves where youth and maturity can interpenetrate?

For Hillman, the negative senex is the senex split from its own puer aspect. It has lost its own sense of youthfulness. The rule of the negative senex is fraught with destructive potentialities. He states:

> So Saturn is in association with widowhood, childlessness, orphanhood, child-exposure, and he attends childbirth so as to be able to eat the newborn, as everything new coming to life can be food to the senex. Old attitudes and habits assimilate each new content; everlastingly changeless, it eats its own possibilities of change.
>
> (ibid., pp. 17–18)

Here, Hillman is evoking the image of Saturn–Kronos eating his own children to safeguard his position as ruler/authority. I hear resonances of this particular style of consciousness in Blos' and Anna Freud's derisive responses to adolescent idealism, heroism, and awakening political and philosophical interests. In a certain sense, what is most magnificent about adolescents, their deep-felt sensibilities concerning beauty and friendship, their illuminating idealism, serves as fodder for the interpretations to the infantile past which fits into a cohesive psychoanalytical system. Is this reductive method of interpretation a kind of senex feeding frenzy for what is vulnerably and shakily coming to life in the adolescent spirit? Doesn't it foreclose the likelihood of taking heed of the tremendous possibilities for growth and refinement in the nascent strivings of the adolescent psyche?

Along these lines, Hillman describes what happens when the senex is completely cut off from the puer. He states:

> Without the enthusiasm and eros of the son, authority loses its idealism. It aspires to nothing but its own perpetuation, leading but to tyranny and cynicism, for meaning cannot be sustained by structure and order alone. Such spirit is one-sided, and one-sidedness is crippling.... Folly and immaturity are projected onto others. Without folly it has no wisdom, only knowledge—serious, depressing and hoarded in an academic vault or used as power.
>
> (ibid., p. 21)

We easily fall into the trap of asking our adolescent clients to hold the underdeveloped, immature, and foolishly vulnerable split-off parts of our own psyches. A clear example of this phenomenon is the unyielding projective identification that occurs when parents see their adolescent children as carriers of unrestrained sexual and aggressive impulses. Unfortunately, as we have seen, adolescents are more than willing recipients of these kinds of projections, knowing them to be an effective way of staying connected to the adult world.

My own experience working on an in-patient unit with severely acting-out adolescents testifies to this kind of splitting. This particular hospital followed a strict behavioral regimen and my colleagues (psychologists, social workers, nurses, and mental health workers) were extremely sensitive to the slightest breach of unit rules. The offending perpetrator was zealously confronted in front of the entire community and treated with severe disdain by the staff. In general, the staff mistrusted the hospitalized adolescents' potentiality for unrestrained sexuality and use of substances on the unit, and, in addition, their sincerity in expressing feelings and forming genuine relationships. These areas were the main subjects of staff gossip and formed the epicenter of treatment goals and expectations.

Once a month, the staff met for a social gathering outside of work. During these parties, I observed a complete reversal of attitude. That which was found to be most abhorrent in the adolescents and was seen to be the whole reason for their hospitalization and need for extended treatment surfaced in the staff members' behavior: rampant substance abuse, unrelated sexuality, communication breakdown. My point is not at all to judge this style of social engagement, but rather to notice how it reflects the profound split that was occurring within those most closely associated with treating adolescents. This split was seemingly invisible and its inconspicuousness only served to increase the polarization between the staff members and the patients they were there to serve.

One of the greatest dangers the therapeutic establishment poses to the adolescent psyche, whether it be out-patient therapy, psychiatric hospitalization, drug and alcohol treatment, or tough love courses for parents, is when this split between the puer and the senex goes unnoticed. When this happens, treatment goals are in danger of deteriorating into an unconscious attempt to break the spirit of the adolescent and force a confrontation with the everyday "realities" of the adult world. In my work on the in-patient unit, this was literally and dramatically played out the first time a patient, male or female, broke the unit's rule against aggressive behavior by punching a wall or striking another patient. When this happened, a code was called and all the available male staff members in the hospital rushed to the scene and the adolescent was physically forced to the ground, carried to a bed and strapped down in full leather restraints.

In the language of archetypal psychology, an attempt to break the willful spirit of an adolescent is characterized as the puer side of the adolescent being persuaded into the temporal world by the negative senex. When the demands of the collective are set over against the adolescent's struggles to define himself as an individual (and it is certainly possible to interpret some forms of psychiatric hospitalization in this light), the puer loses connection with his own source of meaning and becomes the negative puer. This is synonymous with Winnicott's notion of the "false solution" where an adolescent is forced to acquiesce to a situation or a standard that does not feel real to her. Hillman states:

In all this, the greatest damage is that done to meaning, distorted from idealism into cynicism. The puer aspect of meaning is in the search, as the dynamus of the child's eternal "why," the quest, or questioning, seeking, adventuring, which grips the ego from behind and compels it forward. All things are uncertain, provisional, subject to question, thereby opening the soul and leading the way toward further questing. However, if persuaded into the temporal world by the negative senex, within or without, the puer loses connection with its own aspect of meaning and becomes the negative puer. Then it goes dead and there is passivity, withdrawal, even physical death.

(1967, p. 27)

Adolescents, identified with the puer, threaten us with their run-away spirit. They are the living embodiment of the culture's projection of "things gone too far," so that it then becomes our responsibility as ethical and caring adults to rope them back in. However, we must be extremely cautious here, for there is great psychic harm done when we prematurely weigh down the puer spirit with a heavy dose of earthly adult responsibility. Winnicott states:

... but the point about adolescence is its immaturity and the fact of not being responsible. This, its most sacred element, lasts only a few years, and it is a property that must be lost to each individual as maturity is reached.

(1968, p. 147)

Hillman speaks of a "negative turn" in the context of the psychology of the puer–senex archetype. Here, I want to slightly alter his use of this phrase to indicate the process by which the futurity of the puer spirit, its possibility for renewal, is prematurely crushed by the heavy weight of the senex. The puer is forced to turn away from the call to the spirit. If we look at those places where adolescents are in trouble (schools, psychiatric hospitals, detention centers, etc.) there is evidence that, as a culture, we are in danger of fostering this negative turn. This is a subtle and difficult dynamic to observe, thus I will offer several modes of explication.

Winnicott, in his own idiom, makes reference to the difficulty society has avoiding the negative turn in relation to its youth. He states:

But youth will not sleep, and society's permanent task in relation to youth is to hold and contain, avoiding the false solution and that moral indignation which stems from jealousy of youthfulness.

Infinite potential is youth's precious and fleeting possession. This generates envy in the adult who is discovering in his own living the limitations of the actual.

(1964, p. 158) (Italics mine)

Thus, for Winnicott, the "negative turn" happens as a result of our envy of youth's infinite potential. We have seen evidence of this in our quickness to mock an adolescent's persona, point out the inconsistencies of her politics and crush her idealism. The slip from the positive to negative senex happens imperceptibly, outside of awareness. Likewise, Winnicott's notion of preventing the negative turn has a similar intangible quality. In describing the maturational process, Winnicott states, "The process cannot be hurried up, though indeed it can be broken into and destroyed by clumsy handling" (1963a, p. 145).

I am proposing that we read Winnicott's "clumsy handling" in light of the relationship of the adult to the adolescent's spirit. Moore emphasizes the difficulty and danger entailed in this relationship. He discusses Euripides' play *Hippolytus*, which depicts a young man trampled to death by his own horses which he grooms and cares for in total innocence. Hippolytus' name means horse, and a horse spirit is the essence of this youth. He states:

Hippolytus is an image for a puer pattern of consciousness in which this particular beast is let loose, an example of the pathological outcome of rampant horse-power. Just as, in the presence of an actual horse, one feels both the exciting power and threatening force that encircles and therefore inflects the animal's beauty and grace, so the horse of the psyche exhibits both promise and threat.

(1979, p.187)

Moore's description can be read metaphorically, as an account of the strain we feel in the presence of adolescents and the complexities involved in treating them. The force of the adolescent spirit is excitingly powerful and at the same time dangerously threatening. It is just this menacing aspect that makes it so difficult to stay in touch with its grace, beauty, and power.

Moore contrasts the character and function of the imaginal horse which personifies puer youthfulness with another animal which also appears in the play *Hippolytus*—the bull. Of the bull, Moore writes that it is the "consort of all that is material, pragmatic, earthly, fixed, and natural . . . intention is bullish—pragmatic, unimaginative, concerned more for survival than cultural achievement, directed toward satisfaction of instinct and physical comfort" (ibid., p. 194).

Moore goes on to say, "Socially, youthful, puer ideas and imagination are sacrificed regularly to this bullishness, just as in Crete young men and women were sent into the Minotaur's labyrinth to be consumed" (ibid.). This sacrifice of the beauty and spiritedness of the horse for the pragmatism and everyday reality of the bull is Moore's characterization of the "negative turn." This is repeated in therapy whenever we respond to the adolescent wholly in terms of a reality-based pragmatism without giving attention to the imagery and metaphorical meanings of the material that he presents. Our instinctual, gut-level response to an adolescent's far-flung ideas and idealism is to bring him back to the ground, to reality, to be bullish and pragmatic. We cannot ignore the question of what is sacrificed by such a move.

One example of this from my own practice was the work I was doing with a fifteen-year-old client, a Russian Jewish immigrant, who came to see me at his parent's behest after they discovered he had experimented with marijuana. His father, a hard working plant manager who had been living in America with his family for five years, could not accept his son's leather jacket, long hair, rock and roll t-shirts, and his burning desire to take guitar lessons. This boy, Morris, had an electric guitar, and one of the major fights between him and his father centered around his expectation that his father would help finance his guitar lessons. Morris was very earnest about wanting to improve his guitar playing.

In therapy, after we had gotten to know each other over the course of a school year, Morris revealed to me his ambition and dream to be a world famous rock and roll heavy metal guitar player. During this particular session, he was wearing a black Ozzie Osbourne t-shirt.

MORRIS: I want to be as good as Ozzie. He's the greatest heavy metal guitarist around.

THERAPIST: How are your lessons going?

MORRIS: Good. My Mom is sneaking me the money to take them. I practice everyday.

THERAPIST: And you think you are going to do this as a career?

MORRIS: Ozzie did! Why can't I?! If I keep practicing I can be as good as him.

THERAPIST: But Ozzie is one in a million. For every Ozzie there are hundreds and thousands of people who don't make it, can't rely upon their guitar playing to support themselves.

MORRIS: But my teacher says I'm really good. That I show a lot of talent. If I can keep playing, I can be as good as Ozzie.

THERAPIST: Right now you have other things to concentrate on like passing your classes this semester and finding a job for the summer. Your guitar playing will have to wait. Being as good as Ozzie is just a dream.

(Long pause)

MORRIS: (*dejected*) Thanks a lot, Richard.

Thinking back over this session, I perceived that Morris was communicating to me in his last, utterly dejected response, the following thought: "Thanks a lot, Richard, my therapist, someone whom I thought I could count on and trust, also cannot hear my dream." I had let him down. I was unable to hear his ambition to be a great guitar player like Ozzie Osbourne metaphorically, as an expression of where, in the collective, his spirit and desire were constellated. Mistakenly, in a strong negative senex stance, I interpreted this interchange to be a dialogue about the future, about career goals, and Morris' ability to support himself.

To take it one step further, I betrayed Morris by using this dialogue to unreflectively express my anxieties that he was not going to finish up his studies and pass his classes. Morris was doing poorly in school, spending too much time practicing guitar and playing with his band. My concern for Morris' failing school performance was legitimate; however, I took advantage of his vulnerability, rather sadistically, in bringing it up as a topic of conversation at this particular point in the dialogue. It completely ran counter to what Morris was talking about. If I had been able to keep my anxiety in check, reassuring myself that I would have an opportunity to address these concerns at another time, I could have engaged Morris' emulation of Ozzie Osbourne and his passion for the guitar. In that case, I might have explored who Ozzie Osbourne was for him and what it would mean for him to be as great a guitar player as Ozzie. What kind of person would he imagine himself to be under these circumstances, and what would his father think of him with his new found fame? What is it that he likes so much about playing heavy metal music? How does he feel when he is totally engaged with the music and how does that feeling contrast with the rest of his life? This line of questioning stays attuned to the direction of the dialogue and is faithful to the spirit of the material being presented.

Chapter 10

Prohibition and inhibition: clinical considerations

Whenever what is unhealthy is demonized, it becomes irresistible, with all the seduction of vice and the fiery allure of what ought not to come to light. Censorship inevitably incites the very practice it wishes to inhibit and usually makes it more dangerously compulsive, because illicit, in the bargain.

Richard Klein

INTRODUCTION

In Chapter 8, I discussed the theoretical implications of Jung and Hillman's ideas about the nature of conscience and the development of an inner sense of authority in contrast to following collective prohibitions for our study of adolescence. There, I emphasized the connection between individuation, the self-regulating nature of the psyche, and the experience of an impulse having its own inhibitory mechanism. In this chapter, I will describe a model of adolescent psychotherapy based upon these ideas, and illustrate their relevance for the practical concerns of adolescent treatment.

In discussing the tendency to over-pathologize adolescent clients, we pondered the fact that adolescents rarely ask for help, and usually end up in treatment as a result of having bumped up against some kind of deterrent. We examined this dynamic from the therapist's point of view, suggesting that we should differentiate our therapeutic goals and treatment expectations from the collective demand to "fix" a non-functioning, acting-out adolescent. I now want to approach the initial therapeutic encounter from the one who sits in the other chair, examining how the potentiality for transformation appears from her perspective.

When an adolescent oversteps a boundary, he may not find an

adult who is setting clear and consistent limits, but rather one who is angry, expressing his moral outrage, uttering, "I will not tolerate that behavior anymore. I forbid it." The adolescent is sent to meet with a therapist and immediately identifies the therapist with the negative prohibitory force, whether it be a judge, police, school administrator, or parent, who initiated the treatment in the first place. Thus, the stage is set for the antagonism which permeates the beginning stages of treatment. This is yet another manifestation of the "resistance" that arises in the work with adolescents; the therapist must work at differentiating himself from the adolescent's projection of collective morality.

One method of differentiating our concern as therapists from the concerns of those adults who are insisting that the treatment take place is to directly express our interest and curiosity in finding out what ushered in the current situation from the adolescent's point of view. To seriously apply to adolescence Jung's idea that conscience is anterior to the moral code of the time and Hillman's notion of a sui generis inhibitor which is part of the drive itself assumes that adolescents have a far greater capacity than we typically imagine to explore their own internal responses to the behaviors in which they are engaging. Thus, we must maintain an open and receptive attitude toward the web of meanings that comprise their presenting narrative.

One of the guiding principles of this approach to adolescent psychotherapy is to enable adolescents to feel into the problems they are running up against from the inside, from the perspective of inhibition as it relates to the self-regulating activity of the psyche. Psychotherapy, from the perspective of inhibition, impels us to re-think our traditional notions of what constitutes therapeutic transformation. The concrete applications of this approach can be clearly demonstrated through an exploration of the treatment of adolescent substance abusers.

PROHIBITION/INHIBITION IN THE TREATMENT OF ADOLESCENT SUBSTANCE ABUSE

Therapeutically, the theoretical distinction between prohibition and inhibition came alive for me in my work as a counselor in a high school substance abuse prevention program. From the very beginning, I had difficulty determining how I could best benefit the students who were referred to me for mandatory drug and alcohol counseling: fourteen- to seventeen-year-old male and female high school students who were caught buying, selling, or using drugs or drinking alcohol on school grounds. My predicament stemmed from the fact that the substance abuse prevention program had as its mission two separate but related goals: first and foremost, preventing the use of drugs and alcohol; and second, providing counseling for those students already involved with these substances. In trying to integrate these two goals, I found myself caught in what felt like an irresolvable conflict: how does one take a strong stance against substance abuse while at the same time trying, in a non-judgmental manner, to therapeutically engage students who are already using these substances.

The office where I saw students for counseling was small, with one window overlooking a courtyard located next to the art department in an obscure wing of the high school. The students sat opposite a wall lined with shelves packed full of pamphlets and literature on drug and alcohol abuse. A large cardboard display modeling the inside of a human body dominated the room; bold red marks indicated how each major organ system was adversely affected by smoking marijuana. Tacked onto the walls were drug prevention posters proclaiming the dangers of drug use. One extremely macabre poster depicted a black hearse with its back door open, revealing a coffin. The caption underneath chided students that if they ever experimented with cocaine this would be the "carriage" that took them to their high school graduation.

I quickly developed a strong compassion for the students who were sent to me, especially the younger ones. A first time adventure smoking marijuana could lead to their being accosted by school security guards, brought before a tribunal of teachers, school administrators and parents, and sentenced to five sessions with the in-school substance abuse counselor.

Initially, I approached the counseling from the perspective of prevention following the guidelines of the program. I responded to the particularities of each student's contact with drugs and/or alcohol by introducing psychoeducational literature that detailed the health risks associated with marijuana, cocaine, and alcohol, the three most commonly used substances. This approach, however, did not get me very far. Most of the students were not genuinely disclosing the extent of their own use and were biding their time until the mandatory sessions were completed.

In my discouragement, I began to reflect upon the fact that I was asking these students to be open about their drug and alcohol use in the context of a severely forbidding environment. Students entered my office extremely defensive, expecting to hear more of what they had already been barraged with by their teachers, parents and, most powerfully, their television sets as the anti-drug fervor of the Reagan/Bush administration swept across the country. Many seemed uncertain, embarrassed, and ashamed. The clash between the rhetoric of prevention, that is that adolescent substance use is an evil in society and should be eradicated at any cost, and my own intention to therapeutically engage students whose motivation to experiment with these substances seemed multifaceted and overdetermined was profound and forced me to rethink my position.

It was no wonder that many students worked hard during our sessions to hide and distort the true extent of their use. The atmosphere of judgment and disapproval confirmed their worst expectations, reinforcing their sense of shame. It is unarguably true that denial and minimization go hand in hand with people who abuse substances, especially adolescents; however, I cannot think of a better way to perpetuate this denial than to meet those needing help with drugs and alcohol in an atmosphere that moralistically assails them for making a choice to use. This heavy-duty, rigid moralism, where engaging in a particular behavior is equated with sinfulness, is a prevalent attitude of many professionals whose jobs bring them in close contact with adolescents.

An approach to adolescent psychotherapy from the position of prohibition is problematic because adolescents have a legitimate need to be heard in their experience. From this perspective, there is a taboo against empathically exploring with an adolescent drug user the positive, life-affirming sides of her use. Using consciousness-altering substances, especially in adolescence, is a double-sided coin, but by staking out an a priori position that denies a fundamental side of the experience, our credibility as therapists is lost. Our ability to engage dialectically, which is at the heart of adolescent psychotherapy, is diminished. Adolescents are eager for someone to honestly engage with them in a real conversation where they are not being lectured but rather are being responded to seriously, in a straightforward manner. In thinking that we have to robotically repeat the hazards of drug and alcohol use in the name of prevention (like the incessant television commercials), we handicap ourselves in our ability to fruitfully engage the matter; it's like going into the ring with one hand tied behind our back. Almost surely we will be beaten. Our rhetoric is weak. Adolescents will ferret out the contradictions in our argument and throw them in our face. And we must remember that for these adolescents who are using drugs and/or alcohol, the messages of prevention have failed. It is unrealistic to think more of the same is going to help them. Once again, our job as therapists is to provide an alternative dialogue around these matters that an adolescent is not going to get anywhere else.

The most common question asked by adolescents to therapists doing substance abuse counseling is: "Have you ever tried x, y or z yourself?" That question has a variety of implications on many levels, (and I do not believe we need to literally answer it), but certainly one of its significations reflects the adolescent's yearning to know whether or not they can be heard and understood in the context of what they have experienced. Do we, who they identify as adult and other, "really" understand what it is like. Somewhere in our response to that question, even if it is asked with the concealed intention of finding a way to rationalize their own abusive relation to a substance, we must communicate our willingness to listen and engage the full spectrum of experience.

Without a receptivity on our part toward acknowledging the pleasurable sides of being "stoned" or "wasted," an adolescent has a far greater difficulty making a bridge toward a meaningful relationship. This is why the anti-drug campaign in its one-sidedness is so sinister and ineffective. Teen-agers who have experimented with these substances know from their own experience that the claims about drugs are grossly one-sided. There is an insane assumption that we can somehow trick them into believing that there is some correspondence between our anti-drug and alcohol rhetoric and the actual everyday experiences they are having with these substances. This constitutes a betrayal of trust and severely complicates the intention of realistically conveying the actual risks associated with these substances.

My approach to the counseling shifted as I began to disengage from the clamor of my own prohibitive voice, taking a stronger interest in the genesis of the students' own use. For example, I asked those who had become habitual marijuana smokers to think back and recollect the first time they ever got high. These descriptions were ripe with initiatory symbolism. Although each story was unique, a typical scenario went something like this:

*I was with a group of my closest friends. Someone loaded a bowl
and passed it around. I was a little scared of how it might affect
me. I took two or three puffs, and before I knew it, I got the feeling
of light-headedness. It was like nothing I ever felt before. I was so
glad to be with my friends. I laughed harder than I've ever laughed
in my life. Everything was so funny and took on a new meaning.
Afterwards, we munched.*

The first few experiences with marijuana can be priceless. A
person may experience a state of relaxation and merriment unlike
anything he has ever known. Worries and tensions seem to vanish. I
found it essential never to underestimate the pleasure that smoking
marijuana brings. It was useless to try and ignore a student's subjective experience by beating him over the head with medical evidence
that smoking marijuana is dangerous. It was essential not to lose
connection to the tale that was being spun.

By likening these initial experiences to an initiatory event, I
found myself empathically attuned to the deeper meanings in the
students' narratives. The story begins with an invitation to participate in a group event that is illegal and therefore has an
unmistakable element of danger. In those opening moments after
the decision to participate is made, there is no turning back. One
feels fearful, apprehensive, and excited. A communal ritual is
enacted as a joint is passed around the group. The inhalation of
smoke produces a significant shift in consciousness. One feels as if
one is a different person.

I would ask students to describe this exact moment. Who do they
imagine that they have become and what parts of themselves have
they left behind? Through participation in this communal act, one
has crossed a threshold and entered a different world. New bonds
form between friends. I would inquire into the connection to the
group from the perspective of being an insider, having participated
in the ritual, as opposed to the feeling of being an outsider. What
experiences in the past led one to feeling like an outsider? One's
relationship with parents and family is altered as a result of having
crossed this line. How has it changed? Is one in a different place in
terms of wanting more independence from family? What has
happened to one's feelings of dependency?

Further details emerged about the ritual of "scoring some pot,"
going to a special place to smoke it and the sensuousness of
cleaning and preparing it. To hear the hunger for ritual in these

stories, speaking to the event as search for initiation, provides the adolescent a context in which to integrate its meanings at a more profound level. It bestows value and credence upon the event.

I found it therapeutically effective to engage these students who were habitual pot smokers to reflect upon their current habit of smoking marijuana, in contrast to the stories they were telling about their initiatory experiences. Here, their own sense of inhibition came into play. I heard things like: "It's not so fun anymore;" "We don't laugh the way we used to;" "I can't get my homework done;" "If I smoke after school, I'm spent for the rest of the day;" "I don't communicate as well with my boyfriend;" "It makes me want to withdraw from everyone." The juxtaposition of these statements to the memories of what it was like in the beginning impelled them to re-think the status of their current use. It led them into the ambivalence that was at the heart of what had now become habitual. Stumbling upon these painful insights into their current behavior opened the way for them to make a change.

Each of the above admissions, in adolescent vernacular, speaks to the hazards of habitual marijuana smoking. However, there is a crucial difference between an adolescent arriving at these insights herself versus an outside source pointing them out to her. This moment of self-discovery produces a shift in which an adolescent is apt to initiate a discussion with a therapist about the troubling sides of her use. What is crucial is that the desire for change arises within herself, out of a developing awareness of the pain that her habitual drug use is causing her.

With alcohol, the body clearly communicates its inhibitory response to excess drinking. Adolescents typically throw up the first time they experiment with alcohol, vowing the next morning, in the midst of an awful hangover, never to drink again. This has valuable therapeutic applications when working with adolescents who are consistently drinking to excess every weekend. The first thing to explore is the system they have come up with for outwitting their own bodily inhibitory responses. With some experience, maybe six months or a year of steady drinking, they know how to drink right up to the point of vomiting. They know when to drink—those nights when they have no responsibilities the next day and can sleep through a bad hangover. They know where to drink—at a friend's house close by so that they don't have to drive home drunk. They stay out late enough to avoid encountering their parents after a night of heavy drinking.

One can also ask adolescent alcohol abusers questions about their drinking from the perspective of the body. In doing so, the darker side of their drinking experiences begins to emerge. For example, they report just how lousy it is to feel so sick from too much drinking, how embarrassing it is to wake up in one's own vomit, and how agonizing it is not to make it home on time and face being grounded by parents. In addition, they may describe how horrible it feels to face one's friends after a night of being hopelessly drunk and not being sure what was said or done to them: "Mr. Hyde was loose last night and now I am in deep shit."

After tuning into the body's inhibitions, many adolescents make the move of recognizing, in a more global way, the pain and hardship their present drinking behavior is causing them. Their initial denial, their attitude of "I've got it all under control, drinking doesn't hurt me, I'm just having fun," fades. For example, those involved in athletics talk about the toll drinking is taking on their bodies in the context of diminished athletic abilities. One young man I worked with couldn't run as fast as he used to; and for another, Saturday morning practice after a night of drinking was nearly impossible. As these insights emerge, I find it especially important to stay present to what is being said in a non-judgmental way, letting the adolescent discover for himself what effects the alcohol is having on his life. It is at this point, only after having discovered the truth that alcohol is harmful from his own experience, that he can begin to ask for some assistance in changing his relationship to drinking. The potentiality for success in making such changes increases dramatically when it draws upon these inward sources.

With adolescents who are actively caught up in an abusive relationship to drugs or alcohol, a split in consciousness occurs between the pleasure of the experience and the pain, hardship, and suffering which they face as a result of their use. When leading adolescent substance abuse groups, I am always astonished by the disparity between an adolescent's sensitive and moving description of the deleterious effects of alcoholism on her family and her anticipation of an upcoming party where she is gleefully planning to drink until she passes out. These opposing perspectives are kept far apart from each other. Adolescents are not accustomed to holding both perspectives in mind at the same time.

I have developed an exercise for adolescent substance abuse groups aimed at addressing this split. I begin by discussing with the group the enjoyable and painful sides of drug and alcohol use. I list each attribute on the board so that by the end of the discussion we have a fairly comprehensive list of the group member's positive and negative associations. I then ask each participant to draw one picture that in some way captures both sides of the experience. When they are finished, I go around the room, asking if there is a story that goes along with the picture they have drawn. Describing her drawing (see Figure 10.1) one young woman talked jubilantly about how much she liked going to the liquor store, copping some beer, and getting drunk. Her voice and mannerism changed, although, when she explained the second side of the picture which she described as the aftermath of a night of partying. This second image led her to report a memory of finding her father in a pool of blood, having cracked open his head on a curb from passing out after a bout of drinking. She spoke of her fear that he might be dead and began crying as she described calling the ambulance and watching him being taken away. Likewise, a young man shows in his drawing (see Figure 10.2) how he feels like a king, strong and powerful, having the whole world in his hands and yet, alongside of that, has crazy, frightening thoughts that come into his mind whenever he drinks too much. He described a time when he got very drunk and participated in a robbery that to this day he regrets, one in which he would not have been involved had he been sober. By working with the drawings, we were better able as a group to hold both sides of the experience together. The image served the function of concretizing the juxtaposition of the two perspectives, and dwelling with the tension between them caused the release of memory and affect.

CONCLUSION

A prohibitory approach to the dynamics of teen-age substance abuse rests upon a set of assumptions that are in sharp contrast to an approach that emphasizes inhibition.

The prohibitive approach takes a stand against the use of alcohol and drugs for adolescents because of their addictive nature (and the negative health risks involved) as well as the inherent immorality that goes along with the act of using such substances. The voice of prohibition sounds something like this: "We, as adults, knowing better, are telling you that what you are doing is immoral and wrong. It is not only dangerous to your health and well-being, but

Figure 10.1 Aftermath of a night of partying

there is a good chance you will become addicted. Therefore you should, at all costs, practice abstinence."

In contrast, from the perspective of inhibition, the therapeutic task is to awaken consciousness of the lived bodily and emotional responses to one's usage. This approach attempts to meet an adolescent where he is in terms of his use by asking: "Is your current experience of using drugs and alcohol truly meeting your expectations in terms of what you initially hoped for when you began?" Therapy originates in the gap between what an adolescent is yearning for in his desire to use drugs and alcohol and what he is actually getting.

The yearnings of the adolescent substance abuser evoke the image of the puer. Drug and alcohol use produces a state of mind that frees one from the pull of earthly responsibility. Getting high/wasted/stoned/shit-faced etc. offers a moment of experiential transcendence—the high flying puer, soaring through the spirit

Figure 10.2 The whole world in his hands

world. The puer knows no other way of coming down to the earth except by sudden descent and crash. Adolescent substance abusers mimic this pattern in their attempt to stay up as long as possible. One way of assessing the severity of use is to probe the level of desperation that is entailed in wanting the altered state to continue. How self-destructive does an adolescent become in needing to maintain the high? In the most severe cases, one does not come down willingly—it takes the body's intolerance of the mass infusion of whatever is being drunk or smoked or sniffed to force a crash. Then the whole cycle repeats itself in the renewed desperation for transcendence and escape. What if substance abuse counseling was envisaged as a method for helping an adolescent suffer the descent to earth, assisting the client in finding a way down? Such a method requires the therapist to investigate what the adolescent finds so intolerable about the everyday experience of living and help him recognize those moments when the desire to take flight suddenly erupts.

Looking at substance abuse from the psychology of the puer is in conjunction with an inhibitory approach. For example, without having to explicitly communicate anything about the psychology of the puer aeternus, the following set of questions can structure the treatment of a habitual marijuana smoker: "What is it that you are seeking when you light up a joint?" "What part of you is desperate to get high?" "Do you ever come close to this experience in any other activity in your life besides partying?" "Is there a part of you that has no desire to get high when you make the decision to party with your friends?" "If so, what does the voice of this inhibiting one sound like?" "What prevents it from being heard?" "What feelings are you able to escape when you make the decision to light up?" "Can you begin to notice what is going on in your life during those times when the desire to smoke is the strongest." "What would happen if you did not immediately fulfill it?"

This approach assumes that within the adolescent substance abuser there is a nascent sense of restraint and inhibition. Psychologically, one gets at this place by working through the desire for these substances in the imagination. This is what it means to imaginatively engage the puer. A prohibitive approach freezes the imagination. There is an underlying fear of it due to a basic mistrust of the adolescent's ability to hold the metaphorical apart from the literal. Imaginative engagement is dangerous from the point of view of prohibition because it has the potential to open the floodgates of unrestrained instincts and impulses. This is exemplified in the rhetoric about marijuana being a gateway drug. Experimenting with marijuana even one time will lead, so the argument goes, to using increasingly powerful drugs until one ends up as junkie on a street corner. A similar fear exists in the arguments that if we properly educate adolescents about human sexuality this knowledge will set loose upon the world their unrestrained sexual appetite.

Chapter 11

Prohibition and inhibition: cultural dimensions

Generally it was true that in my own life so far I myself had not done anything just because my mom or stepfather or teachers I have had or any of the adults who had me in their power told me it was for my own good. No fucking way. And whenever somebody told me that, there was like this alarm that went off under the hood and all I could hear was whoop-whoop-whoop, somebody's trying to steal something valuable, I'd think so I'd usually do the opposite. Most of the time that didn't turn out so hot either but I'd've never done it in the first place if somebody hadn't've been out to get me for my own good to do the first opposite thing.

Russell Banks

Having looked at the prohibition/inhibition dynamic from the perspective of adolescent substance abuse, I now want to explore its broader psychological and philosophical implications at the level of culture in terms of our contemporary responses to youth. As a culture, we transmit forceful messages, spoken and unspoken, to adolescents regarding their place in society and our willingness to tolerate their developing struggle to form an identity. A covert equivocalness underlies the prohibitory declamations aimed at preventing adolescents from engaging in "dangerous," "immoral" and "illicit behaviors." This ambiguity and ambivalence contained in our prohibitory warnings speaks to the fact that adolescents, in their very nature, dramatically expose those places where we as a culture are in conflict. In this chapter, I will inquire into the impact of our unspoken cultural conflicts on the developing adolescent. More specifically, I will examine how the existing cultural conditions narrow the adolescent's range of possibilities for coming to terms with his own inhibitory responses.

Winnicott (1966), in his essay "The Absence of a Sense of

Guilt," contends that one of the most devastating results of inconsistent parenting is that the child does not form a connection between her impulses and her self and therefore acts without a sense of responsibility. In such cases, therapy is aimed at helping the child realign herself with the inward arising of her impulses, including the destructive ones, so that she can begin to experience them as integral to who she is as a person. In the process, she also discovers a sense of guilt, which Winnicott terms inhibition, and the wish to mend. This new-found awareness heals the split between impulse and responsible action. Here, Winnicott is invoking the tension between impulse and action which I characterized in Chapter 8 as one of the central dynamics of adolescence. How this dynamic gets played out in adolescence has significant implications for adult life.

The search to discover a sense of self that feels real in the world is at the center of identity formation. Adolescents can be " . . . seen searching for a form of identification which does not let them down in their struggle, the struggle for identity, the struggle to feel real, the struggle not to fit into an adult-assigned role, but to go through whatever has to be gone through" (Winnicott 1963a, p. 152). Thus, for Winnicott, adolescents, in an almost instinctual way, resist the premature weighing down of their spirit which we characterized earlier as the negative turn. He names this act of resistance "a refusal of the false solution," in other words, their refusal to take actions and participate in events that are disconnected from a deeper sense of self. And it is here, in this highly personal and individual struggle, that we again encounter the distinction between prohibition and inhibition.

What we disparagingly call "adolescent acting-out" and "teen-age rebellion" can now be re-envisaged as a purposive clash with the prohibitions laid down by parents and the larger culture. The teleological meaning of adolescent rebellion is the search for an individual solution to the complex collective questions which fully engage the psyche.

Adolescents are vitally engaged in these questions, which touch upon matters of morality, integrity, and justice, and are wholly unwilling to accept prepackaged solutions. Personally challenging a prohibition awakens consciousness of inhibition. One has the abiding satisfaction of having worked through the matter for oneself.

Which cultural conditions foster the striving of the adolescent to confront a prohibition in an attempt to extricate its personal meaning? As I have shown, it is the very encounter with desire and its limitations that leads to a sense of personal conscience and autonomy. Thus, what must be investigated is the relationship between the limitations and restraints inherent in an adolescent's impulse for action and the prohibitive commands of the culture. Is there enough harmony between them so that an adolescent is not completely overwhelmed by the restrictive quality of collective morality and can begin to discern his own moral voice? This idea of bringing into harmony the limits we set on adolescents and their own internal sense of restraint is at the heart of enabling them to avoid the false solution.

We falsify an adolescent's inward consciousness of limitation/guilt/inhibition by unequivocally proscribing from the outset, without regard to context, what is right and wrong. It is striking how ingrained this phenomenon is, how it penetrates so many different levels of our educational, legal, religious, and family institutions. There is a great anxiety that without strongly voiced prohibitions, children, when they reach adolescence, will run amuck. Freud wins out here as the development of conscience is viewed merely as the internalization of external forbiddings. There is nothing else inside to rely upon.

I found numerous examples of this anxiety in my clinical work with families when an adolescent living at home temporarily stopped functioning in a predictable way. To illustrate, I worked with a sixteen-year-old girl, a junior in high school, who was flunking all of her classes, staying out all weekend with friends, and was on the verge of being kicked out of school for poor attendance. Her parents were in such a panic about her behavior that every evening she spent at home they assailed her for hours on end about the mess she was making of her life. No doubt, on her own, this young woman was creating chaos for herself. Compounding that with the chaos her parents put her through on a nightly basis, it was nearly impossible for her to sense her own reactions. Thus, she was unable to ascertain what she truly wanted in relation to school, family, and friends at this critical juncture. In addition, her parent's nightly attacks encouraged her to project the cause of all her problems onto them; they provided an immensely appealing hook. Being caught up in the family cycle of rage, disappointment, and regret, this young woman had little opportunity to discover her own emotional and cognitive responses to the events of her life.

The difficulty of harmonizing the prohibitive commands of the culture to an individual's inner sense of restraint can be clearly seen in the phenomenon of juvenile delinquency. As was noted in the discussion of shadow in adolescence, delinquent behavior is typically either completely ignored or responded to harshly, without compassion. Another example of this discordance can be found in the overblown responses we sometimes make to common, non-violent adolescent behaviors such as defacing property with graffiti or shoplifting. It is as if there is no room anymore in the culture for teen-agers to come into contact with the destructive and rebellious impulses within themselves without seriously getting hurt or paying a stiff penalty. For example, in my town, I witnessed a thirteen-year-old girl being handcuffed and dragged to jail amidst three police cruisers for stealing a pack of cigarettes from the local grocery store. This is an example of the "scared straight" mentality which believes that if we can scare an adolescent enough the first time they break the law, we will prevent them from becoming career criminals. It assumes one has to be bullied into making moral choices. Prohibition that imagines there is no inhibition always goes to extremes.

Another example of this was in my work with a fourteen-year-old girl whom I will call Kelly. Kelly was brought in by her mother because she was doing poorly in school, fighting with other girls and being flirtatious around boys. This girl's mother was fourteen when she had Kelly and her greatest fear was that the tragedy of teen-age pregnancy was going to repeat itself with her daughter.

Kelly was struggling with questions about restraint and inhibition. In the course of therapy, we talked about her developing sexuality and her sense that if she and her boyfriend went as far as having intercourse together things between them would dramatically change. In her heart, she did not believe what all the boys said about sex: "That it's no big deal, let's just do it" or the instructions she received from some of her girlfriends, "You do it so a guy will stay with you." She also recognized that in the heat of the moment "What you decided beforehand, that you are not ready to have sex with this boy, seems to vanish and you end up double crossing yourself."

As all of this was being discussed in therapy, Kelly's mother decided in a panic, after discovering Kelly's journal in which she articulated her sexual thoughts and fantasies, to put her daughter on birth control pills. Even though birth control grants sexual freedom, somehow this move by Mom seemed in the spirit of a prohibitory response to teen-age sexuality; there was no trust that her daughter might work out for herself her own sense of what was right and wrong in regard to her sexuality, and an external control was needed to assure she did not end up pregnant. The effect of this, I believe, was to drive Kelly faster into becoming sexually active. It speeded everything up. One moment she was thinking about, imagining, exploring journalistically the ramifications of her sexuality and the next, at Mom's urgings, she was taking a pill everyday that psychologically has the effect of making literal something she was trying to work through imaginally.

For Kelly, the feeling of inhibition in response to her sexuality brought forth an increased capacity for reflection. This was evidenced by her daily practice of writing in her journal (ironically, the very journal, whose discovery by mother, resulted in Kelly being put on the pill), and illustrates the connection between the experiencing of an inhibition in the impulse and the activation of the imagination. This is an extremely valuable connection to be aware of when practicing psychotherapy with adolescents because it provides a crucial passage into their internal world. I will present one final clinical example which makes this connection clear.

I worked with a seventeen-year-old male whom I will call Tommy, who looked five or six years older than his age. He was referred to me by his school principal for his angry outbursts and violent behavior toward other kids and teachers. His principal stated that if he did not get counseling he would be permanently thrown out of school. We worked for many months, talking about Tommy's anger and the types of situations that caused him to lose control. In these initial discussions, Tommy became completely identified with his anger as soon as we got close to it and could only focus on letting it out, letting someone else have it.

As time went on, Tommy was able to feel a sense of inhibition in relation to his anger. Now, when he became rageful at school, he could feel a part of himself holding back, not automatically swearing, screaming and swinging fists. As a result, he was no longer getting into trouble everyday for fighting. As we talked more about his growing awareness of an inhibitory force, dialoguing with the part of him that was not completely identified with the anger, an important memory erupted. He described an incident which had happened two years ago when he was living in New York. He was hanging out with his best friend who went into a phone booth to make a call. A gang member, mistaking his best friend for someone else, came out of nowhere and shot and killed him before Tommy's eyes. Tommy had not spoken about this incident with anyone other than his mother in the two years since it had happened. His grief and rage over his best friend's death found a place in our conversations and allowed Tommy to disidentify with the rageful one inside who was always looking for a fight. What struck me so powerfully about this experience was the way in which his feeling into the inhibition in his impulse to anger led to the release of this traumatic memory. The inhibition gave us access to a deeper place of feeling that underlay much of his violent behavior.

CULTURAL REJUVENATION

The ceremonies marking adolescent initiation were highly valued in traditional societies as significant religious rites. The ritual passage into adulthood was celebrated for the benefit of the entire culture; the ceremony was understood as a form of collective regeneration (Eliade 1958). In a similar vein, Winnicott speaks of the potential adolescents have to rejuvenate contemporary society. He states:

> Immaturity is a precious part of the adolescent scene. In this is contained the most exciting features of creative thought, new and fresh feelings, ideas for new living. Society needs to be shaken by the aspirations of those who are not responsible.
>
> (1968, p. 146)

Winnicott's acclamatory praise of the new and fresh ideas that adolescents can bring to the culture stems from the fact that they are freed from having to think through a long-term, overarching analysis of the world's troubles. In other words, adolescents possess the vision to see the injustices and inequities in society without the burden of having to come up with a solution. While I have shown the value of this for the political development of the adolescent, Winnicott speaks of its benefit for the adult world; it is a wake-up call, shaking us out of our habitual, taken for granted views. In the language of archetypal psychology, the puer provides fresh insights and perspectives on matters that the senex has long ago assumed to be over and done with. The puer spirit takes wing in senex certitudes.

In our culture, it seems that instead of celebrating the potential life-energy and fresh vision that adolescents can bring, the opposite is true. Youth are blamed for the degeneration of society. They are held responsible for causing the mayhem and destructiveness that characterizes much of modern life. According to this fantasy, all would be well if only the young would straighten up and behave. Instead of allowing their fiery energy to renew society, adolescents and young adults have become the scapegoat. Instead of being welcomed into communities, we create ever-new barricades to keep them shut out.

Perhaps part of our contemporary disdain for adolescents can be attributed to their uncanny ability to reveal those aspects of adult life which remain hidden in shadow. Ventura comments on the adolescent's inherent faculty for dredging up from the depths what we as adults hoped to have buried:

> Our secrets, our compromises, our needs, our lacks, our failures and our fears that we're going to fail again—all this stirs and starts to growl somewhere deep inside when the young look hard into our grown-up eyes. It's as though in some dark way, they are privy to our secrets, even to what we don't know or want to know about ourselves, and when they so much as glance toward those parts of us, oh, our old panics resurrect, those demons we thought we'd dealt with, grown out of, transcended, escaped—it only takes this goddam kid, and the beasts awake. As a parent, you measure your fears by the extent of your distance from that kid.
>
> (1993, p. 28)

Hence, our outrage at the adolescent may be a displacement of our rage at having our shadow exposed. Unlike children, adolescents are worldly enough to perceive with exacting precision the inconsistencies between what we say and think and how we act. What Ventura describes at an individual level between parents and their adolescent children also plays itself out culturally. Adolescents mirror the culture's shadow; they embody and live out those places where we as a culture are most unconscious. For example, argue with an adolescent about his use of marijuana and he will gleefully point out the contradiction between the massive amounts of energy and resources put into the war against illegal drugs that are destroying society and the ever-increasing preponderance of legal drug use: sleeping pills, tranquilizers, alcohol, anti-depressants, diet pills, etc. Many of the prescription drugs we consider to be safe and non-recreational, especially psychiatric medications, are hot commodities on the adolescent black market. This forces us to reconsider our smug and somewhat arbitrary distinction between those substances that the psychiatric and pharmaceutical industry consider medicinal and those deemed illicit, for recreational use only.

An adolescent who has been smoking marijuana regularly to combat depression is well aware that the legal drug, Prozac, which she is now being prescribed, serves the same function. She says, "I used to smoke pot, now the psychiatrist has me on Prozac. What's the difference? A drug's a drug." Another example of adolescent behavior exposing our cultural shadow centers on the outrageous amount of Ritalin that is being prescribed in America for children and adolescents. What has been happening over the past few years is that young people are discovering that by crushing these pills and sniffing the powder, they can partake of its powerful amphetamine effect. I knew of a fourteen-year-old who was sniffing crushed-up Ritalin on a regular basis. As a result, his teachers complained about his inattentiveness at school so his mother took him to see his pediatrician who then diagnosed attention-deficit/hyperactivity disorder and prescribed Ritalin.

As illegal drugs become more difficult to obtain, adolescents, desperate to alter their consciousness, turn to common household items for a quick high: they sniff White-Out, glue, and paint thinner and raid their parents' medicine cabinets for prescription tranquilizers or pain killers. Why do we refuse to examine how the current state of the culture is implicated in these troubling patterns of behavior? Our focus on prevention and prohibition inevitably fails to look at what children and adolescents may be hungering for in their compulsion to get high. As we have seen, initiation in traditional societies exposed adolescents to the world of ritual, mystery, spirit, and ambiguity—all the elements which have no place in a highly technicized, hyper-rational culture such as our own. Isn't it time we came to recognize the connection between the crisis of meaning in our culture and the desperation with which adolescents attempt to make contact with that other world? Can this awareness and understanding be brought to bear upon our current debates about the growing youth crisis in this country?

CONFLICTING DEMANDS

The following clinical vignette explores the factors that led an adolescent into deciding to use drugs and alcohol and provides an example of the conflicting demands which lie concealed in our common, everyday adolescent prohibitions. The rhetoric states: Avoid peer pressure; Decide for yourself. But is this possible? What is ultimately influencing those decisions that on the surface look like individual choices? Is the pressure only coming from one's peers?

Will was a seventeen-year-old who had dropped out of high school, and, in a last ditch effort to get a diploma, enrolled himself in his town's alternative high school program, which offered a no-nonsense approach to education with shortened school hours and no homework. After being in therapy for a couple of months, it became evident that Will had a serious substance abuse problem; he smoked marijuana almost daily, and had done so for the past two years. It was very difficult for him to get out of bed in the morning and make it to school on time, and when he was there, he had trouble staying focused. As a result of his poor attendance, his chance of graduating, which was something he desperately wanted, was in jeopardy. Coming to realize the costs of his marijuana habit through our work together, Will resolved to see how his life might be different without marijuana and decided to give it up for one month.

Three weeks into it, I was attending a school meeting with his teachers, and when his name came up, they began assailing me with stories about how, in the last few weeks, Will had become intolerable. In the past, before his self-initiated treatment with me began, they never had a problem with him; outside of his poor attendance, he was a model student. Now, he was irritable, moody, angry, mouthing off, being cruel to other students, and according to the teachers, almost impossible to be around for more than five minutes.

"What are you doing with that kid!" the director of the alternative school turned to me and said. "I don't know what you two talk about during your therapy sessions, but let me tell you it's not working. Can't you do anything about this?" I sat there dumbfounded, unable to respond. And the quieter I was, the more delight his teachers took in describing just how horrible Will had become and in a way, pointing blame at me, his therapist.

I thought to myself how, in confidence, Will and I were working together with the expressed goal of helping him to abstain from using marijuana so that he could find a way other than anesthetizing himself to deal with those emotions that he found so chaotic and troubling. Simultaneously, here were his teachers, the adults in his life with whom he spent the majority of his waking hours, instructing me, in essence, to return him to who he used to be. I received their message loud and clear: "We support whatever it takes for him not to manifest those angry, irritable, affect-laden impulses and outbursts so that he can become the go-along, get-along kind of kid we were once comfortable having in our school." And if they were communicating this to me, I wondered about the unspoken pressures they were putting on Will to subjugate those parts of his personality they found so intolerable. Now it was clear that Will was going through withdrawal and some of his behavior was symptomatic of reducing his psychological dependency on marijuana. However, Will himself had described to me that before he started smoking marijuana it was these same behaviors which were responsible for the conflicts that caused him to drop out of the town's regular high school and his subsequent involvement with the police.

Consequently, I began to see that Will's decision to smoke marijuana in the first place was not a wholly personal one. Larger collective forces, in this case, the educational system, were bombarding him with tacit and oblique messages that communicated something to the effect of, "Your changing, developing, youthful energy is not wanted here. Do what you will—but keep it under wraps. We, as a school system, collectively cannot tolerate it and we won't." Or, in other words, "the intense psychic cacophony" which is adolescence is not welcome (1993, p. 30).

What if the current crisis surrounding the rising use of illicit substances among adolescents was seen in this light? Would it not force us to reconsider the pathologizing of their behavior solely in terms of individual will power and abdication to the pressures of the crowd? In addition, the explanation that Will was merely self-medicating fails for the same reason. It puts the onus of responsibility too squarely on his shoulders. What was behind his desperation to self-medicate? Why did he feel it so necessary to anesthetize certain aspects of self and where was he implicitly getting support for that decision in the cultural surroundings? Isn't self-medication one avenue adolescents have discovered for shifting their chaotic energy into something more tolerable, thus allowing them to maintain a connection with the adults in their lives and function more smoothly in society. I cannot count the number of times I have heard some version of the following statement from adolescent clients: "Yeah, he used to be real violent, but now he smokes pot and everything is cool. It's mellowed him out." They see it, they know it. They are as aware of the anesthetizing effects as anyone.

What a crazy-making, jumbled message we end up sending. On the one hand, there is all the hype about staying away from drugs and just saying no, and yet at the same time the subverted message about conforming to a certain way of being that does not give any place for the despair, rage, sexuality, and pandemonium of the adolescent psyche. The more emphatically this underground message is delivered: "We can't tolerate this kind of energy and if it is displayed, we cannot tolerate you," the more drugs and alcohol become the object of adolescent fascination and abuse. Which gets back to Winnicott and how difficult it is to allow adolescents to have their phase of the doldrums. What would it mean culturally to be more welcoming and engaging of these states of being? How might that influence our structuring of the institutions in which adolescents spend most of their time? And to come full circle to the beginning of this section, how do we revision our notions of adolescent psychopathology so that we follow the thread of origins not only to childhood but to our collective cultural and institutional responses to what we find most terrifying and abhorrent in the passage through adolescence?

Epilogue

In our practice as therapists, it is crucial to supplement and extend the psychodynamic and developmental models to include the impact of culture on adolescence. To gain an appreciation for how the current state of the culture both promotes and denies living out the possibilities inherent in adolescence requires that we focus a psychological eye on the books, television shows, movies, and music that adolescents find so appealing. Such an inquiry seeks to understand which components of the popular culture an adolescent draws upon for life-power and which play a life-negating role. In taking heed of the powerful cultural forces impacting adolescence, we re-contextualize what at first glance looks like individual pathology.

Both Gentry (1989) and Ventura (1993) assert that we are living in an adolescent culture. They point to the congruity between those places where the culture is breaking down and the plight of contemporary adolescents: addictions, failing schools, increasing crime and violence on the streets. Indeed, there is an eerie symmetry between what we find to be the most unsavory characteristics of contemporary adolescents and the pathologies of the culture. For example, our consumer economy reflects the worst tendencies of adolescence, its hedonism and self-indulgence. Our current compulsion to possess ever-more powerful forms of technology (more memory, more speed) to expand our realm of autonomy and control mirrors the adolescent's impoverished ego desperately trying to buoy itself up by any means available. Our failure to take into account the long-term impact of our environmental policies on the fate of the planet reflects the pathological consequences of the puer's inability to consider the future, living only for the now. Our individualistic focus on the self, at the expense of community, parallels the tendency in adolescence for narcissism and self-preoccupation. And finally governmental and corporate regulation of increasing domains of contemporary life echoes the adolescent's alienation from a self-regulating force so that constant external monitoring and surveillance is needed.

Another manifestation of the adolescent nature of our culture lies in our relation to the puer–senex archetype. We project the puer onto adolescents, insisting that they carry that energy and, in turn, blame them for it. In the process, we unfairly identify the adolescent with a slew of derogatory characteristics: they are crazy, self-centered, dumb, wild, ignorant, immoral, destructive, and dangerous. In being so quick to vilify the adolescent, we fail to see how our projections have narrowed our vision and caused us to perceive him in a distorted light. In an adolescent culture, actual adolescents are the ideal projective screen. We see a microcosm of this in families. What is unconsciously enacted by the parents, split off and unacknowledged, suddenly takes root in the perceived behavior, actions and thoughts of the adolescent child. We are familiar with the devastating effects of this form of projective identification for an adolescent growing up in such a family. However, it is important to recognize that a parallel process occurs as our culture's own unresolved conflicts dramatically impinge upon adolescent life.

As a case in point, our discomfort with moral complexity is crystallized in the discordant and one-sided messages we impart to adolescents in regard to what we deem as permissible and impermissible behavior. We severely prohibit adolescents from engaging in certain behaviors in one context yet these are contemporaneously fostered and promoted in another. For example, street drugs are considered undeniably bad, but the use of psychiatric medications to control mood, attention, and anxiety is unquestionably beneficial. Adolescents are told never to resolve conflicts through the use of physical aggression, while, at the same time, the culture mesmerizes them with violent imagery in film, television, and video games. They are cautioned to restrain their sexual impulses while being urged to freely partake as developing consumers in society's obsession and saturation with sexual imagery and erotic titillation. Our struggle as a culture to withstand the tension that these complex moral and ethical dilemmas create is revealed in the extreme and inflexible stances we take with adolescents.

The adolescent psyche is bombarded with loud and conflicting judgments of value, an assault that originates in childhood: for example, the constant warnings which begin now as early as kindergarten, about the dangers of cigarettes, drugs and alcohol. Have we ever stopped to consider the long-term psychological effects of these preventative practices? What does it do to a child/adolescent to hear these repetitive tirades, year in and year out, against the evils of the very substances that may play a central role in the life of family members and relatives and are promoted by the media and the advertising industry? Does this create a confusion about who is telling the truth which leads to curiosity and experimentation—behaviors that our preventative practices are trying to eradicate in the first place? Or does it create an attitude of self-righteous intolerance as witnessed by children who are the recipients of the current anti-smoking campaign? The message that ends up being distilled is that those who smoke cigarettes are in complicity with the devil. One may wonder if cigarette smokers are the real enemy we need to be warning our children about.

The turn toward culture to deepen our analysis of what appears to be an individual or family problem leaves room for us to consider the impact on adolescence of our culture's difficulty in accepting the reality of aging and death. How can we welcome adolescence as a time of symbolic death and rebirth when, as a culture, we worship "youthfulness" and harbor the fantasy that with modern medical technology we can live forever? Doesn't the mind-set of a death denying culture preclude the possibility of accepting the images and feelings related to death and dying which we have found to be an integral part of adolescence?

From the viewpoint of individual adolescents, we have examined the prospective meaning of their symptoms and pathologies as attempts to establish a link with a transcendent order of meaning. This was evidenced in our reading of traditional initiation rites and in our interpretation of adolescence as a time of individuation. Collectively, the symptomatology of adolescence reveals those places where society is in conflict. Given the vulnerability that comes with this transitional stage of development and the adolescent's profound need to connect with a larger circle of meaning, the culture, in meeting this archetypal need, has the potential to be transformed. Left unmet, it is in danger of being torn apart by the conflicting impulses embodied in adolescence.

Being in touch with the suffering of contemporary adolescents forces us to face head on the current cultural pathologies affecting us all. We must widen our scope if we want to comprehend what is boldly asserting itself today in the alarming statistics on adolescent suicide, the spread of AIDS in the adolescent population, teen pregnancy, drug use, violence and murder. To stay narrowly confined in a view of adolescence as a recapitulation of childhood does not allow us to perceive who the adolescent is in her own right and thereby we forgo the opportunity to learn from her. It is important to challenge the traditional habit of mind that reads adolescence reductively. This affords us the opportunity to perceive the very important, yet neglected, link between the suffering of the adolescent and the suffering of the culture, the link between the adolescent psyche and the soul of the world. With this link in mind, we can detect what is being covered over whenever the adolescent is scapegoated as the cause of our cultural ills as well as hear the disparagements about adolescents with a different ear, as revealing something about our own suffering.

Notes

INTRODUCTION

1 For the sake of inclusiveness, I alternate feminine and masculine forms throughout the book whenever the antecedent could be a person of either sex.

1 PSYCHOANALYTIC APPROACHES

1 See Jean Baker Miller, *Toward a New Psychology of Women*, Boston: Beacon Press, 1986; Jessica Benjamin, *Bonds of Love*, Pantheon Books, 1988; Nancy Chodorow, *The Reproduction of Mothering,* Berkeley: University of California Press, 1978; M. Belenky, B. Clichy, N. Goldberger, and J. Tarule, *Women's ways of Knowing*, New York: Basic Books, 1986.

2 John Allan illustrates the impact writing and storytelling can have in the therapeutic work with a physically abused adolescent in his book *Inscapes of the Child's World* (1988). Also, for writing exercises for adolescents see his *Written Paths to Healing* (1992) (Co-authored with J. Bertoia). For an overview of the use of the creative arts in therapy see Seonaid M. Robertson's *Rosegarden and Labyrinth: A Study in Art Education* (1982).

2 DEVELOPMENTAL ANALYTICAL PSYCHOLOGY

1 Robert Stein cautions against interpreting the incest archetype (the psyche's need to lose itself in merger with another) as a literal desire to regressively reunite with mother. He states:

Contemporary psychoanalysis has moved its theoretical focus from the oedipal fantasy to the pre-oedipal fantasy; damaging developmental wounds occur in the process of the child's separation from its original symbiotic union with mother. The transference, so goes the fantasy, recreates this mother–child symbiotic merger, thus offering the possibility of a healing reconstruction of the personality. An important consequence of identifying the origins of the experience of oneness and wholeness with the literal mother–child symbiosis is that unifying experiences tend to be seen as regression. Viewing the trans-ference/countertransference primarily from this perspective plunges the analyst into an identification with the all-embracing, containing mother archetype and the patient into an identification with the innocent, needy, abandoned, helpless, dependent child archetype. Not only does this perpetuate a split in the Mother–Child archetype, but also the analyst becomes inflated by this identification with the all-powerful, all-nourishing, all-containing Great Mother.

(1984, p. ii)

In an intentional move away from the parent–child archetype, he offers the image of the Sacred Marriage (hieros gamos) of the divine brother–sister pair as model for the incest archetype. The implications of such a move for understanding the incest wound and an archetypal view of the transference are worked out in his book, *Incest and Human Love*.

2 See Gilligan's (1982) essay "Woman's Place In Man's Life Cycle" in *In a Different Voice: Psychological Theory and Women's Development*; Stiver (1986) "Beyond the Oedipus Complex: Mothers and Daughters"; Gilligan *et al.* (1990) *Making Connections: The Relational Worlds of Adolescent Girls at Emma Willard School*. For a psychotherapeutic approach that emphasizes a relational perspective with female adolescents, see Gilligan *et al.* (1991) *Women, Girls and Psychotherapy: Reframing Resistance*.

3 *Reviving Ophelia: Saving the Selves of Adolescent Girls* (1994) by Mary Pipher is a New York Times paperback bestseller. For film see Peggy Orenstein's (1996) article "The Movies Discover the Teen-Age Girl." For literature see recent works by Mary Kerr, Dorothy Allison, Maya Angelou, Alice Munro, Alice McDermott, Bobbie Ann Mason, Julie Edelson, and Jamaica Kincaid.

4 See Barbara Greenfield's "The Archetypal Masculine: Its Manifestation in Myth, and Its Significance For Women" in *The Father: Contemporary Jungian Perspectives* edited by Samuels (1986).

5 Winnicott calls this approach "The Therapeutic Consultation." He states:

I am trying to show that in a very common type of child psychiatry case there is a possibility of doing effective and deep psychotherapy by making full use of one, or a limited number, of interviews.

(1965, p. 137)

See also Winnicott's (1977) *The Piggle: An Account of the Psychoanalytic Treatment of a Little Girl* and his *Therapeutic Consultations in Child Psychiatry* (1971). Both works display Winnicott's intrinsically time-limited orientation to child and adolescent psychotherapy.

3 THE ARCHETYPE OF INITIATION

1 For a description of current attempts to revive such rites see Mahdi, Foster and Little (eds) *Betwixt and Between: Patterns of Masculine and Feminine Initiation* (1987) and Mahdi *et al.* (eds) *Crossroads: The Quest For Contemporary Rites of Passage* (1996). For an example of creating such rituals in the context of psychotherapy, see Quinn, Newfield, and Protinsky's article, "Rites of Passage in Families with Adolescents" (1985).

4 LIFE AND DEATH IMAGERY IN ADOLESCENCE

1 For more on the connection between female initiation and Artemis, see Karl Kerenyi's "A Mythological Image of Girlhood" in *Facing the Gods* (1980) edited by James Hillman, and Ginette Paris's *Pagan Meditations: The Worlds of Aphrodite, Artemis and Hestia* (1986).

5 BODILY, IDEALISTIC, AND IDEATIONAL AWAKENINGS

1 A re-imagining of the contours of same-sex love, from a Jungian perspective, can be found in Hopcke *et al.* (eds) *Same-Sex Love and the Path to Wholeness* (1993).

6 THE INDIVIDUATION TASKS OF ADOLESCENCE

1 This orientation is described in Hillman's "Anima Mundi: The Return of the Soul to the World" *Spring: A Journal of Archetype and Culture* (1982).
2 Personal communication, Dr. Joseph Cambray.
3 Mahdi and Bosnak's travels throughout Russia, Japan, and Switzerland interviewing adolescent's about their dreams regarding living in the nuclear age and the possibility of apocalypse are documented in an upcoming film by Mark Whitney scheduled to be released by Mystic Fire Video in 1998.

7 PERSONA AND SHADOW IN ADOLESCENCE

1 For a compelling description of how the self's multiplicity is engaged in adult psychotherapy, see Chapter 12: The Fish Lady and the Little Girl: Case History Told From the Points of View of the Characters in Mary Watkins' (1990a) *Invisible Guests: The Development of Imaginal Dialogues.*

8 THE DEVELOPMENT OF CONSCIENCE

1 I am indebted to Robert Bosnak's (1977) unpublished Diploma Thesis for the C.G. Jung Institute for Analytical Psychology in Zurich entitled "The Cooking-Pot of Conscience: On Emancipation, Ethics and

Marriage". I am adapting his psychological reading of conscience for an understanding of its development in adolescence.

2   The "Self Chart" technique was invented by Jackie Schectman, a Jungian Analyst in Boston whose practice includes children and adolescents.

3   In this connection, Hillman writes:

> The compulsion–inhibition ambivalence shows in ritual, in play, and in mating, eating, and fighting patterns, where for each step forward under the urge of compulsion there is a lateral elaboration of dance, of play, of ornamentation – a "breather," which delays, heightens tension, and expands imaginative possibility and aesthetic form, making patterns, delightful and devious, cooling the compulsion of inborn release mechanisms for direct fulfillment in relation to the stimulus object – whether it is to be copulated with, eaten, or killed. The opus is elaborated into a gestalt even while the gestalt is being closed by the elaboration. The indirect movement is not a pattern of flight, though it may be intertwined with the reflective. It is not, essentially, a bending-back or a turning-away from the object; it is rather a continued advance upon it, but indirectly and with a different timing, and it overcomes compulsion, yet fulfills its need in another way.
>
> (1972, pp. 75–6)

For a further elaboration of this process as an inherent aspect of Eros, see Stein *Incest and Human Love* (1984), especially Chapter 11: The Transformation of Eros.

Bibliography

Aichorn, A. (1925) *Wayward Youth*, New York: Viking Press.
Allan, J. (1988) *Inscapes of the Child's World: Jungian Counseling in Schools and Clinics*, Dallas: Spring Publications.
Allan, J. and Bertoia, J. (1992) *Written Paths to Healing: Education and Jungian Child Counseling*, Dallas: Spring Publications.
Banks, R. (1995) *Rule of the Bone*, New York: Harper Perennial.
Bernstein, J.S. (1987) "The Decline of Rites of Passage in our Culture: The Impact of Masculine Individuation," in L.C. Mahdi, S. Foster and M. Little (eds) *Betwixt and Between: Patterns of Masculine and Feminine Initiation*, La Salle: Open Court.
Bettelheim, B. (1961) "The Problem of Generations," in E. Erickson (ed.) *Youth: Change and Challenge*, New York: Basic Books.
—— (1962) *Symbolic Wounds: Puberty Rites and the Envious Male*, New York: Collier Books.
—— (1975) *The Uses of Enchantment: The Meaning and Importance of Fairy Tales*, New York: Vintage Books.
Birkerts, S. (1994) *The Gutenberg Elegies*, Boston: Faber and Faber.
Bloch, H. and Niederhoffer, A. (1958) *The Gang: A Study in Adolescent Behavior*, New York: Philosophical Library.
Blos, P. (1962) *On Adolescence: A Psychoanalytic Interpretation*, New York: The Free Press.
—— (1967) "The Second Individuation Process of Adolescence," *The Psychoanalytic Study of the Child*, 22: 162–86.
Bosnak, R. (1977) "The Cooking-Pot of Conscience: On Emancipation, Ethics and Marriage," unpublished Diploma Thesis, C.G. Jung Institute for Analytical Psychology, Zurich.
Boss, M. (1983) *Existential Foundations of Medicine and Psychology*, New York: Jason Aronson.
Canada, G. (1995) *Fist Stick Knife Gun: A Personal History of Violence in America*, Boston: Beacon Press.
Dostoevsky, F. (1874) *The Adolescent*, New York: W.W. Norton, 1971.
Eliade, M. (1958) *Rites and Symbols of Initiation: The Mysteries of Birth and Rebirth*, New York: Harper and Row.
Fordham, M. (1957) *New Developments in Analytical Psychology*, London: Routledge and Kegan Paul.

——— (1994) *Children as Individuals*, London: Free Association Books.

Frank, A. (1952) *The Diary of a Young Girl*, New York: Simon and Schuster.

Freud, A. (1958) "Adolescence," *The Psychoanalytic Study of the Child*, 13: 255–78.

——— (1966) *The Writings of Anna Freud*, vol. II: *The Ego and the Mechanisms of Defense* (rev. ed.), New York: International Universities Press.

Freud, S. (1905) "Three Essays on the Theory of Sexuality," in *The Standard Edition of the Complete Psychological Works of Sigmund Freud*, vol. VII, pp. 125–245. Trans. J. Strachey. London: Hogarth Press, 1953–74.

——— (1923) "Two Encyclopaedia Articles," In *The Standard Edition of the Complete Psychological Works of Sigmund Freud*, vol. XVIII, pp. 235–259. Trans. J. Strachey. London: Hogarth Press, 1953–1974.

Gentry, D. (1989) *Adolescence in a Post-Adolescent World*, audiotape of a lecture by David Gentry, presented at a conference of the Dallas Institute of the Humanities and Culture: Cultural Psychology: Healing the World Soul, Dallas, Texas.

Giegerich, W. (1991) "The Advent of the Guest: Shadow Integration and the Rise of Psychology," *Spring: A Journal of Archetype and Culture* 51: 86–106.

Gilligan, C. (1982) *In a Different Voice: Psychological Theory and Women's Development*, Cambridge: Harvard University Press.

Gilligan, C., Lyons, N.P. and Hanmer, T.J. (eds) (1990) *Making Connections: The Relational Worlds of Adolescent Girls at Emma Willard School*, Cambridge: Harvard University Press.

Gilligan, C., Rogers, A.G. and Tolman, D.L. (eds) (1991) *Women, Girls and Psychotherapy: Reframing Resistance*, New York: Haworth Press.

Greenfield, B. (1986) "The Archetypal Masculine: Its Manifestation in Myth, and Its Significance For Women," in A. Samuels (ed.) *The Father: Contemporary Jungian Perspectives*, New York: New York University Press.

Guggenbühl, A. (1996) *The Incredible Fascination of Violence: Dealing with Aggression and Brutality among Children*, Woodstock: Spring Publications.

Guggenbühl-Craig, A. (1971) *Power in the Helping Professions*, Dallas: Spring Publications.

——— (1980) *Eros on Crutches: On the Nature of the Psychopath*, Dallas: Spring Publications.

Hall, G.S. (1904) *Adolescence*, New York: D. Appleton and Company.

Hall, N. (1989) *Broodmales*, Dallas: Spring Publications.

Henderson, J.L. (1967) *Thresholds of Initiation*, Middletown: Wesleyan University Press.

Hillman, J. (1964) *Suicide and the Soul*, Dallas: Spring Publications.

——— (1967) "Senex and Puer," in *Puer Papers*, Dallas: Spring Publications, 1979.

——— (1972) *The Myth of Analysis*, New York: Harper and Row.

——— (1975a) *Loose Ends*, Dallas: Spring Publications.

—— (1975b) *Revisioning Psychology*, New York: Harper and Row.
—— (1977) "Puer Wounds and Ulysses' Scar," in *Puer Papers*, Dallas: Spring Publications, 1979.
—— (ed.) (1980) *Facing the Gods*, Dallas: Spring Publications.
—— (1982) "Anima Mundi: The Return of the Soul to the World" *Spring: A Journal of Archetype and Culture*, 71–94.
—— (1990) "The Great Mother, Her Son, Her Hero, and the Puer," in P. Berry (ed.) *Fathers and Mothers*, Dallas: Spring Publications.
—— (1992) *Emotion: A Comprehensive Phenomenology of Theories and Their Meanings for Therapy*, Evanston: Northwestern University Press.
—— (1995) "Pink Madness, or, Why does Aphrodite Drive Men Crazy with Pornography" *Spring: A Journal of Archetype and Culture* 57, 39–72.
Hillman, J. and Ventura, M. (1992) *We've Had a Hundred Years of Psychotherapy and the World's Getting Worse*, San Francisco: Harper.
Hopcke, R.H., Carrington, K.L. and Wirth, S. (eds) (1993) *Same-Sex Love and the Path to Wholeness*, Boston: Shambhala.
Hume, E. (1996) *No Matter How Loud I Shout: A Year in the Life of Juvenile Court*, New York: Simon and Schuster.
Illich, I. (1982) *Medical Nemesis: The Expropriation of Health*, New York: Pantheon Books.
Jacobi, J. (1965) *The Way of Individuation*, New York: New American Library.
Jones, E. (1922) "Some Problems of Adolescence," *British Journal of Psychoanalysis* 13: 39–45.
Jung, C.G., *Collected Works* (*CW*), by volume and paragraph number, ed. Read, H., Fordham, M., Adler, G. and McGuire, W., trans. in the main by Hull, R., Routledge and Kegan Paul, London; Princeton University Press.
Kaplan, L.J. (1986) *Adolescence: The Farewell to Childhood*, Northvale: Jason Aronson, Inc.
Kegan, R. (1982) *The Evolving Self*, Cambridge: Harvard University Press.
Kett, J.F. (1977) *Rites of Passage: Adolescence in America: 1790's to the Present*, New York: Basic Books.
Kincaid, J. (1983) *Annie John*, New York: Farrar, Straus and Giroux, Inc.
Klein, R. (1993) *Cigarettes are Sublime*, Durham and London: Duke University Press.
Laufer, M. and Laufer, M.E. (1984) *Adolescence and Developmental Breakdown: A Psychoanalytic View*, New Haven: Yale University Press.
Lifton, R.J. (1979) *The Broken Connection*, New York: Simon and Schuster.
Mahdi, L.C., Christopher, N.G. and Meade, M. (eds) (1996) *Crossroads: The Quest for Contemporary Rites of Passage*, La Salle: Open Court.
Mahdi, L.C., Foster, S. and Little, M. (eds) (1987) *Betwixt and Between: Patterns of Masculine and Feminine Initiation*, La Salle: Open Court.
Mahler, M.S. (1963) "Thoughts About Development and Individuation," *Psychoanalytic Study of the Child*, 18: 307–24.
Marin, P. (1974) "The Open Truth and Fiery Vehemence of Youth," in C. Shrodes, H. Finestone and M. Shugrue (eds) *The Conscious Reader*, New York: Macmillan Publishing Co.

Meade, M. (1974) "Rites of Passage at the End of the Millennium," in Mahdi, L.C., Christopher, N.G. and Meade, M. (eds) *Crossroads: The Quest for Contemporary Rites of Passage*, La Salle: Open Court.

Mishima, Y. (1965) *The Sailor Who Fell From Grace with the Sea*, New York: Alfred Knopf.

Milosz, C. (1988) *The Collected Poems*, New Jersey: Ecco Press.

Moore, T. (1979) "Artemis and the Puer," in *Puer Papers*, Dallas: Spring Publications.

Nietzsche, F. (1888) "Twilight of the Idols," in W. Kaufmann (ed.) *The Portable Nietzsche*, New York: Penguin Books.

Orenstein, P. (1996) "The Movies Discover the Teen-Age Girl," *New York Times*, August 11.

Paris, G. (1986) *Pagan Meditations: The Worlds of Aphrodite, Artemis and Hestia*, Dallas: Spring Publications.

—— (1990) *Pagan Grace: Dionysos, Hermes, and Goddess Memory in Daily Life*, Dallas: Spring Publications.

Pipher, M. (1994) *Reviving Ophelia: Saving the Selves of Adolescent Girls*, New York: Ballantine Books.

Pollack, R. (1996) "Breaking the Will of Heaven: The Abduction/Marriage of Hades and Persephone," *Spring: A Journal of Archetype and Culture* 60, 55–74.

Quinn, W.H., Newfield, N.A. and Protinsky, H.O. (eds) (1985) "Rites of Passage in Families with Adolescents," *Family Process* 24: 101–11.

Racker, H. (1968) *Transference and Countertransference*, New York: International Universities Press.

Rilke, R.M. (1949) *The Notebooks of Malte Laurids Brigge*, New York: W.W. Norton.

Robertson, S.M. (1982) *Rosegarden and Labyrinth: A Study in Art Education*, Dallas: Spring Publications.

Rychlak, J.F. (1991) "Jung as Dialectician and Teleologist," in R. Papadopoulos and G. Saayman (eds) *Jung in Modern Perspective*, Bridport: Prism Press.

Salinger, J.D. (1945) *The Catcher in the Rye*, New York: Bantam Books.

—— (1955) *Franny and Zooey*, Boston: Little Brown and Company.

Samuels, A. (1985) *Jung and the Post-Jungians*, London: Routledge and Kegan Paul.

—— (ed.) (1986) *The Father: Contemporary Jungian Perspectives*, New York: New York University Press.

—— (ed.) (1991) *Psychopathology: Contemporary Jungian Perspectives*, New York: Guilford.

—— (1993) *The Political Psyche*, London: Routledge.

Samuels, A., Shorter, B. and Plaut, B. (eds) (1986) *A Critical Dictionary of Jungian Analysis*, London and New York: Routledge.

Scott, C.E. (1982) *Boundaries In Mind: A Study of Immediate Awareness Based on Psychotherapy*, New York: Scholars Press.

Sidoli, M. (1989) *The Unfolding Self*, Boston: Sigo Press.

Sidoli, M. and Bovensiepen, G. (eds) (1995) *Incest Fantasies and Self-Destructive Acts: Jungian and Post-Jungian Psychotherapy in Adolescence*, London: Transaction Publishers.

Spencer, S. (1979) *Endless Love*, New York: Alfred Knopf.

Stein, R. (1984) *Incest and Human Love*, Dallas: Spring Publications.

Stiver, I. (1986) "Beyond the Oedipus Complex: Mothers and Daughters," *Work in Progress*, Wellesley: Stone Center Working Papers Series.

Sullwold, E. (1987) "The Ritual-Maker Within at Adolescence," in Mahdi, L.C., Foster, S. and Little, M. (eds) *Betwixt and Between: Patterns of Masculine and Feminine Initiation*, La Salle: Open Court.

Surrey, J. (1984) "The Self-in-Relation: A Theory of Women's Development," *Work in Progress*, no. 13., Wellesley: Stone Center Working Papers Series.

Van Gennep, A. (1960) *The Rites of Passage*, Chicago: University of Chicago Press.

Ventura, M. (1993) *Letters at 3AM: Reports on Endarkenment*, Dallas: Spring Publications.

Von Franz, M.L. (1970) *The Problem of the Puer Aeternus*, New York: Spring Publications.

Watkins, M. (1990a) *Invisible Guests: The Development of Imaginal Dialogues*, Boston: Sigo Press.

—— (1990b) "Mother and Child: Some Teachings of Desire," in P. Berry (ed.) *Fathers and Mothers*, Dallas: Spring Publications.

Wickes, F. (1927) *The Inner World of Childhood*, New York: Signet.

Winnicott, D.W. (1939) "Aggression and its Roots," in C. Winnicott and M. Davis (eds) *Deprivation and Delinquency*, London: Routledge, 1990.

—— (1956) "The Anti-Social Tendency," in C. Winnicott, R. Shepherd and M. Davis (eds) *Deprivation and Delinquency*, London: Routledge, 1990.

—— (1963a) "Struggling Through the Doldrums", in C. Winnicott, R. Shepherd and M. Davis (eds) *Deprivation and Delinquency*, London: Routledge, 1990.

—— (1963b) "Communicating and Not Communicating Leading to a Study of Certain Opposites," in *The Maturational Processes and the Facilitating Environment*, Madison: International Universities Press, 1965.

—— (1964) "Youth Will Not Sleep," in C. Winnicott, R. Shepherd and M. Davis (eds) *Deprivation and Delinquency*, London: Routledge, 1990.

—— (1965) "The Concept of Trauma in Relation to the Development of the Individual within the Family," in C. Winnicott, R. Shepherd and M. Davis (eds) *Psycho-Analytical Explorations*, Cambridge: Harvard University Press, 1989.

—— (1966) "The Absence of a Sense of Guilt," in C. Winnicott, R. Shepherd and M. Davis (eds) *Deprivation and Delinquency*, London: Routledge, 1990.

—— (1968) "Contemporary Concepts of Adolescent Development and their Implications for Higher Education," in D.W. Winnicott, *Playing and Reality*, London: Routledge, 1991.

—— (1971) *Therapeutic Consultations in Child Psychiatry*, New York: Basic Books.

—— (1977) *The Piggle: An Account of the Psychoanalytic Treatment of a Little Girl*, Madison: International Universities Press.

Zinner, J. and Shapiro, R. (1972) "Projective Identification as a Mode of

Perception and Behavior in Families of Adolescents," *International Journal of Psycho-Analysis* 53: 523–30.

Zoja, L. (1989) *Drugs, Addiction and Initiation: The Modern Search for Ritual*, Boston: Sigo Press.

Index